CELEBRITY ADVOCACY AND INTERNATIONAL DEVELOPMENT

Celebrity advocacy is a curious phenomenon. It occupies a significant proportion of the public domain, but does so without engaging particularly well with much of the public. Yet this may not matter very much. Many people at the core of advocacy, and in political and business elites, simply do not notice any lack of engagement. In these circles celebrity advocacy can be remarkably effective.

Celebrity Advocacy and International Development examines the work of celebrity advocacy and lobbying in international development. Its purpose is to understand the alliances resulting, their history, consequences, wider contexts and implications. It argues that celebrity advocacy signals a new aspect of elite rule. For populist celebrity advocacy can mark, ironically, a disengagement between the public and politics, and particularly the public and civil society. Recognising this poses new challenges, but also presents new opportunities, for the development movement.

This book gives students and researchers in development studies and media studies a wealth of original empirical data, including interviews across the NGO sector, media and celebrity industries, newspaper analysis, large surveys of public opinion, and focus group research.

Dan Brockington is Professor of Conservation and Development at the Institute for Development Policy and Management, University of Manchester.

Rethinking Development

Rethinking Development offers accessible and thought-provoking overviews of contemporary topics in international development and aid. Providing original empirical and analytical insights, the books in this series push thinking in new directions by challenging current conceptualisations and developing new ones.

This is a dynamic and inspiring series for all those engaged with today's debates surrounding development issues, whether they be students, scholars, policy makers or practitioners internationally. These interdisciplinary books provide an invaluable resource for discussion in advanced undergraduate and postgraduate courses in development studies as well as in economics, politics, geography, media studies and sociology.

Popular Representations of Development
Insights from novels, films, television and social media
Edited by David Lewis, Dennis Rodgers and Michael Woolcock

Celebrity Advocacy and International Development
Dan Brockington

International Aid and the Making of a Better World
Reflexive practice
Rosalind Eyben

CELEBRITY ADVOCACY AND INTERNATIONAL DEVELOPMENT

Dan Brockington

LONDON AND NEW YORK

First published 2014
by Routledge
2 Park Square, Milton Park, Abingdon, Oxon, OX14 4RN

and by Routledge
711 Third Avenue, New York, NY 10017

Routledge is an imprint of the Taylor & Francis Group, an informa business

© 2014 Dan Brockington

The right of Dan Brockington to be identified as author of this work has been asserted by him in accordance with sections 77 and 78 of the Copyright, Designs and Patents Act 1988.

All rights reserved. No part of this book may be reprinted or reproduced or utilised in any form or by any electronic, mechanical, or other means, now known or hereafter invented, including photocopying and recording, or in any information storage or retrieval system, without permission in writing from the publishers.

Every effort has been made to contact copyright holders for their permission to reprint material in this book. The publishers would be grateful to hear from any copyright holder who is not here acknowledged and will undertake to rectify any errors or omissions in future editions of this book.

British Library Cataloguing in Publication Data
A catalogue record for this book is available from the British Library

Library of Congress Cataloging-in-Publication Data
Brockington, Dan.
  Celebrity advocacy and international development/Daniel Brockington.
  pages cm. – (Rethinking development; 2)
  Includes bibliographical references and index.
  1. Economic assistance. 2. Economic development projects.
  3. Humanitarianism. 4. Poverty. 5. Celebrities – Political activity.
  6. Social advocacy. I. Title.
  HC60.B677 2014
  338.91 – dc23
  2013039658

ISBN: 978-0-415-70719-0 (hbk)
ISBN: 978-0-415-70721-3 (pbk)
ISBN: 978-1-315-88697-8 (ebk)

Typeset in Bembo and Stone Sans
by Florence Production Ltd, Stoodleigh, Devon, UK

Printed and bound in Great Britain by
TJ International Ltd, Padstow, Cornwall

Dan Brockington has written an important book, exploring the convoluted world of celebrity advocacy. He carefully analyses the evidence and exposes the phenomenon; and just when you think Brockington has delivered his measured conclusions, there comes a powerful 'afterword' which no-one should miss and which suddenly transforms the whole topic.

Michael Billig, Loughborough University, UK

Sharp, clear and fully engaging, this is one of the most comprehensive and insightful accounts of celebrity advocacy that have been written so far. It will no doubt define the field for many years to come.

Lilie Chouliaraki, London School of Economics and Political Science, UK

Dan Brockington emerges from several years of intelligent, evidenced-based interrogation of the role of celebrities in international development with a genuinely insightful and surprising argument. This book will profoundly change the way we think about celebrities and development.

Martin Scott, University of East Anglia, UK

Dan Brockington's excellent book explores the contradictory effects of celebrity populism on international development. He utilizes post-democratic theory to conceptualize the 'authenticity' of the affiliations between celebrity activists, non-governmental organizations and public opinion. This is a major resource for anyone who is concerned with the democratic implications of celebrity advocacy.

Mark Wheeler, London Metropolitan University, UK

For Adela and Adela, in memory.

And for Juli, Justini, Bahati, Reena, Restituta, Redimna and Ambrose, in hope.

CONTENTS

Illustrations

List of figures	*xiii*
List of tables	*xiii*
List of boxes	*xiv*

Abbreviations	*xv*
Preface	*xvii*
Acknowledgements	*xix*
Definitions of key terms	*xxi*

Fame and celebrity	*xxi*
Celebrity advocacy	*xxii*
Development and humanitarianism	*xxii*

1 Introduction   1

The context and purpose of this book   7
The argument   9
Unpopular celebrity?   10
Authentic advocacy?   10
Methods   12
An outline of the chapters   12

2 The terrain of development advocacy   17

Seeing suffering, seeking justice   18
Public awareness of, and giving to, development causes   24
Conclusion   31

x Contents

3 Celebrity advocacy and post-democracy 34

Post-democracy 35
Celebrity, the media and democracy 38
Studies of celebrity advocacy 41
Conclusion 46

4 A brief history of celebrity advocacy for development and humanitarian causes 51

Celebrity 52
Development and humanitarianism 54
The rise and fall of celebrity and international development 56
Overseas development returns to fame 61
Make Poverty History and the Save Darfur Coalition 65
Conclusion 68

5 The current state of celebrity advocacy 75

Systematic celebrity–NGO relations 76
Mapping celebrity advocacy 82
Evaluating celebrity advocacy 83
Conclusion 91

6 'Getting it': Producing authentic celebrity advocacy 95

Developing authentic relationships 97
Coping with constraints 100
Working with the celebrity industries 102
Representing celebrity advocacy 103
Performing authentic advocacy 106
Conclusion 109

7 Elites and celebrity advocacy 113

The corporate interest in celebrity advocates 114
Celebrity and elites 117
Belief in celebrity power 122
Conclusion 126

8 The witches' pond 131

The limited consumption of celebrity media 133
Consumption of celebrity media: a reality check 136
Engagement with celebrity advocacy 138

Contents **xi**

Popular belief in celebrity power and approval of celebrity advocates 142
The charitable frame 144
Talking about celebrity advocates 145
Conclusion 147

9 Changing the world through celebrity advocacy 152

Development representations 153
Inequity and accountability 155
Working with celebrity elites in post-democracies 160
Conclusion 162

Afterword 165

Appendix one: Methods 169

Interviews 169
Surveys 170
Focus groups 171
Newspaper and magazine surveys 173
Limitations 174

Appendix two: Research on celebrity endorsers 176

Appendix three: Trends in reporting on celebrity advocacy 181

References 184
Index 203

ILLUSTRATIONS

Figures

2.1	UK charitable donations for overseas development and total household income: 1978–2004 (constant 2007 prices)	28
5.1	The cumulative growth of NGO celebrity liaison officers and UN Goodwill Ambassador programmes	76
8.1	Survey respondents (2005) grouped according to the things they keep up with	134
A3.1	Trends in reporting celebrity and charity	181

Tables

2.1	Evidence of public awareness of development	26
2.2	Trends in giving to development charities	29
5.1	Celebrity ambassadors and supporters of major development and humanitarian NGOs	84
7.1	Costly charitable occasions	116
8.1	Media use clusters from the 2011 survey	135
8.2	Engagement with celebrity news in a typical week	135
8.3	Clusters of celebrity news consumption	136
8.4	Awareness of famous people working with development organisations	139
8.5	Specific light responses to charitable endorsements by the famous	140
8.6	Deeper reactions to charitable endorsements by the famous	140
8.7	Beliefs in other people's responses to celebrity advocacy	142
A1.1	Country and organisation experience of the interviewees consulted in this research	170
A1.2	The characteristics of the focus groups	172

xiv Illustrations

A2.1	Distribution of effects of celebrity advertising from Amos *et al.*, 2008	177
A2.2	Citation count of different sample types	177
A2.3	The sampling of different countries and populations over time in the celebrity advertising literature	178
A3.1	Trends in celebrity appearance in a sample of British newspapers	182

Boxes

| 5.1 | Samples of Red Pages bulletins | 78 |
| A1.1 | Interviewee responses to circulated papers | 171 |

ABBREVIATIONS

BBC   British Broadcasting Corporation
EMI   Electrical and Musical Industries
ESRC   Economic and Social Research Council
IDS   Institute of Development Studies
IMF   International Monetary Fund
LSN   Landmines Survivors Network
MAG   Mines Advisory Group
MSF   Médecins Sans Frontières
NGO   non-governmental organisation
RGS   Royal Geographical Society
STC   Save the Children
UNDP   United Nations Development Programme
UNHCR   United Nations High Commissioner for Refugees
UNICEF   United Nations Children's Fund
WEF   World Economic Forum
WWF   World Wide Fund for Nature

PREFACE

Perhaps you know little about celebrity. You may be discouraged from reading further because you feel excluded by it. Your impression is that most people know more than you and are more interested in it than you are. Well, please read on. I will argue that you may well be in the majority. Most people believe celebrity to be a vibrant and vigorous pursuit embraced by the general populace. But I believe that they are mistaken in that belief. Part of the purpose of this book is to look beyond the smoke and mirrors that can constitute the very substance of celebrity advocacy, and to understand the political consequences of the confusion it has generated.

Take heart even if you cannot recognise many of the names I must mention. In this respect you cannot be alone. There are tens of thousands of celebrities on the professional contact bases, and many more people who used to be celebrities but who have stepped out of the public eye. It is impossible to recognise the vast majority. Moreover, if the context does not make it clear, I explain (in parentheses) why you might have heard of any famous name mentioned whenever I first use it. I make no exceptions, however important that figure may be, be they David Beckham (a soccer player), Steve Bull (another soccer player), or Madonna (a singer) or Aunt Molly Jackson (also a singer). We cannot assume that anyone is so famous that everyone will know them. If you spot occasions when I have mentioned a name without explanation, then that will be either my mistake, or because the individual was mentioned earlier in the text (or chapter endnotes), or because I am referring to someone who is not famous at all, but is probably an academic writer whose works are listed in the references.

Alternatively, you may know a good deal about celebrity and about celebrity studies. You will probably know that this is my second attempt to understand celebrity advocacy (the first being a book called *Celebrity and the Environment*). You may be wondering why I am having another go. The books have different foci

xviii Preface

and source material. The first explored the varieties of celebrity support for environmental causes, and some of their consequences. In it I tried to map the types of celebrity environmentalism, to understand what sorts of environments they defended (or produced) in the process and what sorts of social forces created them. My main source material for it was readings of celebrity environmentalism. The present book is a very different beast. It focuses on development and humanitarian causes, and in the main it eschews textual analysis. It draws instead on interviews, newspaper surveys, focus group and questionnaire data to understand better the production and consumption of celebrity advocacy.

ACKNOWLEDGEMENTS

My thanks first to the many people in the non-governmental organisations (NGOs), the celebrity industries and the media who generously gave their time to talk to me about this topic both during interviews, and when discussing the notes and findings that emerged. Their co-operation and challenges have made this research both enjoyable and thought-provoking.

I would like to thank the Economic and Social Research Council (ESRC) for sponsoring this research (through a fellowship RES 070–27–0035), the University of Manchester for employing me, my colleagues there for the interest they have shown in it, and to Deborah Whitehead, Kellie Gallagher and Marta Foles for their administrative support, and good humour, during it. Thanks to Andreas Scheba and Surya Fazel-Ellahi for entering data from the *Red Pages*, Rachel Tavernor for her work in the newspaper archives at Collingdale, and the staff of Bodleian Library for their help. Thanks also to Celia Braves for producing the index and my editor, Helen Bell, for her support and advice.

I have benefited greatly from encounters with Matt Baillie Smith, Charlie Beckett, Doug Bourn, Lilie Chouliaraki, Andrew Darnton, Mike Goodman, Jennifer van Heerde-Hudson, Spencer Henson, David Hudson, Joanna Lindstrom, Jo Littler, Cheryl Lousely, John Micklewright, Stefano Ponte, Lisa Ann Richey, Martin Scott, John Street, Alex de Waal, Jaffy Wilson, Mark Wheeler, all the participants of the symposium on 'Capitalism, Democracy and Celebrity Advocacy' held in Manchester in June 2012, and the participants of the Spectacular Environmentalism's network hosted by Mike Goodman and Jo Littler. Thanks to Lisa Ann Richey for hosting me for a most productive week at the University of Roskilde, and to her and Stefano Ponte for looking after me in Denmark, to Doug Bourn, Bina Agarwal and colleagues at Manchester for hosting presentations of this work and listening to early versions of the findings. Thanks to Uma Kothari who helped to design the 'Representations in Development' course, and teach so inspiringly on it at Manchester.

xx Acknowledgements

Elements of the data presented in Chapter 6 have been published in Brockington, D. (2014) 'The production and construction of celebrity advocacy in international development' Third World Quarterly 35(1): 88–108, and are reproduced here under a creative commons license (http://creativecommons.org/licenses/by/3.0/#). My thanks (again) to Lisa Richey and Stefano Ponte for the work they put into the collection of which that paper is part.

In addition to talking to me at length on this topic, Tony Bebbington, Bram Büscher, Lilie Chouliaraki, Jim Igoe, Cheryl Lousley, Katja Neves, Lisa Ann Richey, Martin Scott, John Street, Sian Sullivan and Mark Wheeler read portions (or even all) of the manuscript. The mistakes that follow remain my own.

My parents read the work too, and kept me in touch with important bits of celebrity news they would not otherwise have read, while my siblings were ever vigilant lest I talk too much about it. Thanks to Charlotte and Ger, Paul and Robin, and David and Alison who looked after me on trips to London. My colleagues on the VIVA! collective (you know who you are) have formed a supremely valuable sounding board, source of support, musical inspiration and bucket of cold water at all the right moments.

Thanks to Tekla, Rosie and Emily who will still never be my celebrities and for making the writing time so joyful.

And finally thanks to my in-laws who have been so tolerant, supportive and fun to be with over the last year. I wrote this book in a remote part of Tanzania, surrounded by maize and bean fields, and perched rather high up a large extinct volcano. Puzzling over *Hello!* magazine extracts, statistical analyses of UK public opinion polls and histories of glamour and celebrity, which is odd enough in itself, became more bizarre when I would close the computer to attend my local microfinance self-help group, or weed my mother-in-law's maize field. I have loved being welcomed further into this family, to watch my children learn to talk and play with their cousins and to take a deeper part in its joys, grief, quarrels, plans and hopes. I dedicate this to Adela, her children and her grandchildren.

DEFINITIONS OF KEY TERMS

Fame and celebrity

Defining celebrity is surprisingly difficult. A common strategy is not so much to define, but categorise it. Chris Rojek distinguished between three forms of celebrity: ascribed greatness (enjoyed by royalty), achieved renown (won by great athletes) and attributed glory (afforded by the media to reality TV stars).[1] This echoes Malvolio in Shakespeare's *Twelfth Night*: 'some are born great, some achieve greatness, and some have greatness thrust upon them'. Daniel Boorstin commented that there is now another category who hire 'public relations experts and press secretaries to make themselves look great'.[2]

Graeme Turner defines celebrity according to the nature of public interest in them. A celebrity is someone whose private life attracts more attention than their professional life.[3] This poses the difficulty of quantifying the different sorts of interest. It is difficult to apply to people whose personal life is their profession (royalty or some reality TV stars) or whose profession can dominate their lives such that it becomes hard to disentangle the personal from the professional (some musicians and politicians).

I define celebrity according to the commerce and industry that depends on it. Celebrity describes sustained public appearances that are materially beneficial, and where the benefits are at least partially enjoyed by people other than the celebrity themselves, by stakeholders whose job it is to manage the appearance of that celebrity. According to this definition, members of the public interviewed by roving reporters would not be celebrities. Academics promoting their books in the media would qualify if those media opportunities were provided by an agent promoting their book.

Fame and celebrity are often distinguished in the public mind, generally along the lines that famous people deserve attention while celebrities do not.[4] I do not find the distinction helpful (definitive criteria for such merit are hard to determine);

xxii Definitions of key terms

I will use the terms interchangeably. When I refer to a person as famous that does not mean that they merit attention more than a celebrity. Interestingly, however, the term 'celebrity' can carry those problematic connotations in the celebrity industries themselves. Few celebrities call themselves celebrities; they are stars, artists, talent or personalities.

Celebrity advocacy

It is a social fact that a recognisable category of behaviour exists in the public domain that I and others call 'celebrity advocacy'. It is also known as celebrity charity, celebrity politics, celebrity patronage, etc. Most people seem to be able to recognise it when they see it, and most people call the people doing it 'celebrities'.

Such behaviour requires an inclusive definition. In this book 'celebrity advocacy' refers to any work by famous people in service of some cause other than themselves. They may also benefit in the process, but that does not affect the fact that what they are doing is advocacy. The form of advocacy can vary greatly. Most commonly it involves speaking out, and being seen to speak out, for that cause. This commonly entails collaborating with an organisation, typically an NGO, or non-governmental organisation, which fights for that cause. Such advocacy can involve fund-raising, making films, writing articles, meeting supporters, attending rallies, signing petitions or donating recipes to cook books. The varieties are almost endless. It can also involve less visible work behind the scenes, meeting politicians or policy makers, or arranging such meetings between them and the organisations they support. 'Advocacy' then refers not just to speaking out and literally advocating for something, but to any activities that support the work of a cause or other advocates of that cause.

John Street distinguishes between two sorts of celebrities who advocate for causes: Celebrity *Politicians* and *Celebrity* Politicians.[5] The former are politicians who adopt the trappings of celebrity (Street called them CP1s) and the latter famous people who turn to politics (CP2s). In the pages that follow I shall be mostly focusing on the celebrities who take up other causes.

Development and humanitarianism

Sometimes authors distinguish between 'humanitarianism', concerned primarily with dealing with the problems arising from emergencies, war and disasters, and 'development', dealing with more mundane forms of poverty and the deeper structural causes of misfortune and inequality. Following from this, a fundamental difference between the two is that development is something that you, or your community, can do to yourself or itself. But humanitarianism requires a needy *other*.[6] The history of humanitarianism begins with the recognition of the humanity of distant strangers.

However, when analysing contemporary forms of development and humanitarianism that conceptual division is difficult to apply in practice. Much of the history

Definitions of key terms **xxiii**

of development is precisely a history of intervention in the lives of others, who are regarded as needing change.[7] The very term 'International Development' in the title of this book is recognition of that fact – far from being local, development battles are often fought on international stages and embroil international organisations, states and alliances of different peoples from around the globe. Many NGOs can seek to tackle both development and humanitarianism in their work for needy others.

The conceptual differences are also blurred in writing about these terms. Michael Barnett does not refer to 'development', but distinguishes between two variants of 'humanitarianism': an 'emergency branch' dealing with the symptoms, and an 'alchemical branch' that seeks to tackle root causes.[8] Chouliaraki refers to these two forms as 'solidarity as salvation' and 'solidarity as revolution'.[9]

Perhaps most importantly, development and humanitarianism are united by the contests over them. Both are marked by competing visions as to what their goals should be, and what the means should be of achieving them. And for both there are typically disputes over what the role of states, capital, NGOs and local groups should be in determining and reaching these goals. These disputes are perhaps most vigorous when governments kill people in 'humanitarian interventions' (in Kosovo and Somalia), or when they enrol development NGOs in the reconstruction of countries they have just invaded in the name of progress (Iraq). But such disagreements have characterised both movements since their inception.

To cover all the bases I will talk about development and humanitarianism wherever I can. Sometimes, however, it is easier and simpler just to talk about 'development'. In particular, whenever I refer to 'development advocacy' I include within that advocacy for development *and* humanitarian causes. If the argument requires that I distinguish between development causes (long-term change) and humanitarian emergencies, then I will do so.

In terms of its actual practices, most development and humanitarian activity is performed by governments and large international organisations; NGOs and non-profit organisations are relatively minor players. Yet this book is concerned with the activity of *development advocacy* – of pressing for, executing and supporting change that is believed to make the lives of Southerners more prosperous. This activity is largely carried out in the global North, and is mainly the domain of NGOs; they feature prominently in the story that follows.

In addition to understanding the difference between development and humanitarianism we must also consider what 'development' actually is. Development's potential to be locally defined and realised (immanent change), and its actual history of being externally determined means that development's history of intervention has also been a history of contest, conflict and unwelcome change.[10] So although development is often normatively defined as becoming more prosperous and improving well-being, its critics object that its experience can be far from that. Gilbert Rist defines development as 'the general transformation and destruction of the natural environment and of social relations' in pursuit of the increased production of commodities.[11] At their most extreme, post-development thinkers

xxiv Definitions of key terms

insist that the whole development project has been a sad and violent delusion.[12] They rightly observe that much harm has been committed in the name of development. Other critics point to the unhealthy alliances between development organisations, and state and corporate power.[13] Others point to the fact that economic growth and happiness are just poorly related.[14] Development is often equated with economic growth, but while that may reduce poverty, it does not necessarily improve well-being.

The relevance of that debate for this book is that we cannot equate lobbying for development causes as promoting change that will produce happy outcomes for the world's poor. The paradox here is that, while most people seek to become more prosperous and improve their well-being, 'development' may not always be the best means of doing so. When Dani Rodrik observes that development policy 'has largely failed to live up to its promise' he is referring to the fact that changes that were meant to have improved well-being have not done so.[15] Sometimes when development advocates fail in their goals, poor residents of the global South will remain a little more prosperous than they might have been.[16]

The complexities of development mean that celebrities advocating for apparently good causes, can be promoting bad ones, or failing to tackle the real problems underlying these causes. This can be because the celebrities fail to understand the issues and their interventions, or the failings of the institutions with which they are working, or both. When we examine celebrity advocacy for development we cannot just celebrate their concern for distant strangers. We must also understand what policies their concern promotes. I will explore this in the conclusion of the book.

Notes

1   Rojek, 2001.
2   Boorstin, 1992 [1961]: 45. For useful short reviews of the celebrity literature, see Ferris (2007) and Heinich (2011); for an interesting introduction, see Kurzman *et al.* (2007).
3   Turner, 2004: 3.
4   Epstein, 2005: 9; Gabler, 2001.
5   Street, 2004.
6   My thanks to Jim Igoe for that clarification.
7   Rist, 2008 [1996].
8   Barnett, 2011: 10.
9   Chouliaraki, 2013: 10.
10 Cowen and Shenton, 1996.
11 Rist, 2008 (1996): 13.
12 Escobar, 1992; Esteva, 1992; Sachs, 1992. See Corbridge, 1994 for a critique of that view.
13 Chapin, 2004; Dowie, 2009. Mitlin *et al.*, 2007.
14 Layard, 2006.
15 Rodrik, 2007: 85.
16 Conservation issues provide the clearest examples. Some conservation policies require the eviction and displacement of people, which causes poverty. Advocates endorsing such displacement are promoting impoverishment.

1

INTRODUCTION

Let us begin with a lie told to a princess.

The princess was important. Princess Diana, recently departed from the British Royal Family, was then at the height of her fame. It was also an important lie. For, as a result of it, Diana became involved in The International Campaign to Ban Landmines, collaborating with the Mines Advisory Group (MAG) and the Landmine Survivor's Network (LSN), among other organisations. Her interest in the cause, visits to minefields and meetings with landmine survivors, won it tremendous publicity and moved landmines up the political agenda. According to Kenneth Rutherford, the co-founder of the LSN, 'Princess Diana's involvement helped MAG and LSN transform the landmine debate from a military to a humanitarian issue in many people's minds, including those of many diplomats'. He also states that her lobbying encouraged the then British Prime Minister, Tony Blair, to honour his party's election promise to ban mines.[1]

Diana's last public appearance in August 1997 was with landmine survivors in Bosnia. A few weeks later she died in a car accident just days before the international conference convened in Oslo to negotiate the treaty banning landmines. As Rutherford notes, this meant that the conference 'came on the heels of an emotional week of outpouring for the death of Diana'. More attention focused on the meeting, and pressure increased for a satisfactory resolution. Her influence was apparent in the rhetoric of those present. The Norwegian Foreign Minister, speaking in the first session, stated that 'We shall spare no effort . . . to achieve the goals she set for herself'. The British Foreign Secretary said that the treaty's 'achievement is due in part to the work of Diana . . . who did so much to focus the attention of the world on the horrific effects of anti-personnel landmines'. The US did not sign the treaty after its attempts to water down some of its provisions were defeated. This prompted US President Bill Clinton to complain that his proposals 'were rejected, partly because the Landmine Conference was determined

2 Introduction

to pass the strongest possible treaty in the wake of the death of its most famous champion, Princess Diana'.[2]

It is impossible to gauge what Diana's impact was on the Campaign or the treaty negotiations.[3] Indeed, it would be misleading to focus too much on any one person. The treaty to ban landmines was the work of many social movements and many individuals. The six founding organisations of the Campaign grew to over 1,000 groups; 130 NGOs attended the Oslo conference, and 350 the signing ceremony.[4] In October 1997 the Campaign and its co-ordinator, Jody Williams, were awarded the Nobel Peace Prize. It was accepted for the Campaign by Rae McGrath, who founded MAG, and by Tun Channareth, a Cambodian landmine survivor. They did so on behalf of a multitude.

Nonetheless, even though she joined the campaign late, and was just one of many, Diana's individual contribution was considerable. And for that reason we need to get back to the lie. For it explains how she got involved with the campaign – with the momentous consequences I have described. To understand how it came about we must listen to Rae McGrath's account of a meeting he had with her.

Rae is an unassuming recipient of the Nobel medal. I once invited a Nobel laureate to talk at my university and was told this normally commanded a $50,000 speaking fee, plus expensive air tickets. Rae, in contrast, met me for our interview at the train station near his home in an old and battered car. He was then still pursuing his profession, managing programmes in refugee camps in dangerous parts of the world. The Nobel medal hangs unobtrusively on the wall amid other pictures and memorabilia and he did not seem to mind that I was unaware that he had received it. Rae also has a felicitous mix of pragmatism, opportunism, a good sense of humour and a delight in the ridiculous that has given him many interesting stories to tell, and a good way of telling them. The story of Diana's recruitment to the cause is best told by him partly for that reason – and partly because it was he who told the lie. I therefore quote extensively from my interview with him below.[5]

Diana had visited Angola with the British Red Cross in February 1997, and pictures of her walking in a minefield in full protective gear had covered the world's papers. It was a wonderful publicity coup for the landmine cause. However, when speaking to reporters on that trip Diana said that she thought the landmines should be banned. This was not then the UK government's position, and ministers accused her of meddling in politics. The iconic images suddenly seemed to portray a celebrity out of step with the issues and their politics.

Rae, however, noted her words. He had found it difficult to get the campaign's view into the tabloids and was frustrated because the UK government's position was prominent in the popular press. He was keen to engage Diana's powers of obtaining good media coverage.

His opportunity came when he attended a conference in Japan starting the national campaign to ban landmines there. Diana had been invited but, unable to come, had written to send her apologies. The conference organisers asked Rae what the protocol was for conveying their thanks for her letter. He advised them that it should be sent in person and that he was prepared to take it to her. The organisers accordingly asked Michael Gibbons, Diana's secretary, if she could receive Rae in order that he might convey their thanks to her. This was arranged and Rae had his invitation to Kensington Palace.

It was a rather daunting prospect: 'I took some gifts from the Japan campaign and the conference report to Kensington Palace to meet Diana. It was like *Coronation Street* and *EastEnders* all rolled into one.' And it was a meeting with a problem, because it was meant to be a simple gesture of thanks, but Rae wanted to use it to invite a publicity-conscious person to get involved in a cause in which she had already been somewhat humiliated publicly. Neither Rae nor Diana was well prepared for it:

> I roll in there, this complete anti-royal, and no idea what I was going to say or how I was going to twist this thing round to make it work. She came in and as you'd expect was very charming and everything but probably had no idea what this was about. She'd have had a briefing document on me, so she'd know a little bit about me, she knew about MAG and she thought I was going to give a report about the Japan thing.

As it turns out, when Rae made his pitch, it may well have been better for its spontaneity:

> So I shook hands with her and we sat down on these remarkable ancient sofas they had there. [We had] a cup of tea and I got rid of the Japanese conference in two or three minutes. [I said] 'It was very good and they asked me to bring you these' and put them on the table. She said 'How lovely' and everything. And then there was just this moment where I realised that this was going to end two minutes later or I was going to be able to do it and I just said 'So how much are you interested *really* in landmines?' And I deliberately said it quite bluntly as a challenge. And she became quite defensive and said 'This was the most terrible thing I've ever seen.' She didn't talk about the minefield at all, she talked about the hospital wards. And she said 'Have you ever seen it?' and I said 'Yes, absolutely, that's why I asked you. You said you thought that landmines [should] be banned, can you help us?' She said 'I wish I could. What can I do?'
> So then we started a discussion. I said 'Well, the first thing is that you have got to know more, because you saw one minefield but they are all over the place and that's [just] one country.' I just gave her a very quick briefing about the countries and the problems and particularly the impacts on youngsters and the fact that these things were just growing, and they were making more. They were becoming less controllable because they were air delivered and then add to that the problem of cluster munitions and I painted this picture very, very quickly and I said 'We need help.' And I bluntly said 'I can talk to the *Guardian* and I can talk to the *Telegraph* [but I cannot talk to the tabloids].' She then completely opened up, rang the bell got more

4 Introduction

tea, had a word with Michael Gibbons, which was obviously cancelling whatever was next and we got into it.

So Diana was now really interested in helping, but her input needed a focus. This is when Rae's pragmatic streak took to the fore.

> I realised that this couldn't go on for ever and I needed to bring it to what's going to happen next. And she said 'I have been wanting to make a keynote speech; something that really says what I feel about this.' And I just lied through my teeth and said 'But that's perfect because we are in the process of organizing an NGO seminar on landmines and we don't have a keynote speaker and I don't want it to be someone political.' And of course it was just complete lies I was just inventing it.

It was only a brief lie. For at the very moment he spoke it Rae was rather actively planning that seminar. He had to. For a start he needed to conjure up some more details about this meeting to make it an attractive and realistic prospect for Diana to attend.

> She said 'Well, where will it be?' and I thought 'Oh fuck' because I knew that instantly if I said the wrong place it wasn't going to happen because anything where royalty goes takes months and months to actually approve. They have to send security people to check it. I had walked past the Royal Geographical Society on the way there so I said 'The Royal Geographical Society' because Prince Philip talks there. She said 'That's wonderful because they have everything.' I said 'Yeah, it would be great if you could do it.' She said 'What date?' I said, 'Well, we've got a couple of dates at the moment but because we didn't have a speaker we have been trying to keep it loose, but it's in about a month's time.' She said 'We'll sort that out in a minute.' We went out and saw Michael Gibbons [who] gave me two dates.

Well, Diana was on board. But unfortunately none of the other participants were. Nor yet was the rather prestigious venue aware that it was going to host this gathering. Rae had a realistic approach to the challenge, as he put it: 'I'd given myself a massive fucking problem.' And in such a situation it helps to appeal to other people's pragmatic streaks.

> First of all I called MAG and I spoke to my brother and said to him [we need] a seminar on landmines. He said 'That's a bit short notice.' I said 'Yes, Princess Diana is going to be the keynote speaker.' He said 'OK, right, we'll get everything moving.'

Two other NGOs quickly joined the meeting. This is technically called 'convening power' in the celebrity literature. It describes the ability famous people

Introduction **5**

have of making all the rest of us abandon our plans to fit around their agenda and needs.

But NGOs hungry for publicity are easy to enrol. Booking out the Royal Geographical Society (RGS) at just a month's notice was going to be a harder prospect. Rae knew this and after finishing the call with his brother, he quickly called the RGS.

> The bookings co-ordinator started to be negative and I said, 'I'm just up the road can I come and see you' because I knew on the phone I was just going to get a 'no'. So I went and explained the whole thing, about MAG and about the work we had been doing and I *didn't* mention Diana. And the co-ordinator said 'Well, what are the dates?' And I gave the two dates and the co-ordinator opened the book and said 'No, they are both [taken]'. And I said 'O damn, I am going to have to somehow sort this out because these are the only dates that Diana can do it.' And the co-ordinator said 'Diana?' I said 'Yes, Princess Diana, she's going to be the keynote speaker. I've just come from Kensington Palace, she's agreed, but these are the only two dates.' And of course the co-ordinator said 'Hmm, well these people haven't confirmed; they should have confirmed two days ago. OK, well we'll pencil you in.'

Convening power, it seems, could even work with the RGS. A conversation over a cup of tea had blossomed rather remarkably. In the space of a couple of hours, as Rae put it, 'I had the RGS, I had three NGOs, I had Princess Diana'.

The seminar, moreover, occurred in June 1997, just a month after the new Labour Government of the UK had taken office. They were keen to adopt a different stance from their Conservative predecessors. Clare Short, the Minister of the newly created Department for International Development also spoke as the second speaker (Rae recalls 'I absolutely loved telling her she wasn't the keynote'). Diana's speech was written by the late Lord Bill Deedes, a patron of MAG, based on key campaign themes and emphases agreed by Rae and Princess Diana. That speech, the seminar of which it was part and Diana's subsequent involvement are credited by Rutherford as helping the campaign to move the landmine issue from being a military problem to a humanitarian cause. A mountain of publicity and a determined, motivated Oslo conference all derived from one small but momentous 'lie'.[6]

But the story is not quite complete. For if we see this as merely a piece of brilliant opportunism by media hungry NGOs we will only see their side of it. We will miss Diana's own needs and skills. According to Rae: 'She had this extraordinary understanding of how the whole media mechanism [worked].' She delivered the speech on the day very well:

> She was a very clever speaker. She broke down the speech into a number of sectors she felt comfortable with. She had this ability to deliver a speech

6 Introduction

very well, she was very clear about the optimum length she could give. She learnt it [and] knew when to look up at the press.

She was also thoroughly, and, in Rae's experience of public figures, unusually engaged:

> What was important about her and what made her a good personality in that way was that she understood that what she was talking about was something important. It is not enough to go and see a hospital ward to do that. I don't think that it comes with intellectual capacity or cleverness or education. [The landmine cause] was something that made her angry and upset and she believed that she could make a difference and so she gave time to it. That to me is quite rare.

Furthermore, while MAG and other organisations could inform her about important issues, she had to put all this into her voice and in a way that would appeal to the people she knew listened to her.

> We needed her to say the right things *but* at the same time in her voice. If she was going to say the same things that I said or that MAG said or anyone else it was just a princess. And for me that was not useful. You needed to use her personality, her voice and her world. Who are the people who listen to her who don't listen to us? What would she be interested to say and what would they be interested to hear her say? What would make them engage with what we were doing?

This was a task she clearly achieved.

Moreover, Diana combined that skill and passion with a more personal reason to take up this cause. She explained all of this to Rae at their first meeting in Kensington Palace.

> One of the extraordinary things was that she completely opened up then and was completely honest in the way that I tend to be and just said 'Look, I'm not pretending. I care about this but I also realise that if I am going to survive, in the situation I am in, I have to be visible, I have to be engaged. I'm engaged on AIDS. I need to be engaged with things that people care about.'
>
> Basically she knew that, if you fuck up the Royal Family, if you are to survive, you need to have the right sort of profile. And in that way she did not come across as fluffy headed. She was able to put the two things together in a very logical way and then talk business about it.
>
> Author: 'The two things being?'
>
> 'Well, her personal need to do it and the fact that she cared about it.'

Introduction **7**

Her 'personal need' refers to her need for a good public image and favourable publicity with causes that mattered to the public. This mix of motives strengthened her ability to serve the campaign:

> The two things [are] to me perfect. You have got somebody who has a personal commitment, a survival commitment, and at the same time they really do care about it and they've seen something of it. Fantastic, that was all I wanted.

The context and purpose of this book

This book examines celebrity advocacy for development and humanitarian causes. I began with the story of Diana's (re)recruitment to the landmine campaign because it captures some of the book's key themes. First, and most importantly, it demonstrates the central role that NGOs have played in pursuing and developing relationships with public figures, even reorganising their operations to work better with them. Diana's advocacy is significant because it marks the beginning of a new era of intensified relations between NGOs and celebrity – and probably even contributed to that intensification.

Celebrity advocacy has now become an important part of the constitution of humanitarianism and international development. It is systematically organised by development and humanitarian NGOs with potentially significant repercussions for public understanding of development and fundraising. It affects their politics and policy decisions. Celebrity advocates are significant new actors within the terrain of development advocacy and their work is recognised as a discrete social activity by the British public.[7]

The prominence of celebrity advocacy in development is visible in numerous ways. Most of the major development NGOs devote web space to their celebrity ambassadors, and they have permanent full-time celebrity liaison officers among their staff. This is part of a shift within the practices of the NGO sector that allows it better to accommodate and work with celebrity supporters, and corporate interest in those supporters. Relationships between NGOs and these supporters have become systematic and organised. They constitute an established niche of the celebrity industries. Most celebrities, and the vast majority of the most famous celebrities, publicly support charitable causes.[8] All this has happened relatively recently but the relationships had begun to prosper so thoroughly that in 2005 *Time* magazine was talking about the 'year of charitainment'.[9] In his analysis of development campaigns from 1991 to 2011 Brendan Cox included a special section on the impact of celebrity because he said that 'every single one of the case studies mentioned celebrity as a core element of their influencing strategy'.[10]

Part of the purpose of this book, then, is to explore what the rise of celebrity advocacy has achieved for international development. But this advocacy is not just important for what it does to development issues, or to development and humanitarian NGOs. It is part of a bigger struggle. For the story of celebrity

8 Introduction

advocacy, of the work of the famous in good causes, indeed the very activities of 'development' itself, are part of a long battle within the democracies that govern us. The battle is about the ability of elites to determine the character and structure of our societies. Celebrities are, by definition, members of those elites. At the same time, some of them can be populist and popular; they can join with and speak 'for the people'. This ambivalent terrain is contested. Corporate and political elites will want celebrities to speak for them and to reinforce their views, legitimacy and privilege. Other groups will want them to challenge such inequalities. Celebrity advocacy matters because it is a means of speaking to power.

But there is an important twist here, a peculiar ambiguity at work in celebrity advocacy. It attempts to engage the public, but the public can be nonplussed by these efforts. The very act of public engagement in the form of celebrity can alienate. This response, however, is not widely recognised. For the most part it is accepted that celebrities engage the public. In particular, those who are most invested in this belief in celebrity's popular power are the elites themselves. Celebrity advocacy works with elites, *despite* its lack of resonance with much of the public, because elites believe it to. Celebrity advocacy, then, is not just a means of working with elite-dominated politics, it is a reshaping of politics according to the imagination of the elites who dominate it.

This complicated situation provides another reason to start with the story about Princess Diana. For Diana's role in the International Campaign to Ban Landmines illustrates one of the central issues, and paradoxes, that celebrity advocacy raises for the function and characteristics of democracy. For her role appeared, to most of us, to be about raising public awareness. But her work was part of a broader strategy that Cox characterises as 'a predominantly elite-level campaign'.[11] Popular support was important, and, with Diana's influence, clearly provided a powerful imperative to the treaty negotiators. But much of the work was done behind the scenes with elites. Moreover, Diana's influence clearly worked there. Her convening power extended to the RGS. And, as Rutherford reported (p. 1), it was her influence on 'many diplomats', who were doing the actual negotiation, that was vital.[12]

Diana's example is also important because it is frequently mentioned as an emblematic case of celebrity advocacy. But it is an example that must be used with care because it is unusual. Diana's popularity can disguise the general lack of engagement that I contend characterises many responses to celebrity and celebrity advocacy. My point here is that we cannot extrapolate from Diana's popular advocacy to celebrity advocacy generally.[13] She was plainly exceptional. When we consider public responses to celebrity advocacy it is not reasonable to use her example as a model for others.

In this book I want to look beyond unusual cases and distracting individuals. My purpose, the book's purpose, is better to understand the economic and political circumstances surrounding the rise of celebrity advocacy, and thus also better understand its consequences, at home and abroad. As I will make clear in Chapter 3, central to that understanding are concepts of 'post-democracy'.[14] Post-democracy describes politics that are characterised by a loss of democratic verve and the corresponding rise of government by elite, and particularly corporate elites. The task of government becomes managing societies and economies in the interests of corporate power – and they do so with at least the passive consent (little more is possible) of most of the electorate.[15] The contribution of this book is to consider how celebrity advocacy helps us to grasp the nature and form of this elite rule.

The argument

The argument of this book hinges on four paradoxes of celebrity advocacy. The first paradox is that celebrity advocacy occupies a significant proportion of the public domain, but does so without always engaging particularly well with much of the public. Celebrity is populist in form, but not always popular in character. Second, that failure to engage the public does not really matter. Celebrity advocacy can be a remarkably effective tool for working with corporate and government elites. It works partly because they experience closer, less mediated, encounters with celebrity advocates and partly because these elites, and the NGO elites lobbying them, are unlikely to notice any lack of engagement by the general public. It would be hard to. Good evidence of what public engagement with celebrity constitutes is scarce. The assumption that celebrity advocacy is popular is deeply rooted. What matters, however, is that they *believe* that celebrities are embodying the affective will of the people.[16] Third, it is not just elites who may be deceived as to the nature of celebrities' influence; in the glare of publicity we, the viewers and consumers of celebrity spectacle, are also blinded. We may think that the publicity is the important aspect of celebrity, but publicity can be a sideshow; what matters goes on behind the scenes.

My argument, therefore, is that celebrity advocacy, which is now so well organised by NGOs, marks, ironically, a disengagement between the public and politics, and particularly between the public and the civil society organisations that try to represent development and humanitarian needs. It is not an expression of the popular will because the evidence indicates that interest in celebrity seems rather thinner and more variable than we might expect. Its rise has not been fuelled by popular demand but by corporate power. Celebrity advocacy is by and for elites. It provides a means for NGO elites to work more effectively with corporate and policy elites, not the broader population. As such, celebrity advocacy is part of the lived practices of post-democracy.

And what are the consequences of this state of affairs for the achievements of celebrity advocates for development? My argument here is that thus far the influence of celebrity on development issues and problems per se has been relatively limited. Celebrity is rather good at sustaining an NGO sector, but not necessarily good at tackling inherently problematic development issues. However, I will also argue that the new development actors that celebrities constitute could be used more imaginatively, and progressively, than at present. The final paradox is that the very post-democratic politics that can make elites oppressive may also contain within it the possibilities of making celebrity advocacy progressive.

10 Introduction

Unpopular celebrity?

The astute reader will have noted some apparent contradictions in the lines above. I seem to think that celebrity is both a vital and important part of our societies *and* that it is significantly overrated. Its influence, I seem to be saying, is both widespread and exaggerated. Other readers may struggle with my suggestion that celebrity might be populist, without being popular. This will probably sound odd, if not just plain absurd. Since celebrity fills the news and media all around us, surely most people must be interested in it?

The contradiction disappears if we distinguish between the nature of celebrity's influence, and *belief* in its influence. It is precisely because celebrity's influence is exaggerated that it is widespread. One of the clearest results of the surveys I conducted is that a majority of Britons say they are not taken in by celebrity advocacy, but that most people believe, falsely, that most other people are. The force of celebrity derives from the perception of its power. It is because so many people, and particularly so many members of elite groups, are mistaken as to celebrity's actual influence that it becomes so influential. There is, therefore, no contradiction here. Rather, we have a paradox that constitutes the very possibilities for celebrity politics.

As for the idea that celebrity is populist but not popular, I admit that celebrity is all over the news, but surely the relevant question here is 'how do people consume this material?' It is surprisingly hard to discern what people might think about celebrity.[17] Those data that I have been able either to find suggest that if you ask Britons about their consumption of celebrity, many seem to pay much less attention to it than you might first expect.

Note, too, the key word 'Britons' in the preceding paragraph. My work was conducted among the British public, and I am talking about the reach and influence of celebrity primarily in British politics and public affairs. The prominent role of British-based organisations in development affairs internationally makes the country a good case study. But it means that we have to extrapolate to other countries with caution, just as we should be cautious about extrapolating from others (particularly the US) to Britain.[18] I will make some observations about other countries, but in the main, with respect to audience responses, I can only talk about Britain.

Authentic advocacy?

My final reason for beginning with the story of Princess Diana and landmines is that it gives me the opportunity to distance this book from the debate about whether celebrities 'really' care about the charities they support or whether they are just after the publicity. I do not find the authenticity of celebrity altruism a particularly interesting issue. But given its prevalence I need to say why.

In part the problem is that this debate misrecognizes the nature of the need for publicity and its significance for celebrity supporters. Many famous people do not need the extra publicity that charitable activities can bring – Diana least of all. But even Diana had, as we would say nowadays, to manage her 'brand'. Her work for charity was part of the public persona she cultivated. And, as those close to her work with landmines testified, cultivating that public persona was compatible with caring deeply about an issue. Mixing publicity considerations with her desire to oppose landmines did not compromise her support. It simply demonstrates that she, as almost all other supporters of any cause, had more than one motive for working with the campaign.[19]

The debate about celebrity motivation somehow imagines celebrities might be an exceptional form of volunteer who are only altruistic. But research on volunteers demonstrates clearly that their motives are mostly mixed. Pure altruism, oddly demanded of celebrity advocates, is rare. Sean Kelly's master's thesis provides a useful corrective here. He surveyed 169 celebrity advocates who he was able to contact via their shared interest in the charity Sparks, finding a mixture of altruistic and egotistical motives at work, with the altruistic ones dominant.[20]

But perhaps most importantly, this issue entails a problematic use of ideas of 'authenticity' itself. There is not space to do justice to this topic here but suffice to say that the nature of authenticity has changed over time.[21] In Victorian times being authentic meant internalising a set of ideal values. Self-realisation was achieved by becoming a model character and embodying ideals of honesty, politeness and self-control. By the later decades of the twentieth century this was reversed. Authenticity was about expressing one's true inner core, despite the constraints of social demands. Somogy Varga argues that this has in turn been replaced by a form of authenticity based on performance.[22] Inner qualities are important, but what matters most is how they are performed, for demonstrating your difference makes the authentic 'you' visible. In this respect authenticity is non-referential. It does not refer back to an ideal type, but rather collates and creates a plausible 'performance of difference'.

As I will demonstrate in Chapter 6, authentic celebrity advocacy is not given within people's character, experience, history or expertise. It is a potential that is recognised and brought into effect. It is also, and this is crucial, *performed* to the media for broader public consumption. Authenticity therefore is constructed, negotiated and mediated over time, and between people and institutions. Authentic celebrity advocacy is not about internalising a required set of advocacy norms, nor is it about expressing one's real self. Neither of these can suffice. It is about collating a plausible set of associations, experiences, connections and insights.

Whether celebrities 'really' care or not is the wrong question to ask. Instead, we need to ask how potential advocates are recognised and enrolled. We need to ask how they perform. For the rise of celebrity advocates in recent years denotes neither a new compassion, nor a new celebrity hunger for publicity. Both are rather old. It reflects the changing circumstances and organisation of celebrity advocacy.

We need to see authenticity as constructed and performed in order to understand the power and function of celebrity spectacle in post-democratic politics.[23] Authentic celebrity advocates provide resources for politicians and NGOs who need to be seen to be popular, or populist. Likewise, associating with politicians and

12 Introduction

policy-makers lends celebrity advocates gravitas and significance. The construction of authenticity is an integral part of the lubrication and manipulation of elite-dominated politics.

I am therefore not interested in this book in trying to sift 'genuine' support from publicity-driven support. I will not try to determine what motive is pre-eminent in the minds of celebrity advocates. These considerations have little bearing on my argument. Instead, I will try to understand the processes constructing celebrity advocacy.

Methods

I have drawn upon numerous sources that I summarise briefly here and discuss in more detail in Appendix One. One of my most important activities was a series of interviews with over 120 NGO staff, journalists, employees in the celebrity industries and other researchers. I promised all interviewees anonymity and refer to them as numbered sources in the text below. I explored attitudes to celebrity in the British public by means of two large surveys (to 1,111 and 1,999 people respectively) administered to the UK Public Opinion Monitor. The Monitor is a panel database, which means that successive surveys are posed to the same group of people – it is not composed of two random samples. I also conducted nine focus groups to explore responses to celebrity advocacy. Finally, I undertook surveys of newspapers and magazines, using electronic records and library deposits.

There are significant omissions in these methods (discussed in Appendix One). Nevertheless, I believe they make a contribution to what Nick Couldry calls, following Bourdieu, 'a practice approach' to the use and production of media forms, and to Graeme Turner's call to improve understanding of the production and consumption of celebrity.[24] I look at how media, celebrity and NGO professionals are constructing and creating diverse forms of celebrity advocacy across all sorts of media. I also enquire as to how publics in Britain, and corporate and political elites respond to these representations and relationships. The result goes some way to meet Couldry's desire to explain the power of the media (in this case celebrity advocacy) in ways that take into account the 'plurality of practices' surrounding celebrity advocacy on the ground.[25]

An outline of the chapters

In brief, the book proceeds as follows: the next two chapters discuss the important ideas and writings with which any study of celebrity advocacy has to engage. I then review the history of celebrity advocacy (Chapter 4). Chapters 5 and 6 examine respectively the current state of celebrity advocacy and how it is co-ordinated and managed by NGOs. Chapters 7 and 8 explore the different responses to celebrity advocacy in elite groups (Chapter 7) and British publics (Chapter 8). The Conclusion (Chapter 9) examines what we have learned from all of this and its implications for development and post-democratic politics.

Introduction **13**

In more detail, the substance of the chapters is as follows. I begin by examining the problems of portraying the needs of distant strangers, and the sorts of public awareness of development with which NGOs are wrestling and producing (Chapter 2). This review demonstrates the limited public understanding of development with which celebrity advocacy must contend, as well as emphasising the importance of looking at celebrity advocacy with elites. Chapter 3 examines debates about celebrity advocacy more specifically, and the broader debates about media and democracy of which they are part. I discuss thinking about the role of elites and elite lobbying in post-democracy, and contrasting views about the democratic implications of new media forms of which celebrity is part, focusing specifically on critiques of celebrity advocacy. I argue that these critiques have not sufficiently got to grips with the anatomy of celebrity advocacy– the nuts and bolts of how it is done. Chapters 2 and 3 cover the main theoretical ground with which we need to be familiar if we are to understand and analyse the phenomenon of celebrity advocacy for development and humanitarian causes. Each chapter ends with the important questions that I distil from the literature, and which I will attempt to answer in the Conclusion.

I then offer a short history of celebrity interventions in development and humanitarian causes (Chapter 4). This, rather surprisingly, goes back a long way. In fact, it is arguable that the real peak of celebrity advocacy for development occurred in the Victorian era. I will show that the relationship between fame and development has been patchy and intermittent since then, but has become increasingly intense in the last ten years. But in describing that long relationship I also show that the current crescendo of celebrity philanthropy differs from previous eras, and particularly from earlier decades. The change derives from the changing nature of the contest over what development means. For that contest is now marked by the dominance of neoliberal thinking, which in turn both engenders and is nurtured by post-democratic politics. Thus, a political space for celebrity interventions in development and humanitarianism is forged.

We can then review the current state of celebrity advocacy (Chapter 5). This chapter makes two important points for the argument as a whole. First, I make plain that behind the crescendo of celebrity advocacy in the last 10–15 years there lies a profound reorganisation and systematisation of the relationships between the celebrity and NGO sectors. Second, when we evaluate the achievements of celebrity advocates, personal, unmediated, encounters between NGO supporters and celebrity supporters appear particularly useful. This will help us to understand celebrity advocacy's effectiveness with elites later.

Having explored how interactions have changed over time, and what sort of celebrity advocacy is now going on, we can examine how these interactions are constructed. Chapter 6 traces a number of common experiences and practices that shape the interactions of NGOs and the celebrity industry which are now taught by celebrity liaison officers in workshops and disseminated in blogs and websites. It then examines the forces shaping the presentation of celebrity advocacy and particularly celebrity field-trips overseas. This chapter explores in more detail the nature of the authenticity that celebrity advocates for development display.

14 Introduction

Chapters 5 and 6 constitute one of the three key pillars of this book, for they make the case for a systematic and organised set of NGO relations with celebrity among the largest development and humanitarian NGOs. Effective lobbying in post-democracies has required new forms of civil society organisation and operation. These chapters explain how celebrity advocates are organised and marshalled to enable development and humanitarian NGOs to work more effectively in post-democracies.

Crucial to the shaping of celebrity advocacy practices with NGOs, and their workings in post-democratic polities, are the way in which celebrity advocates and elites interact, and these are explored in Chapter 7. Business elites are keen to encounter and work with public figures, political elites love meeting them and being seen to do so, celebrities love meeting other elites, and media elites need access to all these groups. On the basis of interview data examining when and with whom celebrity works, and by drawing on grey literature from elite gatherings, this chapter explains how well celebrity advocacy works in elite-dominated politics.

Chapter 7 provides the second pillar of the book, for it demonstrates the importance of corporate interests in shaping NGO strategies, the effectiveness with which celebrity ambassadors then work with political and corporate elites, and how thoroughly elites believe in the power of celebrity advocacy. It also shows that relationships between celebrities and NGOs are constitutive of post-democratic elite governance, particularly with respect to international development.

But what are different audiences making of all of this? Chapter 8 examines how Britons respond to celebrity advocacy using the survey data and focus groups. These data show that interest in celebrity is a minority affair, but that it is popularly, and falsely, believed to be popular. Nonetheless, Britons help to build its edifice because they demonstrate widespread *belief* in its efficacy. That belief is founded on celebrity's place in the glamorous 'media world', and because they believe charitable donations are an effective way of engaging in politics.

This chapter provides the final pillar of the book. For it presents the evidence that celebrity is not as popular as it might at first appear. It shows that celebrity advocacy can signal a form of disengagement from publics, not populist engagement with them. Celebrity advocacy is thus one of the components of the separation of the demos from the institutions that rule them.

And so we come to the issue of what all this means for international development. What does this study add to our understanding of celebrity, to development and the world that celebrified development is creating? What does it portend for international development itself? I examine in the Conclusion how celebrity advocacy affects public understandings of development and what prospects there are for using celebrity effectively to combat international economic inequities. Here I present the argument that in post-democratic politics more celebrity lobbying, elitist though it is, may well be required. I suggest that those who argue for more powerful democracies and democratic deliberation of development policies need to consider the character of the public sphere in post-democracies for their recommendations about globally just economic policies to take effect.

Finally, in my last word, the Afterword, I present a more personal reaction to all that I have just written, and its prospects for international development.

Notes

1 Rutherford, 2011: 102–3.
2 All cited in Rutherford, 2011: 107–14.
3 A treaty signing ceremony had already been announced before Diana joined the campaign, and the process to negotiate the clauses that would be discussed in Oslo in September 1997 was underway when she first went to a minefield in Angola. Diana's posthumous influence was on the negotiation of those clauses. According to Rutherford, the sessions were recorded but he has been unable to find copies of the tapes, and it is not clear where they are held (personal communication, 27 June 2012). Without them it will be difficult to determine what lies behind the rhetoric of ministers proclaiming her influence. With respect to her influence in setting the political agenda and facilitating dialogue and meetings Rutherford writes: 'In my personal day-to-day dealings on landmines during that time period, the words "Princess Diana" were on everyone's lips [with] regards to landmines . . . agenda setting, opening doors, attracting political and media attention, were less challenging with her involvement period' (personal communication, 27 June 2012). On reading a draft of this introduction he wrote: 'At the Center for International Stabilization and Recovery, we all personally think your conclusion should be that her influence continues today. Almost everyone we meet who knows where we work brings up Princess Diana; she was a huge influence on the world on this topic' (personal communication, 28 September 2012). Brendan Cox's analysis of the campaign notes Diana's influence, but does not assign it a crucial role. Instead, he emphasises the importance of the close working relationship the campaign enjoyed with the Canadian government (Cox, 2011: 46). See also Scott (2001) and Huliaris and Tzifakis (2010).
4 Cox reports over 1,000 groups being part of the ICBL (2011: 34); Rutherford reports attendance at the treaty negotiations and signing ceremony (2011: 110, 117).
5 I have smoothed the transcript of the interview, missing out 'erms', 'you knows', 'sort ofs', and occasional asides and I have not indicated with '. . .' where those cuts fall. This polished version reads better, and is thus a more accurate experience of listening to Rae's well-told story. Rae has also checked this version. I am grateful to him for permission to use it.
6 More well-known lies in celebrity advocacy, which were also momentous, were those told by Bob Geldof (a musician) to the managers of the bands he was persuading to make the record *Feed the World* in aid of famine relief to Ethiopia in 1984. He told them that the other bands were on board, when in fact they were not. Collectively deceived, they all joined in (Geldof, 1986).
7 Note that advocacy has an interesting homogenising effect across different types of celebrity. For example, Joanna Lumley (an established actress) and Olly Murs (a less established X Factor finalist) may appear under the same organisation's website as 'celebrity advocates' (see entry to SightSavers in Table 5.1); other organisation websites (such as the Red Cross) lists consecutively different public figures of different renown.
8 Thrall *et al.* found that 63 per cent of a random sample of 147 celebrities on Celebopedia, and 90 per cent of the Forbes top 100 celebrities in 2006 were engaged in celebrity advocacy (Thrall *et al.*, 2008).
9 Poniewozik, 2005.
10 Cox, personal communication, 8 January 2013.
11 Cox, 2011: 10.
12 In October 1996 (months before Diana's first involvement) the Canadian government announced unilaterally that it would host a treaty-signing ceremony in December 1997, thereby precipitating the intense diplomatic activity required to produce the clauses for

16 Introduction

negotiation in Oslo. Hence influence on diplomats involved in that negotiation was important.

13 cf. Brown *et al.*, 2003: 601.
14 Crouch, 2004. 'Post-democracy' is also described by Jacques Ranciére and Chantal Mouffe (Nash, 1996; Ranciére, 1998; Mouffe, 2005).
15 Ranciére, 1998: 113.
16 My thanks to Lisa Richey for that phrase.
17 cf. Turner, 2006 in the notes of which there is mention of a discussion with Nick Couldry about what evidence there is as to the actual grassroots appetite for celebrity.
18 cf. Couldry, 2001: 173; 2012: 179. The US has dominated research on celebrity, particularly, but not only with respect to marketing research, as we shall see in Chapter 7 (and Appendix Three). We need to see US engagements with celebrity as specific to that country, not typical of others. The histories of celebrity and cinema in the US suggest that it is an unusual case (Barbas, 2001). Central to Laurie Ouellette and James Hay's intimate and detailed study of Reality TV in the US (2008) is the fact that such TV can only be understood in the context of broader political, social and economic contexts found in their country – and that other Reality TV programmes in other countries need to be understood according to those contexts. Cooper has also recognised that the significance of celebrity advocates differs between the 'Anglosphere' (i.e. US and UK) and continental Europe (Cooper, 2008b). Grainger and colleagues' analysis of celebrity sports advertising hinges on the different way different celebrities are received around the globe (Grainger *et al.*, 2005).
19 For example, Diana once told Ken Rutherford that she went to Bosnia because 'reporters and photographers have made my life horrible, so I would like to make their life horrible by taking them to places they normally otherwise would not visit and covering issues they normally would not cover' (Rutherford, 2011: 108). Tempting the paparazzi to stray into a minefield may have made walking through one about as pleasurable as it can get, but it was unlikely to be her only reason for going.
20 Kelly, 2012.
21 For detailed discussions of the concept, see Goffman, 1959 [1990]; Berman, 1970 [2009]; Trilling, 1971; MacCannell, 1973; Taylor, 1989, 1991; Benjamin, 1999; MacCannell, 1999 [1976]; Lindholm, 2002; Guignon, 2004; Lindholm, 2008; MacCannell, 2008a, b; Varga, 2011.
22 Varga, 2011.
23 cf. Chouliaraki, 2013: 114.
24 Turner, 2010; Couldry, 2012: 37.
25 Couldry, 2012: 65.

2

THE TERRAIN OF DEVELOPMENT ADVOCACY

> [A]pproaching the theatricality of humanitarianism in its full ambivalence . . . treat[s] its paradoxes not as a priori disabling facts that define the meaning of solidarity once and for all but as productive tensions that may settle the meaning of solidarity in different ways, at different moments in time.
>
> Lilie Chouliaraki[1]

Most of the actual activities involved in development – the planning, projects and constant immanent change – happen in poorer parts of the world. But the advocacy, driven and stimulated by global inequalities, mostly happens in rich parts of the world.[2] Celebrity advocacy for international development is no exception. While often hinging on field-trips overseas, it does not happen 'over there'; it happens 'here'. It takes place in fundraising meetings, private lobbying and media events, on the pages of magazines reporting field-trips, and in the consumption of websites, news items and tweets in our homes, offices and trains.

The representations and reception of development and humanitarian issues constitute what I call the 'terrain of development advocacy'. This chapter examines two key issues of that terrain. First, I look at the challenges facing the portrayal of poverty and inequality of distant strangers in the media and the difficulty these portrayals face in building relationships, empathy and acknowledgement of others' needs. I do this by discussing theoretical contributions to this issue, and also by examining actual trends in the portrayal of development issues in the British media. Second, I examine the levels of development awareness the British public tends to display. The awareness is rather thin and combined with a tendency to try to address development causes through charitable giving rather than political action. In the conclusion I consider the implications of this terrain for analyses of celebrity advocacy and the questions we must ask of it.

18 The terrain of development advocacy

Seeing suffering, seeking justice

I will not recite the statistics of deprivation that normally begin books like this. The deaths and illnesses of young children, the want of clean water, education or safe homes – all are documented regularly in the reports of the United Nations Development Programme (UNDP), World Bank and annual publications of leading development organisations. I will assert that the key problem that development and humanitarian organisations address, which is driving the appearance of those other evils, is the problem of inequality.

Inequality matters for three reasons. First, in many forms it can be evil in itself. Inequality is frequently iniquitous. It is associated with lower standards of living, life expectancy and environmental performance.[3] It is a bigger problem than poverty in that it is more widespread – afflicting wealthy countries and poor ones. Poverty reduction is faster if inequality is also reduced, whereas inequality's increase is associated with more unhappiness, resentment and civil disturbance. Or, put differently, there is little point in countries becoming wealthier if the proceeds of wealth are not well distributed.

Second, inequality matters because defence of privilege has driven regressive change and policies for centuries. Inequality does not merely describe circumstances that will be miserable for most people and happy for a few. Inequality can become an active force preventing beneficial change. As we shall see when exploring ideas of post-democracy, it can strongly shape the character and deficiencies of our democracies. International trade relations and the negotiations of the World Trade Organisation, to take another example, are dominated by controversies over the rules that privilege wealthy countries. Creating fairer trade rules is one of the enduring calls of the development movement, and one of the most strongly resisted.

The third reason is that, paradoxically, the practical love that humanitarianism and international development entail, and the solidarity they seek, can only be produced by inequality. Our attitudes to inequality at home and abroad are fundamental to the possibilities of cultivating what the late Stan Cohen might have called 'cultures of acknowledgement', in which citizens are alive to the needs of their neighbours – be they compatriots or more distant strangers. But those attitudes have to negotiate, as Didier Fassin has explored, a 'tension between inequality and solidarity, between a relation of domination and a relation of assistance, [that] is constitutive of humanitarian government.'[4]

Resolving that tension requires that humanitarian assistance tries to tackle not only the symptoms of the problems (the sickness, hunger, want) but also the forces that drive these depredations. It matters therefore a great deal whether the impulse of humanitarian responses is about tackling the structures producing need, or dishing out palliative remedies that can only ease present suffering. Both are necessary, but only offering palliatives is deeply unsatisfactory. The triumph of humanitarianism and development is that they can confront injustice; their terror is that they can make us feel that we are tackling great ills, when we might not be, or worse still, adding to them.[5]

The terrain of development advocacy **19**

Amid such great expectations and responsibilities one of the most common ways in which celebrity advocacy seeks to make a difference is by making problems visible, by publicly endorsing attempts to address injustice. However, its ability to do so may be constrained from the outset. This is because of the dominance of pity, not justice, in the modes of representing others' needs and because of the sorts of distance this maintains between spectators and the needs they view.

The distinction between a 'politics of pity' and 'politics of justice' is developed by Luc Boltanski, following Hannah Arendt.[6] The politics of justice is concerned with equity, with resolving disputes over distributions of resources, or fortune and misfortune, according to ideals of fairness. In terms of the distinction I offer above, between structural causes and palliative remedies, it is concerned with the causes. Pity is concerned less with causes and more with outcomes. Its mandate, and sole sphere of activity, is the existence of the unfortunate.

Boltanski also takes up Arendt's distinction between pity and another form of concern, which she labelled 'compassion'. Compassion is local, it is not merely voiced, but is practically expressed in actions by people who physically meet each other. Pity, in contrast, generalises. It voices its concerns and it hinges on distance: 'it is inherent in a politics of pity to deal with suffering from the standpoint of distance since it must rely upon the massification of a collection of unfortunates, who are not there in person.'[7] Pity depends on the spectacle of suffering, on the fortunate being able to observe the problems and difficulties of the unfortunate.[8]

Cohen's book *States of Denial* could be taken as a devastating account of lives, the spectators' lives, lived under a regime of the politics of pity. Cohen's question is 'what is it that enables us to see, recognize, acknowledge and respond to other people's needs?', whether those be our relatives, partners, neighbours, compatriots or strangers who we will never meet and with whom we may never communicate. He also poses the corollary: 'what it is, and how it is possible, to live in denial of those needs?'

To me, his book recalls a famous exchange recorded in Luke's gospel between Jesus and a religious lawyer.[9] The lawyer, testing Jesus, asked what he had to do to inherit eternal life. Jesus asked him what was written in the law, and the lawyer parsed it correctly: 'Love God with all your heart, soul, mind and strength, and love your neighbour as yourself.' But then the lawyer asked his supplementary question: 'And who is my neighbour?' Jesus's answer was deliberately insulting and outrageous, telling a parable of how the most revered men in Jewish circles, a priest and a Levite, avoided helping an injured man (whose blood would have ritually sullied them), but how a Samaritan, reviled by Jews for their heretical beliefs, aided him. The implication was that these holiest of men were not acting in a way that deserved eternal life. The lowliest, who by definition of his faulty understanding of the law should not be getting anywhere near heaven, somehow was.

That conversation took place in a different media environment from the present. Distant needs were often unknown, they could not be communicated with much speed, and scarcely acted upon very easily. Distance, in the main, was local.

20 The terrain of development advocacy

It was defined by rules of exclusion and separation that meant, for example, that Samaritans were ungodly and defiled.

But the question, 'who is my neighbour?', and its outrageous answer 'those who need you, however distant, alien and offensive to you,' is as troublesome now as then. In our present media environments we can hear of people who might need us, and respond to them instantly, even if they are an ocean away. This is why Cohen's work is so disturbing. He takes some of the worst conflicts and political violence of the last century and asks how people have responded to the demands these disasters have placed on them. How was it possible for tens of millions of people to be complicit in the Holocaust? How can Turkey, and its allies, still deny the genocide its soldiers committed in Armenia during the First World War? How could states not act during the Rwandan genocide? But then he twists the knife. From those unusual situations he then considers much more common dilemmas facing us all. How could we not protest against disappearances in Argentina, or human rights abuses in Iraq, or the poverty on our doorsteps? How could we not take a more vigorous stance on the iniquitous economic, trade, debt and development policies with which rich countries have made the prospects of poor countries difficult for decades? Or, in its most general terms, how do we respond individually and collectively to the needs thrust into our consciousness unremittingly by the media?

With an unrelenting logic, Cohen's argument is that we are all bystanders. We observe and learn about suffering and do not respond. There is always something horrible going on about which we know, but about which we do nothing: 'All of us don't care sometimes or about some things; some of us don't seem to care about anything most of the time.'[10] In fact, acting effectively on problems *requires* denial of others: 'the really effective people are self-consciously selective about which problems they take on. "Doing something" is possible only if they do not allow themselves to be overwhelmed.'[11]

Living a life of complete acknowledgement is impossible, but, Cohen asks, what conditions encourage more denial than others? With respect to our responses to news about suffering he argues that it is not the repetition of these images that is the problem.

> There is, after all, no such thing as love fatigue. And most parents do not become numbed or oblivious to their child's pain and suffering however often she bumps her head or cries. The problem with multiple images of distant suffering is not their multiplicity but their psychological and moral *distance*.[12]

This is why his book is an account of our lives lived under the politics of pity. Distance, as Arendt and Boltanski have shown, is a prerequisite for the politics of pity, which has been the dominant narrative for many decades. It is also, for Cohen, a condition of denial.

How, then, can any portrayal of development promote justice and acknowledgement? Does the dominance of distance and pity render all celebrity advocacy, indeed any form of advocacy, impotent in the face of injustice, and likely to promote denial and inaction?

Roger Silverstone provides one way out of this dilemma. What is required, he observes, is 'proper distance'. Humanity is united, Silverstone argues, by virtue of the fact that we are all different from each other, so 'it is precisely the commonality of difference which is shared'.[13] For the media to facilitate mutual understanding between different peoples it has to cultivate a proximity that promotes understanding and obligation but which is not too close. 'Proper distance preserves the other through difference as well as through shared identity.'[14] Proper distance requires context, an understanding of the circumstances in which people live, and an empathetic imagination.[15]

The problem, however, is that proper distance is only rarely achieved in most media presentations of distant others, and even in the publicity material and campaigns of development NGOs. There are several issues here. On the one hand there are surprisingly fewer chances of hearing about other parts of the world on British media now than thirty years ago. This is visible in the print and broadcast media. In British newspapers the proportion of international news stories has declined as a whole (from 20 per cent in 1979 to 11 per cent in 2009), and within the first ten pages – where the most prominent stories tend to be listed (from 33 per cent to 15 per cent in the same time period).[16] On terrestrial television there has been a continual decline in the amount of time devoted to developing countries, such that in 2010 half as much was shown as in 1989 (when monitoring began). Instead, this content is migrating to the more marginal digital channels.[17]

Then there is the problem of how this world is portrayed when it appears. With respect to television, Lilie Chouliaraki has analysed how different forms of news reporting convey the needs of distant strangers to Northern publics in terms of the distances they develop between observer and observed.[18] She identified three types of news reporting. There are short reports 'without pity' and devoid of agency (persecutors or benefactors). She calls this 'adventure news'. 'Ecstatic news', its opposite, characterises, for example, reporting on the September 11 attacks or the 2004 tsunami. 'Emergency news', news with pity, brings in more agency and possibilities of response by the spectator. It also provides the greatest possibilities for realising the proper distance Silverstone called for as it recognises both the difference of the spectators from those being portrayed and the need for action. Ecstatic news tends to efface difference between observer and the observed.

Martin Scott has applied Chouliaraki's analysis to consider what ways people from poorer parts of the world appear on British television.[19] He found that in 2007 and 2010 the news mostly encouraged responses of indifference or reflective contemplation, not indignation at perpetrators of injustice or pity for those experiencing it. Scott also examined whether audiences responded as Chouliaraki suggested they would, finding that, in the main, they did.[20] He then examined portrayals of distant others in non-news formats (documentaries and especially entertainment) finding that they could provoke much more active and humane

22 The terrain of development advocacy

responses than news.[21] However, audiences have little chance to respond in this way as we very rarely learn about development issues through comedies, soap operas or dramas. Some 3 per cent of such international entertainment is about the developing world, 89 per cent of it about the USA. Instead, we learn about poorer parts of the world almost entirely through factual formats – and these tend to be rather unimaginative, tending to portray particular places in the same sort of ways, showing either conflict (the Middle East) or wildlife (Africa).

With respect to newspapers, articles tend not to communicate the causes of development problems well. Van Heerde and Hudson's study of 112 newspaper articles from eight British papers in 2005 found that 82 per cent of articles studied framed international poverty in self-interested terms, i.e. what this poverty implied for Northern readers, as opposed to moral framings based on, for example, justice or empathy.[22] The majority of articles did not discuss the causes of poverty. They argue that coverage of issues of poverty internationally are 'substantially more sensationalist and episodic than thematic'.[23]

With respect to NGO publicity, Nandita Dogra has examined the content of NGO publicity and campaigns, based on the materials produced by twelve organisations from February 2005 to January 2006.[24] She found a strong 'colonial presence' in the images she analysed that tend to erase the 'diversity, complexity and historicity' of poorer countries. These images did not give a good sense of the histories and politics of colonialism and imperialism that tie the rich world to the poor. The developing world and its peoples appeared historyless, awaiting development. She also shows that these images arise from organisations that are intensely conscious of the need to move away from negative stereotypes – and which have developed codes and practices for the use of good imagery in constructive campaigns – and yet she found the consequences dissatisfying.[25]

Celebrity has not generally featured in the literature above, but there is one detailed examination of the performance of celebrity advocacy for development and humanitarian causes. Chouliaraki has undertaken a comparative analysis of the contrasting performative strategies of the actresses Audrey Hepburn for the United Nations Children's Fund (UNICEF) (1988–93) and Angelina Jolie for the United Nations High Commissioner for Refugees (UNHCR) (since 2001).[26] She shows that the sorts of connection enabled depend on the style and manner of the celebrity's performance. Hepburn's performances drew attention away from her own celebrity and, through her acting skills, highlighted the needs of poor people in poor countries. She drew attention to herself, talking about her responses to what she had seen and her empathy with sufferers (based on her experience of wartime deprivation as a child) but did so as a professional messenger. Chouliaraki names this style ambassadorial/ceremonial because of its reliance on established conventions of representing suffering through rituals of acting. Jolie's work, in contrast, draws attention to her own celebrity status and her personal responses to the suffering she has witnessed. Her work with the UNHCR is part of an extensive repertoire of charitable acts, giving and political engagement that have been enacted prominently in the public eye.[27] They are part of a declared strategy of self-fulfilment, her professed desire to find 'some sense of purpose'.[28] When she talks about her experiences she often breaks down or suppresses tears. Chouliaraki labels this style 'entrepreneurial/confessional'.

The difference is important when it comes to audiences' responses to these performances. The confessional performance 'collapses the voice of the sufferer, invisible, distant and unnamed, with the voice of the celebrity, visible, "intimate" and world famous, and displaces the affective relationship between spectator and sufferer onto a relationship between spectator and celebrity.' [29] This in turn 'encourages the narcissistic disposition of voyeuristic altruism rather than a disposition of commitment to the humanitarian cause.'[30] The result may stymie efforts to produce long-term and meaningful change in that such 'voyeuristic altruism . . . may intensify connectivity with celebrity but does not necessarily facilitate a move to action'.[31]

For Chouliaraki this development is part of a broader trend towards 'post-humanitarianism'.[32] Post-humanitarianism is not so much based on a politics of pity, but a more ironic stance, which is self-focused not other-focused, and which seeks to root support for humanitarianism in personal lifestyle choices. Post-humanitarianism is also manifest – for example, in advertisements for humanitarian NGOs that seek primarily to make viewers aware of these NGOs' brand rather than the needs of distant others.

Note that Chouliaraki does not despair at this development. Post-humanitarianism engages with others' needs, just for different reasons than before. Indeed, she argues that problems such as the authenticity of celebrity testimony and the crippling lack of agency it can bestow on the needy, are inherent in the very *theatricality* of humanitarianism. Or, in other words, they stem from, and will always be present in, any attempt to present the needs of distant others to spectators. What matters, therefore, as the epigraph to this chapter underlines, is how audiences respond to these tensions and how different agencies handle their contradictions.

Nevertheless, examining what representations of needy others entails, and what responses they provoke, remains a sobering exercise. On one hand, we have seen that the dominant form of representing others is cast in a politics of pity, which hinges on the presence of distance, and can encourage denial and a failure to acknowledge others' needs. On the other hand, we learn that the present post-humanitarian alternative is grounded in a narcissistic concern for the self. We have also seen that empirical examinations of the forms of distance in media reports, or even just the simple plain presence of information about other places, are unlikely to promote a deep and rigorous concern for others.

The eminently post-democratic character of development issues begins to emerge from this analysis of the portrayal of development issues, for the way in which they are mediated and represented is not likely to advance empathy, understanding or action among broader publics. Indeed, for the ironic spectators of post-humanitarianism the very concept of a 'broader public' becomes irrelevant. What matters is what it does for me. This means that coherent understanding of distant strangers, and the structural economic inequalities and policies that drive

24 The terrain of development advocacy

development and inequality, becomes the provenance of elites. It belongs to the realm of professionals whose job is to understand the minutiae of policy and economic connections that bind and mutually create the global rich and poor. This fact will be reinforced when we consider public understandings of development in the next section.

Note, however, that there are multiple possibilities for celebrity engagement here. It could well be 'part of the problem' in that it is part of problematic and stereotypical representations, or is narcissistic. Or it could be innovative and novel in its communication. It could be, or become, part of new forms of entertainment that provoke the more desirable responses that Scott described.[33] The depressing nature of the terrain here does not constrain the possibilities of working with celebrity.

Public awareness of, and giving to, development causes

What are the consequences of the current modalities of communicating development issues for public awareness of and attitudes to development issues? The public awareness and understanding of development has animated numerous researchers, producing some reasonably clear findings.[34] I have summarised these below and tabulated the detail and evidence in Table 2.1. The main findings are:

1   International poverty is a low-status issue among the British public. About a quarter are 'very concerned' about it, but most do not think about it much at all.
2   Few people explain poverty in terms of relations between poor and wealthy countries.
3   Instead, there is a strong sense that the poor in the world are damned by their own corrupt and failing governments. This view prevails not only among those hostile or cynical about development but also among people who support development aid and are 'very concerned' about international poverty. Aid in particular is thought to be poorly managed by both recipient governments and NGOs.
4   Despite this, support for aid, or rather the *principle* of aid, is 'strong and stable'. This is consistent with a general trend in the global North since the early 1990s.
5   Note the word principle above. Most questionnaires have asked about support for levels of development aid in the wrong way. They have not told people what current levels of expenditure are, or if they did, expressed that in a meaningful way (dollars per capita) and presented expenditure on other sectors as a comparison. When people are asked about the actual money that should be spent on overseas aid, there are several indications of public ambivalence, if not hostility to development aid.
6   There is considerable ignorance about what aid is. Britons tend to think of overseas aid as something that charities do in the form of disaster relief; the role of British government funding is misunderstood and often neglected. Most

people do not know how much their own governments contribute to development aid.

7   Public attitudes to development are not well correlated to government spending on development. Studies of the relationship between public support for development and government giving for development suggests that there is none. Policy here is not populist.

In these trends are sedimented the consequences of decades of problematic publicity and representation of distant others. The results are a rather poor understanding of the nature of development, development aid and the causes of international poverty. Development, and particularly development policy, is *prima facie* an issue for policy-making elites.[35]

Despite the constancy of attitudes to development over time, giving to development NGOs is increasing. The trends are shown in Figure 2.1. Although only a minority of people give to development causes, giving has risen faster than increases in household income, and giving to the development sector has risen faster than growth in giving to other charitable sectors. Table 2.2 assembles the detailed evidence that lies behind the changes shown in the figure.

The issue of giving, however, is a rather fraught one in the development community. A persistent theme is the strength of the 'charity frame' with which the UK public approaches its relations to poorer parts of the world.[36] By this I mean that most people approach development problems as something that can be solved by giving money, rather than by taking on the tough political issues that cause poverty. Increased giving to development causes may thus reflect more effective use by fundraising departments of this apolitical understanding of development.[37]

Indeed, it seems that giving money is one of the only ways Britons are able to express their concern for distant strangers. When confronted by representations of need we respond through our cheque books, rather than through pressure on our politicians. Andrew Darnton provides a sobering comment on this:

> A further striking example of the public defaulting to giving money even when the context has been designed to rule out that response can be found in a study of the African School documentary [2005], screened as part of the BBC's Africa Lives season . . . Following the series, viewers contacted the producers and the BBC seeking to send in donations to the school, much to the dismay of the programme makers who saw the programme as a piece of development education work, and were aiming only to increase public understanding of the issues.[38]

The dominant patterns of portraying development problems in order to raise money have a lot to answer for here.[39] There is a deliberate avoidance of political issues in order to fundraise. Consider this statement from a mainstream fundraising organisation.

TABLE 2.1 Evidence of public awareness of development

Issue	Evidence	Source
The low salience of international poverty.	In a 2005 British Election Study, 4,789 people were asked an open-ended question: What is the most important issue facing Britain today? Just ten mentioned things relating to global poverty.	Hudson and van Heerde-Hudson, 2012: 3.
Low levels of concern.	Persistently around 25 per cent of people declare themselves to be very concerned about international poverty.	Darnton, 2009.
Aid is something charities do, not the government.	Most people think that the best thing that governments can do is to encourage people to give money to charity.	Darnton, 2009: 11–12.
	In 2009, about 4 per cent of people understood what DFID did.	Darnton, 2009: 11–12.
	Fewer than 5 per cent of UK adults in 2009 and 2010 could spontaneously name DFID as responsible for aid work.	Darnton, 2009: 11–12.
	In 2010, only 62 per cent were aware of any development activity and of these most spontaneously named NGOs (Oxfam, Red Cross, Save the Children (STC), Comic Relief, Christian Aid) or international organisations (UNICEF, UN), as doing aid work.	TNS, 2010: 32.
Aid is equivalent to disaster relief.	Darnton reports McDonnell *et al.*'s 'prevailing understanding of aid as "short term charity for humanitarian relief"' and Creative Research's finding that aid is 'donations to charities in response to disasters'.	Darnton, 2009: 11.
Corruption causes poverty.	About half of people agree with the statement that 'most financial aid to poor countries is wasted', but over 70 per cent agree that most aid is wasted because of corruption. In other words, people who do not otherwise think aid is being wasted will change their minds if you use the word 'corruption' in the question.	Darnton, 2009: 15.
	This concern for wise and proper use of funds extends to aid agencies. Darnton reports that in 'January 2006 . . . 76 per cent of respondents agreed that "Most because it is inefficiently administered"'.	Darnton, 2006: 8.

Support for aid strong and stable.	For 23 OECD countries between 1990 and 2007, between 68 per cent and 92 per cent of the public support development aid.	Hudson and van Heerde-Hudson, 2012.
	Otter reports generally high and stable levels in four other OECD countries (Japan, Denmark, Australia and Canada) over a variety of timespans.	Otter, 2003.
	Note that levels of support tend to be somewhat lower in the US (47–54 per cent). Paxton and Knack argue that this may be in part because US citizens are more likely to think that the high levels of military expenditure, and military expeditions overseas, by their government fulfil their country's obligations of global citizenship.	Paxton and Knack, 2008: 16–17.
Ambivalence to aid.	Surveys that asked if the UK government increase its spending to honour its pledge to spend 0.7 per cent of GDP on aid can find that 40 per cent of respondents to agree, but the same survey can find only 16 per cent of people saying that government spending on overseas aid should increase (as required to meet the pledge).	Darnton, 2009: 14.
	Early results from the Public Opinion Monitor suggest that between 63 and 71 per cent of respondents thought development aid should be cut, but that the overall government expenditure within the UK should be increased.	Anonymous, 2011: 9.
Ignorance of how much governments give.	In the US in 1995, 49 per cent of respondents thought that aid should be cut but believed that their government was spending on average 18 per cent of GNP on aid. When told that aid spending was less than 1 per cent of GNP, 57 per cent of those who thought less money should be spent on aid changed their mind and advocated increasing expenditure.	Otter, 2003.
	In 2001, only 24 per cent of Europeans could accurately estimate the aid budgets of their governments.	Hudson and van Heerde-Hudson, 2012: 9.
Government spending on aid related to public support for it.	Otter found very little correlation between aid given and public opinion about aid in five OECD countries (Japan, USA, Canada, Denmark and Australia).	Otter, 2003.
	Hudson and van Heerde reached the same conclusion for twenty-three OECD countries for 1990–2007, with no statistically significant relationship between public support for development aid and levels of overseas development assistance.	Hudson and van Heerde-Hudson, 2012.

28 The terrain of development advocacy

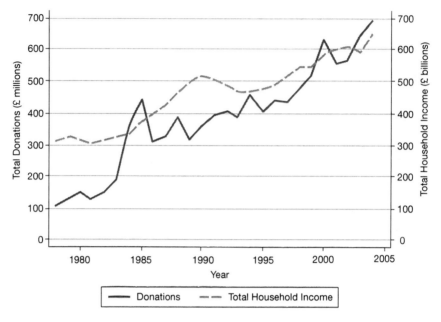

FIGURE 2.1 UK charitable donations for overseas development and total household income: 1978–2004 (constant 2007 prices)

Source: Arulampalam et al., 2009.

> Part of the success [of our fundraising] is that it is so middle of the road, and it's not controversial . . . We know that if we started venturing into . . . injustice and the rights of children . . . everybody would . . . get turned off . . . There is an awful lot of self-censorship . . . [T]he brand is about being inclusive and about being mainstream . . . There is no way you can start talking about the rights of . . . women workers on flower farms. [T]hat will never be the most compelling fundraiser because people are not going to emotionally engage with women's rights who are being abused by exploitative employers . . . We will go for the kind of child in a hospital dying of malaria . . . you have to go into those no brain issues which is what people will feel comfortable giving money to rather than issues where there is perceived rights and wrong, perceived injustice, that is much more complex waters.[40]

It was partly in response to the problems of the dominant charitable frames in Britain that a number of British development NGOs collaborated in a report published as *Finding Frames*, work that was launched in 2011. Building on Tom Crompton's analysis of values and social action the authors expressed considerable

TABLE 2.2 Trends in giving to development charities

Issue	Evidence	Source
Giving to development NGOs has increased in Britain.	Giving now amounts to about £1 billion (in 2004/05) equivalent (then) to 25 per cent of British development aid.	Atkinson *et al.*, 2008: 2; Arulampalam *et al.*, 2009; Micklewright and Schnepf, 2009.
	Donations to overseas charities did not decrease during the recession of the early 1990s. When incomes fell 9 per cent in real terms between 1990 and 1991 and 1993 and 1994, giving rose by 6 per cent over that period.	
	Whereas around 70 per cent of contributions went to the 'big four' (Oxfam, Christian Aid, Red Cross and Save the Children) in the late 1970s, by the mid-2000s that concentration had reduced to around 50 per cent. As Atkinson and colleagues summarise: 'These results are consistent with the notion that while donors have increased their total contribution to development charities, they have also increased the number of charities to which they give.'	
	Government grants to development charities increased considerably from 1985 to 1995, but then slowed. Government grants to charities do not appear to 'crowd out', i.e. discourage giving. If anything, it appears to have a positive effect.	
Giving has risen faster than other sectors.	The increase in average donations from 1978–80 to 2002–04 was nearly 1 per cent higher in the development sector than its nearest competitors, which amounts, over time to £150 million per year. Only growth in support for 'Animal' charities has been higher since 1985, but this came following considerable declines in the first seven years of the study, and from a much smaller base.	Atkinson *et al.*, 2008: 24.
Only a minority of people give to development causes.	Micklewright and Schnepf's analysis of the 2004/05 Omnibus surveys, which covered 9,050 people, found that just over 55 per cent of people gave to some causes in the previous four weeks before the survey, but just over 10 per cent gave to overseas aid and disaster relief.	Micklewright and Schnepf, 2009: 321.
	Moreover, the distribution of giving is such that just 1 per cent of people (90 in the sample) giving accounted for over 50 per cent of the amount given to overseas aid and disaster relief.	

continued . . .

TABLE 2.2 *Continued*

Issue	Evidence	Source
	It is important to point out that this finding is quite dissimilar to that of the UK Public Opinion Monitor. This found that 32 per cent of respondents gave regularly, and a further 32 per cent gave occasionally. It is possible, therefore, that the four-week window mentioned in the Omnibus survey was not long enough to capture people's giving.	
Education increases giving.	People with no qualifications are three times less likely to give than those with university degrees (a probability of giving of 0.06 compared to 0.19) and the chances of giving increases incrementally with different levels of education. Similarly, people employed in a manager/professional role have a 0.16 chance of giving, twice as much as routine/ manual workers who have a 0.07 chance. When included in logistic regression models, the correlates of higher income (education, occupation and home ownership) render the effect of income on giving to overseas development causes insignificant.	Micklewright and Schnepf, 2009: 333–334.
Giving and levels of concern.	Of those giving money 42 per cent are very concerned about international poverty and 48 per cent are fairly concerned, but 10 per cent of those giving expressed no strong concerns. Of those who are not giving anything, 60 per cent declared that donating to charities was an effective way to contribute, more than any other means.	Micklewright and Schnepf, 2009.
Giving has no political agenda.	This is neatly captured by a question in the 7th Public Opinion Monitor about Comic Relief. This found that a notable minority of people (27 per cent) would give more to Comic Relief if all the money went to UK causes. Less than 3 per cent indicated that they would give less. The largest group, however, did not mind where the money went (35 per cent). Giving to Comic Relief (which over 75 per cent of people do) is just something one does, wherever the money goes.	Anonymous, 2011.

dissatisfaction with the values promoted by development campaigns. They sought new ways of 'framing' development issues in the public mind that activate different sets of values.[41]

What this might portend for development organisations was still being debated while I was conducting this research. The authors recommend moving away from 'transactional' engagements (buying things for development), unless it is part of encouraging supporters to embark on personal journeys that would promote greater awareness and understanding of development issues. They were specifically wary of working with celebrity, 'given the strong links between celebrity culture, consumer culture and the values of self-interest'.[42]

Conclusion

Celebrity advocacy for development and humanitarian causes happens in complex and difficult terrain. It is embedded in media practices that are becoming decreasingly cosmopolitan in Britain, and in NGO literature which, though enlightened, is still problematic. Celebrities are communicating to publics who know very little about development. Most people do not know how much aid their government gives or what it is spent on, even if they think development aid is a good idea in principle. They think that most aid is swallowed up by corruption or wasted by inefficient NGOs. The majority, if not the vast majority, have many other things on their minds. They are not encouraged to engage with or learn about poorer parts of the world from much of the media imagery surrounding them.

This situation then suggests an important question to ask of celebrity advocacy. How do celebrity advocates affect public understandings of development? We will consider this question again in the Conclusion at the end of the book.

And yet, in exploring the public response to celebrity advocacy, we must also remember that general public opinion may not be the most important terrain of celebrity advocacy. As I have said repeatedly above, development affairs are an elite issue.[43] Therefore, to understand the work and role of celebrity advocacy we must look beyond the public domain. We have also to look at how celebrity works with elites. We will do this in Chapter 7. First we must examine the specific debates about celebrity advocacy and celebrity media, and consider their place in post-democratic politics.

Notes

1 Chouliaraki, 2013: 43.
2 Hulme, 2010: 107.
3 UNDP, 2011.
4 Fassin, 2012: 3. Fassin speaks of domination because, as he puts it, 'Humanitarian reason governs precarious lives: the lives of the unemployed and the asylum seekers, the lives of sick immigrants and people with AIDS, the lives of disaster victims and victims of conflict – threatened and forgotten lives that humanitarian government brings into existence by protecting and revealing them. When compassion is exercised in the public space it is therefore always directed from above to below, from the more powerful to the weaker, the more fragile, the more vulnerable' (Fassin, 2012: 4).

32 The terrain of development advocacy

5 Of this hope and danger Fassin writes: 'In contemporary societies, where inequalities have reached an unprecedented level, humanitarianism elicits the fantasy of a global moral community that may still be viable and the expectation that solidarity may have redeeming powers. This secular imaginary of communion and redemption implies a sudden awareness of the fundamentally unequal human condition and an ethical necessity to not remain passive about it in the name of solidarity – however ephemeral this awareness is, and whatever limited impact this necessity has. Humanitarianism has this remarkable capacity: it fugaciously and illusorily bridges the contradictions of our world, and makes the intolerableness of its injustices somewhat bearable' (Fassin, 2012: xii). Chouliaraki (2013: 52) makes a similar argument; see also Stirrat and Henkel (1997).
6 Boltanski, 1999.
7 Boltanski, 1999: 12–13.
8 Boltanski, 1999: 3; Chouliaraki, 2012.
9 The Gospel according to St Luke, 10: 25–37.
10 Cohen, 2001: 75.
11 Cohen, 2001: 260
12 Cohen, 2001: 194, italics in the original. Jim Igoe (personal communication, 28 May, 2013) observes that we can become dulled to the pain of even those we love. It can overwhelm us. Without the support networks to help us cope with the grief or material resources to respond to the needs we can experience love fatigue.
13 Silverstone, 2007: 28, 47.
14 Silverstone, 2007: 47.
15 Silverstone, 2007: 121.
16 Moore, 2010: 12, 19. These findings are based on a survey of stories in the *Mirror, Mail, Telegraph* and *Guardian* in the first week of March.
17 Hardstaff, 1991; Cleasby, 1993, 1995, 1996; Lay and Payne, 1998; Stone, 2000; Nason and Redding, 2002; Dover and Barnett, 2004; Padania *et al.*, 2006; Seymour and Barnett, 2006; Smith *et al.*, 2006; Scott, 2008; Harding, 2009; Scott, 2009; Scott *et al.*, 2011. See also Franks, 2010a.
18 Chouliaraki, 2006.
19 Scott, 2011: 190.
20 Scott, 2011.
21 cf. Philo and Henderson (1998), who also argue that different means of communicating foreign needs are already available to media professionals.
22 van Heerde and Hudson, 2010.
23 van Heerde and Hudson, 2010: 396–7. Indeed, such is the relentlessly negative portrayal of poorer parts of the world that they suggest that it is possible that people who are more aware of these portrayals are more likely to be disengaged from poverty issues because they feel that there is so little chance of making any difference.
24 Dogra, 2007, 2011, 2012. See also Manzo (2008). On a similar issue, Cottle and Nolan argue that humanitarian communications (from Australian NGOs) are increasingly being governed by a media logic (Cottle and Nolan, 2007). Chouliaraki (2013), in contrast, would argue that these tensions are inherent in the 'theatricality' of humanitarianism – see below.
25 A somewhat discouraging addendum to Dogra's work is Bruna Seu's research on audience responses to awkward and discomforting images about development needs. She argues that 'a careful reading of more of participants' talk [suggests] that audiences might be turning away from identification with the horrific and destructive potential of the human race. What might also be defended against is having to take responsibility for their country's involvement or at least acquiescence in human rights abuses' (Seu, 2003: 184). But note that Matt Baillie-Smith, in contrast, has a more upbeat view of the potential of development education (Smith, 2004, 2008; Smith and Donnelly, 2004; Smith and Yanacopulos, 2004).
26 Chouliaraki, 2012, 2013.
27 cf. Smith, 2007.

The terrain of development advocacy **33**

28 Chouliaraki, 2012: 11.
29 Chouliaraki, 2012: 15.
30 Chouliaraki, 2012: 17.
31 Chouliaraki, 2012: 16.
32 Chouliaraki, 2013.
33 Scott, 2011, 2013a.
34 These are also summarised in Riddell, 2007.
35 This position is corroborated by recent research based on forty interviews with development policy-makers in the US, UK, Germany and France. The report's authors summarise that 'public opinion seems to have less impact on policymaking in this sector than might have been expected, and most government decision-makers perceive other factors, such as data-based evidence, as considerably more important for policymaking than public opinion' (Anonymous, 2012: 3).
36 In the first five of surveys of the Public Perceptions of Poverty research (from December 2004 to January 2006), between 57 and 59 per cent of over 10,000 respondents thought that the only thing they could do about global poverty was to give money to appeals and charities (Darnton, 2006: 8). According to the Voluntary Service Overseas (VSO), 74 per cent believe that people there 'depend on the money and knowledge of the West to progress', casting themselves as 'powerful givers' and the rest as 'grateful receivers' (VSO, 2002: 5).
37 Analysts are unable convincingly to explain why giving has increased. It might result from stronger corporate giving, which is included among the voluntary donations. If it is due to changing public behaviour it will be hard to work out what is changing because we do not have historic survey data which has asked the right questions. Rising wealth is not likely to be important in itself, given that correlates of wealth have a more powerful impact on probabilities of giving than wealth itself. Instead, Micklewright and Schnepf suggest that, given the association of giving to overseas development with education, 'the recent expansion of higher education in the UK could be favourable for overseas giving' (2009: 334). Arulampalam and colleagues find that fundraising effort has 'a powerful effect on donations' (2009: 22). This suggests a combination of charities that have become more effective in requesting money, and audiences becoming more responsive. Note also that giving does not even seem to be well matched to levels of concern for overseas poverty. Levels of concern are high among those who give, but those who express no strong concerns also give. As Micklewright and Schnepf observe, 'these results can be seen as encouraging for international charities: charitable giving finds very widespread support, including those not giving in the recent past' (Micklewright and Schnepf, 2009: 327). Research on the effects of the recent financial crisis and recession does not suggest that giving will have declined. Giving does decline somewhat, but the impact varies from sector to sector. Giving to development causes continued to increase during the recession of the early 1990s (Anonymous, 2009, 2012).
38 Darnton, 2007: 25.
39 Cameron and Fairbrass, 2004: 739; Darnton, 2009: 14. Otter noted that greater public involvement rather than attention to public opinion had produced better aid performance (Otter, 2003).
40 Source 70.
41 Crompton, 2010. Darnton and Kirk, 2011. Crompton distinguished between 'intrinsic values', which value community, friends and family, and 'extrinsic values' which place an emphasis on admiration from others. Crompton noted that these values tend to work in opposition to each other in that people who demonstrated strong intrinsic values are weak extrinsically, and vice versa. He also noted that when these values are practised, they grow stronger if used. He observed that, in the long term, NGOs that campaign in ways that promote extrinsic values (for example, promoting hybrid cars because they are cool and others will admire them) may well be promoting in the long run behaviours that reinforce values that are antithetical to the sorts of societies many NGOs wish to promote.
42 Darnton and Kirk, 2011: 10.
43 cf. Lancaster, 2007.

3

CELEBRITY ADVOCACY AND POST-DEMOCRACY

> After all these months of activity and the combined fire power of worldwide NGO members and sympathisers you can only muster a fairly small number [of marchers] on your biggest day. Tragic. Do you seriously imagine that could or would have affected the outcome of the Gleneagles summit? The leaders couldn't care less. The marchers were never ONCE mentioned by the politicians in the building. By either the Africans or the G8 guys and girls. Nothing. Not a single shred of influence.
>
> Bob Geldof[1]

Celebrity advocacy is divisive. Ilan Kapoor is unequivocal in his rejection of it. He imagines that celebrity humanitarians might be 'sadists' delighting in others' misfortune, and applauding the death of impoverished African children.[2] Andrew Cooper, in contrast, is almost sycophantically optimistic as to their potential. He contends that celebrity diplomats' interventions can be fresh, fluid and flexible. They consciously and positively shape debate and can mobilise vast resources for effective use.[3]

This chapter explores the issues that underlie these divisions, particularly as they apply to the ability of celebrity advocacy to make a positive difference to development and humanitarian causes. I first look at the broad political context within which celebrity advocacy works, exploring Colin Crouch's writings on post-democracy. I consider what his theories about the power of elites in contemporary politics imply for a study of the work of celebrity advocacy. I then examine writings about the role of new media trends (of which celebrity is part) in invigorating, or diminishing, public deliberation in contemporary democracies. Finally, I focus more specifically on current critiques of celebrity advocacy.

The purpose of this review is to identify important questions that we need to ask of celebrity advocacy if we are to understand it better. I summarise these in the conclusion of the chapter. They derive from its argument that current studies have not explored the anatomy of celebrity advocacy, how it is constructed, and how represented. This makes it hard to tell precisely how corrupt, or emancipatory, it might be in the post-democratic contexts in which it must work.

Post-democracy

Understanding the influence of celebrity advocacy requires some insight into the behaviour and practices of the ruling institutions and governments that advocacy might influence. That requires an understanding of post-democracy. For thinking on post-democracy will allow us to grasp the spheres where celebrity advocacy may be most influential and the social and economic changes underlying that influence.

Following Crouch, 'post-democracy' refers to a state of affairs in many western polities where

> boredom, frustration and disillusion have settled in after a democratic moment; when powerful minority interests have become far more active than the mass of ordinary people in making the political system work for them, where political elites have learned to manage and manipulate popular demands, where people have to be persuaded to vote by top-down publicity campaigns.[4]

Post-democracies, however, are not just characterised by this poor performance of, and participation in, democratic institutions and customs. Post-democracy is also characterised as a particular alliance between capitalist and government elites, which are promoted because liberal democracies tend to privilege the interests of the most wealthy groups. As Rancière describes, political legitimacy comes from ensuring corporate viability: 'the absolute identification of politics with the management of capital is no longer the shameful secret hidden behind the 'forms' of democracy; it is the openly declared truth by which our governments acquire legitimacy'.[5] In that respect, post-democracy is not just a characteristic of democracy alone; it is also a characteristic of current forms of capitalism and corporate alliances with the democratic state.

One of the defining characteristics of current post-democracies for Crouch is their tendency to inequality. This is visible throughout the operations of the state:

> The welfare state gradually becomes residualised as something for the deserving poor rather than a range of universal rights of citizenship; trade unions exist on the margins of society, the role of the state as policeman and incarcerator returns to prominence, the wealth gap between rich and poor grows; taxation becomes less redistributive; politicians respond primarily to the concerns of a handful of business leaders whose special interests are allowed to be translated into public policy; the poor gradually cease to take an interest

36 Celebrity advocacy and post-democracy

in the process whatsoever and do not even vote, returning voluntarily to the position they were forced to occupy in pre-democracy.[6]

Or, to put it rather unpleasantly, Crouch sees post-democratic societies stricken by the 'establishment of a new dominant, combined political and economic class' and in them a return to politics of a pre-democratic age which served the privileged rather than the majority of the citizens. Indeed, in the strong post-democracies, such as the USA, contrasts are such that 'divisions between rich and poor [have] started to resemble those of Third World countries, reversing the normal historical association between modernisation and the reduction of inequality'. Increasing inequality is driven by the character of the elites who are dominating politics, across the parties. They are, principally, corporate elites, and 'one of the core political objectives of corporate elites is clearly to combat egalitarianism'.[7]

There are several factors underlying the rise of post-democracy. Crouch focuses on post-industrial economies and the rise of the service sector which have seen the demise of the manual working class whose demands had been so central to securing egalitarian measures such as better pay, working conditions and state services in the middle of the twentieth century. No significant class or identity group has arisen which can challenge corporate power as effectively. These changes have been compounded by the failure of political parties to represent the new needs created by these conditions, and their closer links to businesses to fund ever more expensive election campaigns.[8]

But perhaps the most important factor for this book is the power that global economic policies have given large firms over states. Firms can threaten to leave or fail to invest in countries if conditions are not right. States therefore are encouraged to shape domestic policies in order to suit the interests and demands of international capital. As Dani Rodrik shows, the policies that have been promoted to improve the efficiency of markets internationally and reduce the transaction costs of conducting business internationally clash with the domestic social needs.[9] Or, as Rodrik glosses it: 'globalisation gets in the way of national democracy'.[10]

Post-democracy is important for the argument of this book for several reasons. First, it helps us to understand the context within which celebrity advocacy has arisen and flourished – and also what challenges it might face should those circumstances change. Put simply, the current form of celebrity advocacy is driven by the dominance of the firm. The rise of NGOs, in which celebrity advocacy flourishes, results from the same economic thinking (and political failings) which promote the market as the best means of addressing social problems.[11] Moreover, as we will see in Chapter 7, the rise of corporate power helps to explain why celebrity has become so prominent within NGOs themselves. Celebrity lubricates and facilitates links between NGOs and businesses. NGOs offer corporate partners routes to celebrity and these partners seek cheap or free access to it through their charitable activities. The rise of celebrity within the NGO sector is partly a manifestation (and a consolidation) of the rise of corporate power in our societies.

Second, post-democracy helps us to understand the ways in which NGO-wielded celebrity power works. Crouch was clear as to the economic advantages to corporate elites of being close to power. Much of this can be counted in concrete economic benefits (influence over policy), but some returns are more indirectly beneficial. They are about producing good images and brands.[12] Forging relationships with celebrity is part of that process, and access to celebrity provided by NGOs, is part of the need, and attraction, of being in the elite. The rise and influence of celebrity among NGOs is part of the performance and display of elite-dominated post-democracies which Crouch describes.

Third, as we have seen in the previous chapter, international development and aid allocation and policy are a prima facie arena of elite policy formation, and therefore are likely to display post-democratic politics in action.[13] Cooper's work on the powers and efficacy of celebrity 'diplomats', and particularly Bono (a musician), Geldof and Jolie, could be read as championing the achievements of particularly skilled and effective celebrity advocates that post-democratic political environments make possible.[14] His optimistic assessment of their achievements, celebration of their role in strengthening Davos and search for a means of extending the reach and origins of celebrity diplomats hinge upon the possibilities of access and influence that celebrity can wield for development causes in post-democracy.

Fourth, ideas of post-democracy help us to understand how celebrity advocacy has changed. As we shall see when we review the history of celebrity advocacy (Chapter 4), there are important differences between the celebrity advocacy practised now and that of earlier decades. Key to that difference is the intensely agonistic struggles that characterised the celebrity advocates of, for example, the 1960s. These feature less prominently in celebrity interventions now. As the epigraph to this chapter makes plain, post-democratic politics signal a change in the way in which governing elites engage with their publics (as we shall see in Chapter 7).

Indeed, post-democracy is convenient for the politics of pity and for post-humanitarianism that I discussed in the previous chapter. The former lends itself to action in the charitable frame, giving money to the needy, but not seeking definitive resolution to the causes of inequality. The latter is more about the self, as Chouliaraki puts it, paraphrasing Silverstone: it 'shares its private passion without its public commitment'.[15] Both will fit relatively easily with an inegalitarian politics.

Post-democracy, therefore, is a crucial lens for understanding celebrity advocacy and trends in celebrity advocacy. But it has been curiously overlooked in many writings about development matters and about the work of the media in democracies. The final reason why post-democracy features so prominently in my argument is that it does not do so elsewhere. Yet we need a theory with this sort of historical, sociological and political scope to comprehend the trends in celebrity advocacy. It provides the framework with which we can understand the rise and current features of celebrity advocacy today.

Celebrity, the media and democracy

To understand some of the potential and tensions of celebrity advocacy we first need to review broader debates within media studies about the implications for democracy of the rise of celebrity. The aspects of democracy that most concern me here are the practices of public debate, communication and deliberation by which choices affecting politicians and electorates are aired. Some of this takes place in official fora – parliament and its committee rooms in the UK, and some of it in the media and social media. Celebrity advocacy needs to be set in the context of these broader deliberative practices.

There is a popular argument that celebrity is anathema to democracy and a healthy society. A steady stream of newspaper articles condemns the shallowness of celebrity culture, the debasing admiration we offer celebrity, and their unauthorised and unearned power. The columnist Marina Hyde has built a substantial reputation for her relentlessly acerbic and perceptive critiques whose only drawback is that they seem to require, and produce, a great deal of familiarity with celebrity.[16] She insists that celebrities' sallies into politics are totally unwarranted, and that 'if the entertainment industry is the solution, then we're asking the wrong questions'.[17]

A strong tradition in academia echoes those views. With respect to celebrity generally, Kerry Ferris was able to devote an entire section of her review of celebrity literature to authors who see celebrity as pathology.[18] With respect to celebrity and politics specifically, Darrell West and John Orman insist that celebrities do not enrich democracy, or help citizens make informed rational choices.[19]

These views are part of a long tradition in studies of the relationship between the media and democracy which are suspicious of the influence of entertainment on politics. It has been most famously expressed in Theodor Adorno and Max Horkheimer's scathing attack on the 'culture industries', which they thought were exploitative in themselves, and whose content they believed stunted consumers' imagination and perpetrated obedience to existing hierarchies. Such entertainment, in this view, stifles dissent, thought and critical democratic debate.[20] Neil Postman has similarly deplored the decline of text and the rise of image in public discourse. Text requires 'ratiocination', judging by reason and logic, but imagery does not.[21] Therefore, a society dominated by imagery will be less reasonable and logical in its decision-making.

Other commentators plead for a more tolerant view of celebrity in political affairs.[22] They recognise the possibility of these deficiencies, but insist that celebrity politics can play a more constructive role. John Street examined the merging of the celebrity sphere with the political sphere and devotes his article to exploring different defences to the accusations that celebrity politics is illegitimate, because celebrities usurp roles for which they have not been chosen, and that they dumb down politics.[23] With respect to legitimacy, he notes that celebrities can sometimes occupy space that politicians create by their inactivity, and their failure to give voice to popular concerns. Live Aid and Band Aid filled a gap left by the government's failure to respond to a Disasters Emergency Committee appeal in the summer of 1984.[24] The activism of musicians in the US in the 1960s was invited by the social movements of the time, and by the laws and policies (the Vietnam War, racist segregation) prosecuted by elected politicians.[25] With respect to dumbing down, he argues that politics is not just about rational communication; it is about style.[26] Without style (adopting the right vocabulary, wearing the right clothes in a press conference, using the right body language at a convention) there could be no possibility of communicating between the electorate and their representatives. 'Adoption of the trappings of popular celebrity is not a trivial gesture towards fashion or a minor detail of political communication, but instead lies at the heart of the notion of political representation.' [27] Street is clear that this does not mean we should welcome all populist styles or all celebrity advocacy. His point is that we cannot dismiss it all.[28]

This position is part of a larger debate about how and whether new political styles, new media engagements and emotively driven politics are potentially liberating. Advocates of the democratic potential of celebrity are sanguine about the parlous state of democratic participation in many countries. Peter Dahlgren, for example, pays considerable attention to problems of declining voter turnout, party membership and trust.[29] But he and others do not see current forms of media engagement as necessarily part of the problem. Rather, they insist on the possibility that these new media engagements – Facebook, Twitter, chat shows and appearances on popular television programmes – and the informal, non-hierarchical style in which they are carried out, offer new opportunities and spaces for democratic engagement.[30] They are 'expanding the platforms for engagement and citizenship' in John Corner's and Dick Pels' words; in Dahlgren's words, 'the field of democracy is in the process of addition not subtraction'.[31]

Underpinning these views is a suspicion of the scope of reason and rational deliberative democracy evoked by models like Jurgen Habermas's public sphere.[32] Many of these authors would insist that this casts too strong a divide between reason and emotion, that passion can be reasonable, and sentiment rational.[33] Affective politics can be just, effective and result in sensible decisions. Indeed, the distinction between emotion and reason, rationality and affect may be misconceived. Affective politics have always been present, but they are misrecognised as rational deliberation when they present themselves in a cold calculative form. We therefore need to foster media that promote effective affective politics. Liesbet van Zoonen even praises television programmes such as *Big Brother* for 'inviting the affective intelligence that is vital to keep political involvement and activity going'.[34] From such a perspective, the distaste of celebrity is not a critique of misplaced style and emotion in politics; it is rather a discomfort with the wrong sort of style. Advocates of the progressive possibilities inherent in celebrity politics could suggest that their critics are not so much wrong, as unfashionable.

Other commentators welcome the possibilities of these new forms of engagement and communication but ask testing questions about the politics they produce. Couldry notes with some concern that the greater space for more voice(s) is not resulting in political stances or parties or debates that coherently address some

40 Celebrity advocacy and post-democracy

of the problematic living conditions created by neoliberalism.[35] There is more short-term protest and disruption, but fewer '*long-term* strategies of positive politics'.[36] He warns against celebrating communication in itself; effective politics for change is built on more than that.[37] Similarly, Michael Marks and Zachary Fischer see in celebrity politics a *simulating* of consent. They see celebrities providing some invigoration of public participation in politics (in the US) but not necessarily to emancipatory ends, but rather to ends that celebrity politicians prefer.[38]

It would be possible to infer that post-democratic writers share the concerns over the quality of public debate that critics of celebrity voice. This would classify these writers as part of an old guard of media theorists who lament a lost and declining rational public sphere, and who see the problems of post-democracy as deriving in part from that decline. Such a classification may be accurate in some cases. The post-democratic concern about passive electorates and the dominance of spectacle easily segues into a concern about the quality of the media disseminating the spectacle and propagating passivity. But it would be wrong to do so in all instances. That inference would miss an important common ground between critics and advocates of celebrity among media theorists. It also elides over an important difference between media theorists and post-democratic writers which can make their perspectives complementary.

The shared common ground of the critics and advocates of celebrity is that they are principally concerned with the *processes* of mediation that characterise the democracies they study. This is common to all sides of the debate, in West and Orman's desire for 'proper information' in electoral debates (which for them precludes celebrity), and in Street's insistence that communicative style needs to be taken seriously (and therefore so do some celebrity interventions).[39] All these analysts are concerned with the way in which information, ideas and issues are debated, discussed and communicated.

But democracy is not just about the quality of mediation, the character of the information with which decisions are made, or the way in which they are debated. Democracies can also be examined according to their *outcomes* with respect to distributions of resources they produce, and the interests which their deliberations favour or reject. If democracy is government of the people, by the people and for the people, it is reasonable to ask what it achieves for them. It is here that writings about post-democracy are so engaging.

The complementary aspect of debates about the potential of new media and the limitations of post-democracy is that one is concerned with *processes*, and the other *outcomes*. Many writers in media studies, concentrating on the processes, have adopted a more optimistic position with respect to the democratic possibilities of better and richer communication which celebrity advocacy can entail.[40] My point, however, is that these richer democratic processes can proceed quite compatibly with increasing inequality and fewer egalitarian policies. We can participate now much more thoroughly in our own marginalisation.[41]

This may seem extreme but the fact is that economic inequality, nationally and internationally, has generally increased. It is one of the most fundamental forms of marginalisation. Therefore, if we have been participating more in politics through these new media opportunities we have been participating in our own marginalisation, at best ineffectively opposing it, but at worst condoning it. The key argument of this book – the idea that celebrity advocacy works because of the belief in it, despite the lack of popular engagement with it – suggests that we may be marginalised even as we appear to be included. My point that belief in celebrity advocacy reshapes politics according to elites' imaginations of the political (see p. 9) goes hand-in-hand with our marginalised participation.

Studies of celebrity advocacy

There are two general sorts of analyses of celebrity advocacy. There are those that take a broadly empirical approach to the sort of influence celebrities wield, and a collection of more radical critics for whom celebrity advocacy is distinctly problematic. The former involves surveys of media and audiences, as well as experiments with large samples of audiences, to examine the influence celebrity enjoys in politics. The latter relies on diagnoses of power relations, often based on readings of celebrity advocacy from reports published in the media, on websites and in books. I will deal with each in turn.

One of the most thorough studies available is that of Trevor Thrall and colleagues who produced unexpected findings with respect to the consequences of celebrity endorsements on publicity.[42] They examined the number of causes supported by celebrities and the coverage these received, based on a quantitative survey of newspapers. They found that celebrity support did not significantly increase newspaper coverage of NGOs, that celebrity gossip magazines did not cover celebrities' causes (even popular ones like the environment). Mainstream coverage of celebrity advocacy could be uneven. They found good coverage in the *New York Times* of Bono's activism (404 stories) but only seven covering Harrison Ford's support for Conservation International.[43] Celebrity, they conclude, may be a much better vehicle for narrow-casting causes, i.e. targeting specific audiences through devices such as websites and YouTube videos, rather than broadcasting on the mainstream media.

There is little work that has tried to measure and quantify interest in celebrity culture, but that which has been undertaken finds it is a minority activity. Couldry and Markham found that only 14 per cent of British adults were preoccupied with it. Moreover, celebrity was their primary interest.[44] They were not particularly politically active; they were interested in celebrities for the gossip, fashion and news, precisely because these were not more serious matters. Couldry and Markham concluded that celebrities are an unlikely vehicle for promoting interest and engagement in political affairs. Ekant Veer and colleagues found the opposite, however, in that their experimental data suggested that celebrity was a good vehicle for targeting people not interested in politics (and a bad one for those who were).[45] We shall be re-examining these findings, and updating them, in Chapter 8.

42 Celebrity advocacy and post-democracy

Findings from the US and Canada emphasise the influence of celebrity in democratic politics. One remarkable paper quantifies the influence of the chat show host Oprah Winfrey's endorsement of Barack Obama's campaign for election in the Democratic Party's primaries in the US. The authors correlate purchase of her magazine with voting patterns and conclude that her endorsement may well have mobilised enough votes to win Obama the election. Experimental evidence suggests that celebrities influence young voters.[46] David Jackson and Thomas Darrow even found that the great Canadian hockey player Wayne Gretzky could make 'it less unacceptable for young Canadians to believe that US President George Bush Jr was a great leader'.[47] Other findings are more ambiguous. Anthony Nownes suggests that celebrities' and parties' brands reinforce each other – those who think poorly of a party will think worse of a celebrity who supports it.[48] Inthorn and Street argue that in the UK celebrities who become involved in politics offer youth an 'alternative' to normal politics which still affirms the privileged discourses of masculinity, maturity and capitalism.[49]

Note the difficulties, however, of extrapolating the general power of celebrity from some of these results. Oprah's influence was interesting (and measurable) because she is an unusually prominent figure in the US (she topped the Forbes ratings of celebrity influence for several years) and her support for Obama was her first political endorsement. Findings from the UK likewise have to be extrapolated with caution.

The important point to draw from this work is that celebrity operates under an aura of populism. The general perception is that it appeals to the masses, and it works globally. Its value in shaping democratic practices of communication and deliberation is that it allows the public to speak through their popular representatives, or because these popular representatives encourage them to speak up. However, this work also shows that the appeal and the responses to celebrity are textured, varying nationally, and according to different population groups (see also Appendix Two). To understand the role of celebrity in democracy, and the broader media changes of which it is part, we need to understand the variety of responses that celebrity provokes. We will do so in Chapters 7 and 8.

The works I have just discussed commonly lack attention to the broader politics of celebrity power, and to its role in perpetuating inequality. Attention to that role and politics, and their hostility to both, unites the second set of analysts of celebrity advocacy. They insist that celebrity is inexpert, illegitimate and upholds injustice.[50] Celebrity advocacy for development and humanitarian causes is at best an oxymoron and at worst an anathema for three reasons. First, that celebrity perpetrates damaging views of needy others and places (especially 'Africa'); second, that celebrity is part of an unjust humanitarian regime, and third, that celebrity is founded on, and implicated in, structural inequalities which it does not challenge. A variant of the last argument is that celebrity reproduces a violent and unjust capitalist global order.

The first reason is visible in Keith Tester's arguments against current versions of 'common-sense' humanitarianism which he sees as being promoted by celebrity advocacy.[51] Common-sense humanitarianism is characterised by its false and

Celebrity advocacy and post-democracy **43**

damaging views about 'Africa' and its needs, and 'Africa's' inability to act on them. Tester likens celebrity humanitarianism to a beautiful plant that looks great but poisons the soil, and has to be eradicated in order to create the political space to think differently about Africa.

The second argument, the problems of humanitarianism, is the main target of Yrjölä, who offers a strong critique of the world view, and world system, which celebrity humanitarianism reproduces.[52] Her dissatisfaction is with humanitarianism generally, not merely the celebrity variant of it. Nevertheless, she is particularly critical of celebrity humanitarians and insists it is 'instrumental in constructing the consensus on the existing world order, where the global South is, and remains in a subordinate position to the West'.[53]

The third, the structural injustices of which celebrity part, and which celebrity must inevitably reproduce, is well set out by Jo Littler.[54] She argues, following Boltanski, that if the cosmopolitanism celebrity advocacy encourages is to be progressive, it must provide a means for audiences to act. Because so much celebrity advocacy is offered within the register of pity, not justice, it rarely offers a means to act in a way that confronts the unjust system of which celebrity is part. Worse still, where it does invoke justice, then it does so, as Cohen would say, in a way that acknowledges it, but does not believe it.[55] That is, it recognizes the truth, but not its implications. As Littler puts it, celebrity advocacy 'can acknowledge the structural inequalities in global social systems whilst simultaneously denying the material implications of the wealth of the star and how they contribute to the spaces where suffering takes place'.[56]

These three arguments, concerning celebrity's representations, humanitarianism and structural violence, have been most aggressively combined in a recent book by Ilan Kapoor. He finds celebrity humanitarianism offensive for it 'not only masks the causes of inequality [the operations of capitalism], but handsomely profits from this deception too'.[57]

I sympathise with these critiques.[58] Their fundamental point – that a world with less celebrity would be more pleasant – may well be correct. But they risk being too sweeping in their condemnation and foreclosing enquiries, which I think are important.

In the first instance we must warn against over-simple, or singular, readings of celebrity. More complex analyses of celebrity advocacy suggest ways of interpreting their performances, work, interventions and roles within society in terms of opposition and resistance to oppression. My methods do not allow me to elaborate on this point; others have made it far better.[59] Suffice to say that critiques that fail to recognise that possibility, that role of stars in society, have too narrow a view of politics.

A further objection, which I am better placed to address, is that we do not learn enough from these critiques about the broader system of which celebrity humanitarianism is part. This means that we cannot be sure that the source of the problem is the celebrity. Dogra's work, as we have seen, shows that the quality of representations of the other is part of a more general problem across the humanitarian and development NGOs.[60] Moreover, it is one with which NGOs

44 Celebrity advocacy and post-democracy

have continually wrestled.[61] Chouliaraki's work locates current forms of celebrity advocacy within broader trends towards post-humanitarianism.[62] Therefore, calling for celebrity advocacy's eradication (as Tester) will not necessarily make things any better. Before we can diagnose how celebrity advocacy contributes to flawed understandings of development or of Africa, we need a better understanding of how that advocacy happens.

I do not see humanitarianism as an extension of Western power, reproducing inequality (as Yrjölä). Following Fassin and Chouliaraki, I see humanitarianism as more paradoxical, complex and ambiguous than Yrjölä, and doing so removes much of the force of her objections to celebrity humanitarianism, for her argument is founded on a broader critique of humanitarianism. If humanitarianism is not the monolithic force that Yrjölä represents, it would be wise to understand the complexities and ambiguities of the politics of celebrity advocacy.[63] Again, this requires exploring its practices and processes.[64]

This brings me to the relationship between celebrity advocacy and capitalism. There are some plain truths in aspects of Littler's argument about the association of celebrity with inequality and injustice. In the first place the practices of celebrity hinge on inequality and hierarchy. Part of the condition of being a celebrity is the access it provides to otherwise inaccessible people, places and events. The hierarchies *within* celebrity circles revolve around what sort of access they can claim or afford. The celebrity industries are driven by controlling contact to famous people's time and person, or news about them.

Celebrity reinforces the hegemony of capitalism's inequalities through day-to-day practices that are riven with inequality and symbolic violence, and which maintain status and privilege.[65] One of the best studies of hegemony in action in a variety of celebrity is Michael Billig's book *Talking of the Royal Family*.[66] Resonating from this account are the multiple strategies, used across class, age and gender, by which relatively poor subjects acclaim and justify the wealth and privilege of one of the most unequal aspects of British society, and then live with the consequences. Billig talks of this ideological work as 'settling accounts' – that is, countering the envy and dissatisfaction that a comparison of stations might produce, with feelings of satisfaction, even superiority at our position over theirs.

For example, Billig writes that Britons cope with the inequalities of lifestyle by considering that they are employing the royal family who are expected to work for their lifestyle in various forms of public service and luxurious visits overseas.[67] He also describes Britons celebrating their own freedoms, which they imagine the royal family, constrained by public expectation and continual surveillance, cannot enjoy. This freedom was often expressed as an ability to 'nip' to the chip shop or pub whenever they wanted. Few actually did so, but they thought they could, and it was the possibility of their freedom thus to nip which excited them. For Billig, Britons' welcome of royalty clearly stymied moves to reduce inequality:

> The movement of time towards progressive equality is seen as threatening.
> Royalty could not survive such equality, so it was said, and if royalty cannot

survive, then the nation will be cut dangerously from its past, from its present and from itself. The premise of 'royalness', which is a premise of inequality, limits the imagining of the future. A future without inequality – and thus, without royalty – is to be feared even dismissed as unimaginable.[68]

To this hegemonic power of celebrity, the ability to make profound inequality right and normal, must be added the role it plays in the inequalities of 'media power'. Couldry argued that one of the ways in which the media structure our societies is to set up a boundary between 'ordinary life' and the 'media world'. The media world is glamorous and exciting. Ordinary life is banal and dull. Being moved into the media world makes someone or an activity, glamorous and exciting, even if that activity, or person, are eminently ordinary. Couldry calls the process of constructing and policing that boundary, and its widespread social legitimacy, 'media power'. He notes that belief in it exalts, and overexalts, the status of the media, and at the same time, devalues our own 'ordinary' lives.[69] Celebrity is an important signifier, and embodiment, of media power. Where the celebrity goes, so therefore goes glamour, and, presumably, excitement and interest in it.

Celebrity therefore is uncontestably bound up in the condition, and reproduction, of inequality. But, nonetheless, there is a lack of precision in Littler's argument as she applied it to development issues. [70] Stars may be 'materially implicated' in poverty, but what does that mean exactly? How directly are they causing poverty, and what levels of poverty are they causing? Most Northerners are implicated in the causes of poverty in some way either through their work (promoting consumer capitalism), consumption (ditto) or simply because they have not objected more thoroughly to the unequal economic relationships their governments have perpetrated. Indeed, it would be rather hard to find any citizen of a wealthy country who can speak out with complete legitimacy and authority. Littler's position, that celebrities are too compromised to speak out, would make it difficult for anyone in the North to protest development issues.

Kapoor's work presents a different problem.[71] Kapoor does not like celebrity advocacy, or celebrity advocates. He makes this reasonably clear. When imagining what might motivate them he writes:

> [P]erhaps they are sadists, secretly enjoying, not just the excessive pleasures of capital, but also the pain and degradation that capitalism inflicts on the Other. Despite public expressions of guilt, perhaps they derive obscene satisfaction and fascination from the global system of inequality which places *them* as the dominant. Perhaps they get off on humanitarianism's ideological deceptions, cover-ups and disavowals.[72]

To understand his thesis it is best to read the book backwards. Towards the end Kapoor argues that the only possible legitimate way out of our present dilemma is through a revolutionary overthrow of the capitalist system.[73] For this reason Kapoor advocates doing nothing in the face of poverty and inequality.[74]

46 Celebrity advocacy and post-democracy

His reason is that the only course of action currently open to us, supporting organisations like Oxfam, or lobbying for fairer trade rules, would also somehow end up sustaining the current system in some ways. That would be self-defeating; therefore it is better not to act.[75]

I find the prospect of such revolutionary inactivity leading to an overthrow of the capitalist system too remote. I prefer a more active approach. For that it is important to engage with the possibilities and practices of celebrity activism, one which, in Mark Wheeler's words, entertains 'a more intellectually curious critique of celebrity politics'.[76]

My explorations will show that all those who see celebrity advocacy as integral to capitalism are more right than they realise. We cannot understand the rise, or current role of celebrity advocacy, without seeing its close connections to corporate sponsorship and corporate social responsibility. However, precisely because of these deep entanglements with capitalism I find that demanding a celebrity-free clean slate provides no better starting point for constructively engaging with celebrity advocacy than bland assertions that celebrity advocacy builds cosmopolitanism. I want to understand the detail of these interactions in order to explore the possibilities of constructively engaging with celebrity advocacy.[77] We may conclude that none exist, and we are likely to find that celebrity is not a good vehicle for tackling structural inequities, but I want to look first.

Conclusion

Celebrity is not a trivial matter. It is indicative, indeed constitutive, of broader powers of elites, and wider problems of inequality. It is intimately implicated in the performance of democracy, and particularly of the media. Post-democratic politics and celebrity politics are deeply intertwined.

But we still need to understand *how* they are intertwined. It is trite to say that both are elites, both are part of the same 'system', both speak out for the same social and political order. Celebrity elites and political elites are often cut from a different cloth, and maintained by different processes. They work differently in the political and in the public domains. Therefore, in order to understand celebrity advocacy, we need to get to grips with the anatomy of how it is done. We need to understand how celebrity advocacy works with elites, and how it contributes to the mechanisms of elite politics which Crouch identified. We will examine this in more detail in Chapters 5 and 6.

And with this knowledge we should also be able to address the more fundamental issues of international development. How does celebrity advocacy affect the economic structures producing and reproducing inequality? What potential does celebrity have to effect meaningful change, or is it too much part of the problem of inequality to make any difference? How egalitarian are the outcomes of celebrity politics and advocacy when applied to international development? We will discuss these questions in the Conclusion at the end of the book.

We have in the last two chapters reviewed theories about how development advocacy works in general and what sort of awareness of distant strangers it produces. We have examined the emancipatory possibilities of celebrity advocacy. In the next four chapters we will explore the history, mechanisms and practices of celebrity advocacy in more detail to see how much of that emancipatory possibility is realised. We will examine how it has arisen, what forms it takes, how it is practised and what responses it produces among elites and the public. Let us turn first to the history of celebrity advocacy for international development cause.

Notes

1 Geldof is commenting on the public marches organised by the Make Poverty History campaign during the G8 summit at Gleneagles in 2005 whose timing clashed with the Live 8 concerts. The words come from a letter available at: www.starsuckersmovie.com/bob-geldof-letter (viewed August 2011).
2 Kapoor, 2012: 34 and 12.
3 Cooper, 2008b: 128.
4 Crouch, 2004: 19–20. Crouch recognises that enthusiasm for democracy will always be uneven over time. There will always be particular democratic 'moments' in the history of democratic societies, when popular verve for democratic power will be strong, and 'the political system has not quite discovered how to manage and manipulate the new demands' (2004: 7). In Europe this occurred shortly after World War II. However, as those moments subside, post-democratic politics have emerged. For the empirical details of democratic performance in the UK, see Aeron Davis, 2010. For doubts about the function of journalists in post-democratic times, see Schlesinger, 2006.
5 Rancière, 1998: 113.
6 Crouch, 2004: 21.
7 Crouch, 2004: 11, 52.
8 Celebrity politics may itself be a factor in the development of post-democratic politics. Marsh and colleagues, summarising Bang's work, observe the rise of 'expert-celebrity' political parties (Marsh *et al.*, 2010). Celebrity politics, in Street's felicitous summary, 'functions to convince electorates that they are being well governed' (2012: 6), with all the passive and marginal roles for electorates that that implies.
9 Rodrik, 2011. Rodrik provides a catalogue of the means by which mobile corporate firms can constrain political choices available to governments including labour standards, health and safety standards, corporate taxes and restrictions on labour policy.
10 Rodrik, 2011: 190. Tom Friedman, whose view of these policies is different from Rodrik's, makes a similar point. He calls them the 'Golden Straightjacket' because, he believes, they promote prosperity but reduce political freedom. 'Once your country puts on the Golden Straightjacket, its political choices get reduced to Pepsi or Coke – to slight nuances of tastes slight nuances of policy, slight alterations in design to account for local traditions, some loosening here or there, but never any major deviation from the core golden rules . . . your economy grows, and your politics shrink' (1997: 87, quoted in Rodrik, 2007: 202). See also Davis, A., 2010, Chapter 8.
11 Edwards and Hulme, 1992, 1995; Fisher, 1997; Hulme and Edwards, 1997; Crouch, 2004, 2011; Igoe and Kelsall, 2005; Bebbington *et al.*, 2008.
12 Crouch, 2004: 21, 26, 27, 103.
13 Hudson and van Heerde-Hudson, 2012. Olsen (2001) studied support to Africa from France, the UK, Germany, Denmark and the EU and concluded that decision-making was elite and top-down.
14 Cooper, 2007, 2008a, b.
15 Chouliaraki, 2013: 137.

48 Celebrity advocacy and post-democracy

16 Hyde, 2010. When the initial findings from one of the UK POM surveys we conducted were released Hyde wrote an article about them that referred to Kim Kardashian's (a US reality TV star) work in reducing poverty (Hyde, 2012). The commentators on that article, of whom there were several hundred, were often keen to demonstrate their ignorance of who Kardashian was, or what she was for. It was clear too that many of them spent some time trying to correct their ignorance. The article decrying celebrity produced a great deal of interest in it.

17 Hyde, 2010: 4.

18 Ferris, 2007: 374–6.

19 West and Orman, 2003.

20 Horkheimer and Adorno, 1972.

21 My discussion of Postman comes from Gabler, 1998. See also Duncombe, 2007, Chapter 5 for a thoughtful discussion on the repressions of celebrity.

22 Wheeler, 2012.

23 Street, 2004.

24 Source 8.

25 Street, 2004: 448.

26 Street, 2004.

27 Street, 2004.

28 Street, 2002, 2012.

29 Dahlgren, 2009.

30 Wheeler, 2013.

31 Corner and Pels, 2003: 10; Dahlgren, 2009: 142.

32 Habermas, 1989 [1962].

33 Marcus, 2002; Dahlgren, 2009.

34 van Zoonen, 2004: 49.

35 Couldry, 2010: 142.

36 Couldry, 2012: 128. Italics in the original.

37 With respect to engagement with media more generally (not just celebrity) and participation in politics, the Public Connection Project of Nick Couldry, Sonia Livingstone and Tim Markham makes an important contribution. They find little support for the idea that the media are dumbing down political debate, rather the media sustain political interest (Livingstone and Markham, 2008). They find that people are well connected via the media, but not necessarily through them to 'communities of practice' which facilitate the move from engaging with media to practising politics. In a discussion that describes post-democracy in all but name, they suggest that not engaging in politics may be a legitimate response to elitist politics (Couldry *et al.*, 2010 [2007]: 188–9).

38 Marks and Fischer, 2002.

39 West and Orman, 2003: 119.

40 Dahlgren, 2009.

41 Crouch makes a similar point 'while the forms of democracy remain fully in place – and today in some respects are strengthened – politics and government are increasingly slipping back into the control of privileged elites in the manner characteristic of pre-democratic times' (2004: 6).

42 Thrall *et al.*, 2008.

43 Thrall *et al.*, 2008: 375. Hawkins (2011) makes a similar argument.

44 Couldry and Markham, 2007. They derived this total from a cluster analysis of two of their questions from a large-scale survey which presented people with a variety of topics and asked them which they were interested in. The questions they used are listed on the research website: http://celebrityanddevelopment.wordpress.com/methods-used-in-the-book-celebrity-advocacy-and-international-development (viewed 25 February 2014).

45 Veer *et al.*, 2010.

46 Austin *et al.*, 2008; Jackson, D. J., 2008; Nownes, 2011; Becker, 2012.

47 Jackson and Darrow, 2005: 92.

48 Nownes, 2011.
49 Inthorn and Street, 2011.
50 For an excellent distillation of these arguments, see Chouliaraki (2013), Chapter 4.
51 Tester, 2010. Tester's whole essay was motivated by his hostility to the power and influence of celebrity (p. x). Problematic views of Africa are also one of the main arguments in Riina Yrjölä's first paper (Yrjölä, 2009). Both these authors base their critique on a detailed analysis of representations employed by Geldof, with Tester also examining Madonna's work and Yrjölä Bono's. Other examples include Anderson, 2008; Magubane, 2008; Niekerk, 2008; Magee, 2009; Davis, H. L., 2010. For a nuanced discussion of this with respect to the Save Darfur Campaign, see Whitlock, 2009.
52 Yrjölä, 2009; Repo and Yrjölä, 2011; Yrjölä, 2011a, b.
53 Yrjölä, 2011: 371. A related argument here is the way in which needy development victims are robbed of their agency by shallow portrayals of them, see Cameron and Haanstra, 2008, and Dieter and Kumar, 2008, but note Cooper's reply to the latter (Cooper, 2008a).
54 Littler, 2008. Other examples are Meyer and Gamson, 1995; Goodman, 2010; Richey and Ponte, 2011; Peck, 2012. Another variant of this argument is the idea that celebrity promotions and particularly cause-marketing associated with celebrity reproduces and strengthens neoliberal thinking and behaviour which are at the roots of inequality, e.g. Biccum, 2007; Anderson, 2008; Kuehn, 2009; Phu, 2010; Biccum, 2011; Njoroge, 2011; Tait, 2011. Farrell, 2012 puts it slightly more subtly, with respect to Bono and Product (RED). He argues that 'the (RED) campaign has sought to construct AIDS in a manner consistent with the ideological views with which it is underpinned' (p. 404).
55 Cohen cites the example of Jan Karski who reported the developing storm of the Holocaust to Western leaders in 1942. Those who heard him did not dispute the facts, but they did not believe him, which I think means that they could not acknowledge or act meaningfully on the significance of what they were being told. There is a difference, Cohen notes, between telling the truth, and being believed (Cohen, 2001: 160–1 and 187).
56 Littler, 2008: 248.
57 Kapoor, 2012: 33.
58 In particular I value the radical role of bearing witness, which they adopt. Imagining what something completely different might be is vital; it is a role I have take on elsewhere, in *Fortress Conservation* (Brockington, 2002).
59 See, for example, Dyer, 2004 [1986]; Brough, 2012; Gotham, 2012; Molina-Guzmán, 2012; Mukherjee, 2012; Trope, 2012.
60 Dogra, 2012.
61 van der Gaag and Nash, 1987; Darnton and Kirk, 2011.
62 Chouliaraki, 2013.
63 Fassin, examining literature on humanitarianism called for 'an approach that would allow us to analyse the effects of domination expressed through suffering . . . at the same time as the construction processes of which suffering is the object – in other words, to consider the politics of suffering in their complexity and ambiguity' (Fassin, 2012: 9).
64 cf. Anderson, 2011: 543.
65 Kate Crehan has made an important intervention in the understanding of what hegemony means, observing that it has been equated with ideology, concerned only with beliefs and ideas. Her intimate understanding of Gramsci suggests a different reading. Hegemony is about how social inequality is lived and practised, in day-to-day life as well as ideas (Crehan, 2002: 176, 200). See also Femia, 1975. As such, the problem of hegemony is echoed too in Pierre Bourdieu's work on the symbolic violence of the gift – in which subordinate people, receiving gifts from those above them in social hierarchies are implicitly (if not also explicitly) affirming these hierarchies, and their lowly position in them, by accepting gifts from above. Bourdieu, 1977 [1972]. cf. Eagleton, 1991 (2007): 156–8.

50 Celebrity advocacy and post-democracy

66 Billig, 1998 [1992]. It is based on his listening to 63 interviews recorded among different families across Middle England in the early 1990s about their views of the Royal family.
67 Billig, 1998 [1992]: 115.
68 Billig, 1998 [1992]: 222.
69 Couldry terms this exaltation of the media an injury because of its 'pervasive misrecognition of everyday life as '"merely" ordinary', which results in 'people's accepting as somehow justified their subordinate position in the distribution of society's *symbolic* resources, the ability to speak and be listened to on what matters to the world at large' (Couldry, 2001: 161–2, italics in the original). See also Couldry, 2012.
70 Compare also Richard Dienst's work here. He observes that 'Bono surely knows that the economic and ideological machinery that creates global rock superstars is inseparable from the vast machinery that creates and maintains global poverty' (2011: 96). This is a truism. These machineries are inseparable. But what matters is their causal relations – and it is harder to discern how poverty in, for example, rural Tanzania, is tangibly and directly linked to U2 album sales.
71 And also note an entertaining discussion between him and Mark Wheeler in the New Internationalist. Available at: http://eewiki.newint.org/index.php/Should_celebrities_ promote_charities%3F (viewed 8 January 2013).
72 Kapoor, 2012: 34. Kapoor repeats similar sentiments when he wonders whether Bono clapping on stage, once every three seconds, in time with the frequency of deaths to poverty in Africa might be 'applause *for* that child's death', for otherwise, no one would profit (Kapoor, 2012: 12, italics in the original).
73 Kapoor 2012: 124.
74 Žižek's writings are riven with violence, the more so for the callous and banal way in which he calls for it and celebrates it. I do not wish to engage with them in this book, for reasons that Gray (2012) captured well in his review. Available at: www.nybooks. com/articles/archives/2012/jul/12/violent-visions-slavoj-zizek (viewed 25 February 2014).
75 Kapoor, 2012: 123–4. Note, by the way, that if Kapoor is right in his criticism, or at least if he still believes that he is right, it would be still fair to expect some changes to Kapoor's own work. After all, he is asking us to abandon our support for distant strangers and to do nothing, because it ends up propping up an evil and iniquitous system. It cannot be reasonable to leave our inactivity there. We would surely need to do nothing a bit more generally, and could, for example, stop writing books for capitalist publishers and training new generations of employees (or, even worse, employers). Kapoor risks living precisely the life he is denouncing.
76 Wheeler, 2013: 171.
77 cf. Street *et al.*, 2008.

4

A BRIEF HISTORY OF CELEBRITY ADVOCACY FOR DEVELOPMENT AND HUMANITARIAN CAUSES

> It is a jail house crime for a poor damn working man to even hold a meeting with other working men. They call you a red or a radical or something, and throw you and your family off of the farm and let you starve to death . . . These songs will echo that song of starvation till the world looks level – till the world is level – and there ain't no rich men, and there ain't no poor men, and every man on earth is at work and his family is living as human beings instead of like a nest of rats.
>
> Woody Guthrie[1]

There is a well-known history of the famous working for development causes and fighting against oppression, poverty and misery. This takes in left-wing artists victimised by the House Committee of UnAmerican Activities during the McCarthy period, Bob Dylan's (a musician) protest song; Geldof's work for Band Aid, Live Aid and Live 8; the musicians who opposed against apartheid and celebrated Nelson Mandela (then a political prisoner); Bono's lobbying around debt, and George Clooney's (an actor) activism in the Sudan. There is also a less well-known one, which has seen the Save Darfur Coalition's celebrities criticised for misdiagnosing the problems in the Sudan; Bono become the subject of hundreds of vituperative comments from development activists; a collection of artists, including black South Africans, release a pro-apartheid single at the behest of the South African government; Geldof berate his fellow anti-poverty campaigners as 'wankers dressed as clowns'; Bob Dylan declare his ambivalence to the Vietnam War and left-wing actors and musicians declare their support for Stalin, which meant that during the Molotov–Ribbentrop pact they opposed war against Hitler and stood alongside far-right voices to do so.[2]

The task of this chapter is to tell the history that unites these diverse and contradictory events.[3] Varied though they are, two important themes emerge. The

52 A brief history of celebrity advocacy

first is that the nature and meaning of development (and humanitarianism) have long been contested, and celebrity has been part of the contest, at times changing the nature of those struggles.[4] The second, as the epigraph to the chapter indicates, is that the current proliferation of celebrity in development and humanitarian affairs reflect the dominance of one of those visions for development – a neoliberal capitalist vision – that obscures other, still vigorous, voices. As development practice and policy in pursuit of that vision have become increasingly the province of elite policy formation and less the terrain of popular struggle (or, in other words, more post-democratic), so the space has opened up for celebrity champions to service this hegemonic formation.

To develop this story I will first recount two histories – that of celebrity and that of development and humanitarianism. Then I will explore how they intertwine. This we can divide into three periods. In Victorian times, good causes (and often good causes overseas) were some of the main drivers of fame. This slowly declined until World War II. After World War II until the 1970s activism around the civil rights movement, anti-racism and the Vietnam War produced some deep involvement in political causes, but not in the international development sector. From the 1980s onwards, international development and international human rights issues became some of the main drivers of changes that saw the celebrity industry and the NGO sector form closer relations. This has become formalised into intensive and systematic relationships that began to blossom at the start of the present century.[5]

Celebrity

Celebrity presents itself as a recent phenomenon. But historians are pushing its history back many more centuries than is normally fashionable.[6] Perhaps the most entertaining contribution is Aviad Kleinberg's suggestion that we could treat twelfth-century saints as a form of celebrity.[7] Living saints could attract large crowds which, like present-day celebrities, could make their lives difficult. Like present day celebrities they found it difficult to appear twice in the same outfit. But this was not for fear of fashion editors' criticisms, but because their clothes could be ripped off them by followers seeking holy relics. Kleinberg reports an event in which one frustrated preacher, known as Fulk of Neilly, wreaked revenge on a particularly ardent admirer who was then ripping off his gown. Turning on the man, Fulk loudly and vigorously blessed his fan's clothes and made the sign of the cross, whereupon 'within minutes the crowd tore the gown of that man to pieces and kept the shreds as relics'.[8]

The dangers of anachronism are plain here, but so too should be the dangers of failing to recognise some of the continuities with the past.[9] We cannot, of course, say when celebrity began, but we can approximately date some its recent attributes. For Chris Rojek, the possibilities for celebrity emerge with modern democracy, which allows, in theory, anyone to achieve anything, regardless of where they are born in the social structure.[10] Tom Mole suggests that development of celebrity is differentiated from fame by its 'fascination with an individual's deeply privatised subjectivity', and dates its separation from achievement or status, to the late eighteenth century.[11]

As an industrial phenomenon, celebrity depends on technologies able to produce and disseminate large volumes of information about individuals to audiences. Initially, these were just texts (not pictures). Mole notes that the improvement of presses in the early 1800s and of distribution networks (especially railways) a little later made it possible for Lord Byron's publisher to sell 10,000 copies of one of his poems in a single day.[12] Other authors have noted the rise of newspapers and, especially, what Boorstin called 'the graphic revolution', which made it possible to circulate images of people and places widely and rapidly through society.[13] While celebrity in its most recognisable form may probably be dated to the rise of film and the cinema in the early 1900s, it built on forms of commodity circulation and consumption forged earlier by industrial societies.[14]

The history of celebrity in the last hundred years has to be understood as a history of controlling appearances (originally of stars in films) and access to these stars as a means of promoting commodities.[15] The commodities were originally the films themselves, but soon spread to other goods, in conjunction with the growing use of signs, symbols and images required to sell an increasing surfeit of commodities.[16] Celebrity has been central to the spread of particular forms of consumer capitalism. That was partly why Horkheimer and Adorno wrote their essay against the culture industries in the first place.[17]

The commercial dynamism of celebrity is responsible for its proliferation in recent years. As the media have become more varied in recent decades with more television channels, more magazines, and the development of the Internet, so there have been many more locations to be seen to be famous, and a growth of celebrity industries to fill the demand. There are now tens of thousands of celebrities. The Red Pages keeps contact details for over 25,000 public figures; Celebrities Worldwide has a similar number. 'Contact Any Celebrity' lists over 60,000 on its books.[18]

We have a limited understanding of the diversity of celebrity culture, and how its nature and form vary from country to country. We know, for example, that television advertisements in South Korea are dominated by celebrities far more than in the US, and that Europeans respond less to celebrity endorsements than do US citizens, but these are rather isolated facts. Comparative celebrity studies is a nascent discipline.[19] One important contribution is Laurie Ouellette and James Hay's study of reality TV programmes in the US. They stress repeatedly that the rise of these programmes has to be interpreted within the context of particular neoliberal politics and economic changes. For example, self-help and makeover programmes in the US such as *Dr Phil*, *Starting Over* and *Judge Judy* need to be interpreted as products of a neoliberal economic rationale that demands people be flexible and dynamic to meet the needs of an increasingly unpredictable economic regime.[20] Problems of job insecurity and lack of state provision for the needy are met with demands, exemplified by make-over programmes, that people take

54 A brief history of celebrity advocacy

responsibility for their own fate within the vicissitudes of that regime. The celebrity that is attendant on reality TV is produced by the failings of an economic system and attempts to fill the gaps it creates. Likewise, my reading of celebrity advocacy as functioning well in post-democracies is an attempt to locate the rise of this form of advocacy within broader political change.

Celebrity, then, is old. It is a product of democracy and the enlightenment, and it is an industrial force. It is part of the system of signs and images with which capitalism has sought to expand the market for commodities.[21] Within the work of celebrity advocacy we should expect to see the guiding hand of commercial interests shaping the development and growth of protest and causes.

Development and humanitarianism

Development and humanitarianism each have an official starting point: development in US President Truman's inaugural address in 1949, humanitarianism in Henry Dunant's epiphany in 1859 on the bloody fields of Solferino, from which the Red Cross dates its origins. But it is more accurate to recognise that each shares celebrity's antiquity and origins in profound social and industrial transformations. Michael Barnett locates the beginning of humanitarianism in the mid-eighteenth century, when the idea that humanity shared something in common, regardless of ties of blood, nationality, or even class and religion began to take hold.[22] Theories of the rights of men, and later women too, forged in revolutionary regimes, produced new sets of obligations. These included an expanding geography of need that recognised ever-more categories of people to be human, and increasingly sought to address the causes of want, not just the symptoms.

Humanitarianism is commonly portrayed as experiencing a sort of crisis because its central tenet of non-interference and independence from state power appears to have been relaxed. Now humanitarian organisations are calling for military interventions (in Kosovo in 1999, which British Prime Minister Tony Blair called a 'humanitarian war'), and states that are intervening militarily are calling for humanitarian organisations to support them in doing so (as did the US in Iraq). The scale of state funding for development and humanitarian organisations makes independence from them difficult to maintain. Relations between humanitarianism and military intervention can now be so close that 'Aid NGOs now work with the military in post-conflict zones assuming responsibility as public service subcontractors for the provision of health and education.'[23] But Barnett insists that it is misleading to think of this crisis as a new chapter in the history of interactions between humanitarianism and state power. Rather, these dilemmas have been present from the start. Aid organisations have always been embroiled in politics. If anything is new about the current era, it is *the idea* that these affairs present humanitarianism with a crisis.

Björn Hettne sets his history of development thinking in the origins of capitalism and the development of nation states in the late Middle Ages in Europe, through which several European countries were able to begin forcibly shaping the world system (then dominated by China and India) to their own ends.[24] Into these thriving new powers were infused ideas of 'progress', developed as thinkers began to try to comprehend the new capitalist economies forming around them. Through the nineteenth century, development became fused with industrialisation, often driven itself by security interests.[25]

The notions and goals of development have been thoroughly contested. Much of the strife of the last century concerned questions about the proper development goals for people to attain and how they could be realised. Development has meant both self-determination by colonised people and more colonial intervention; both freedom from racial oppression and racially segregated (and unequal) polities; both freeing of markets and communist planning; both land reform that restores land to dispossessed peasants, and agricultural change that empowers already rich landlords; and both small-scale self-sufficiency and integration with the global economy.[26] Much of that is hard to appreciate now with formal colonisation virtually over and communism a largely spent force. But radicalism, among scholars, celebrities and politicians alike, was, for the vast majority of the twentieth century, defined by the alternative visions of development it enshrined.

The history of development, then, is part of a geopolitical battle.[27] David Ekbladh's history of the development mission of the US is a demonstration of the presence of state interests in development and humanitarian work overseas. Truman's inaugural speech in 1949 was new not because it created overseas development but because 'it enshrined it as a permanent part of the official foreign policy apparatus of the US government'.[28] In particular, Truman's project was a determined effort to win the affection of peoples all over the world who might otherwise be drawn to the development promises of the Soviet Union. Ross's history of this period documents some appalling travesties in which, despite its goal of making capitalism look attractive, the interests of the rich against the poor prevailed. Theories based on Malthusian thinking about the inadequacies of the poor have obscured the real causes of their difficulties, which lay in the inequities of capitalism.[29]

Since the Cold War, development has been dominated by the rise of neoliberal thinking about the power of markets, the need to cut down the reach and spending of states and a corresponding faith in civil society which has seen NGOs blossom in numbers and size. The consequences of that growth for development NGOs have been traced in a series of conferences held in Manchester over the course of the 1990s. These were first characterised by optimism and hope,[30] then by doubts over NGOs' proximity to states and corporate power.[31] The distinction between civil society and markets blurs as NGOs have become increasingly businesslike in their operation, commercial in their funding, competitive with each other and have formed close relationships with large corporate sponsors. Companies, as we shall see below (Chapter 7), have also increasingly sought to work with NGOs as part of their corporate social responsibility and cause-related marketing campaigns. Corporate leaders and NGO leaders now attend the same global meetings and

56 A brief history of celebrity advocacy

gatherings; they are an element of the same transnational capitalist class.[32] Civil society is marked by its merging and overlap with states and the business sector such that it can be hard to tell where one begins and the other ends. This merging is, as Cooper and Wheeler have argued, crucial to understanding the rising power and influence of celebrity which is able to cross the blurred boundaries of these sectors with ease. [33]

Development and humanitarianism, then, are thoroughly imbricated in state power and have been since their inception. Just as celebrity is fundamentally a commercial force, development and humanitarianism have been, effectively, instruments of political ideology. Yet, at the same time, that role has been strongly resisted by organisations and individuals within the development and humanitarian movements. The political role of development and humanitarianism has been characterised by tension and paradox. The rise of celebrity within development is also one of the means, and indicators, of the way in which development actors, and particularly development NGOs, have come to terms with, and sought to extend the influence of, their changing position.

The rise and fall of celebrity and international development

Celebrity advocacy may well be prominent and organised now, but it is not the high point of the association of fame with good causes overseas. The zenith belongs to the Victorian era. Then, serving good causes, and in particular Britain's self-proclaimed mission to bring civilisation and progress to other parts of the world, was one of the major driving forces creating fame. Some of the most famous Britons of the time were acclaimed because of their support for good causes overseas. The precursors of development – the campaign against slavery, missionary activity, exploration and imperial conquest – produced the household names of the British Imperial Age.

The list here is long and impressive: the missionary explorer, David Livingstone, Henry Stanley (also an explorer) who found him, Colonel Gordon (a soldier) who died defending Khartoum, Captain Scott (an explorer) who died in the Antarctic and Shackleton (an explorer) who ensured that all his men survived it. We could also include Byron, who, having won fame, put it and himself to the service of Greek independence; the politician William Wilberforce, whose moral crusade against slavery constituted part of his renown, and Edward Morel who came to public prominence campaigning against the evils of King Leopold of Belgium's Congo.[34] If we consider good causes more generally and include more domestic issues, then the list expands to include Dr Barnardo for his work with poor British children, William Stead's campaigns against child prostitution and Florence Nightingale who won fame while ministering to British soldiers in the Crimea.

This list includes very different sorts of acclaim. Morel and Wilberforce were fighting oppression. In that respect we could also include Saint-Simon, Comte and Marx among their number, as all won renown for challenging what progress

A brief history of celebrity advocacy 57

(development) meant under nascent capitalist formations.[35] Others, like Livingstone, were on safer ground, if not literally (Livingstone died in Africa), at least with respect to the ideals they advanced.

Many were able to thrive because of the mass-circulating commodities they could create. Explorers' books, and the prestige of speakers at the Royal Geographical Society, bought both money and fame. The potter Josiah Wedgwood produced one of the first mass-circulated commodities in support of a humanitarian cause overseas. He created numerous pottery items portraying a slave kneeling in chains with the inscription 'Am I not also a man and brother'. Another way of putting this is that the commodity-making commerce that fuelled early forms of celebrity also drove the renown of early forms of celebrity advocacy.

It does not matter why or how people took on these public roles. Some were certainly shrewd publicists (Barnardo), energetic social campaigners for whom public support gave greater influence (Morel), or explorers who realised that the stories of adventure and daring meant they could 'sing for their supper'.[36] Others appeared to give no thought to the public reception of their work (Nightingale). More importantly, these people, in taking on substantial ills plaguing their society, or those they perceived in others, both created and benefited from one of the main engines of public renown: being 'do-gooders'[37]. This period differs from others because the British public were seemingly so keen to reward their activities with renown.

The first half of the twentieth century is a chronicle of the slow decline in this association. Prominent figures did emerge to champion humanitarian causes. Eglantyne Jebb worked despite opposition in Britain to support starving children in Eastern Europe. She founded the International Save the Children Union in Geneva in 1920 and the Declaration of the Rights of the Child that she drafted was adopted by the League of Nations in 1924. The Norwegian explorer Fridtjof Nansen became the League of Nations Commissioner for Refugees in 1921 and was awarded a Nobel Peace Prize in 1922. In Britain, Eleanor Rathbone became known as the Member of Parliament for refugees for her work on displacement in Europe. Later, after World War II, Victor Gollancz, a publisher, campaigned vigorously for provisions for Germans suffering hunger and deprivation after World War II. Albert Schweitzer won the Nobel peace prize in 1952 for public health works in Africa.

But the point of this period is that its story can be quickly told. In the first half of the last century there were few great artists, entertainers or athletes who became famous for their political or humanitarian stances, and few humanitarians, do-gooders or campaigners who won renown for their good works. The engines and publics producing fame did not work well with such material.

It may reflect the fact that battle lines over what progress meant were being drawn between massive encampments, dividing liberalism, fascism and communism. In the liberal UK and US, protest and political action against the evils of the day were increasingly anti-establishment. This could mean unpopularity, even notoriety. The pacifism of writers such as George Bernard Shaw and Romain Rolland caused

58 A brief history of celebrity advocacy

both to be vilified during the First World War.[38] Morel's opposition to that war saw him surrender the public approbation he secured in his campaign over the Congo for derision and a jail term.[39] Such protest was not easily captured for commercial purposes. Joe Hill, 'America's first star protest singer',[40] was part of the International Workers of the World whose *Little Red Songbook* was a powerful part of the success of the movement to empower labour in the US at the start of the twentieth century.[41] It was emphatically not a commercial movement.

Alternatively, these dominant creeds tamed and restricted the protest voice. One of the most famous black leaders in an era of white supremacy in America, Booker T. Washington, was acclaimed in part because he sought to accommodate Jim Crow and focus merely on economic advancement for black Americans.[42] Artists who stood out in opposition to dominant creeds in the West were rare. Colin Chambers's book exploring artists' protest concentrates on just three: the dancer and feminist Isadora Duncan; Paul Robeson, an African-American singer and actor who opposed racism at home and oppression abroad, and Charlie Chaplin whose films (like *Modern Times*) caused the establishment such unease that he had to leave the profoundly anti-communist US in 1952.[43]

When the fight between these blocs came to a head in World War II, governments quickly put famous people to work for their causes. Celebrities worked particularly closely with their respective governments during World War II. The boxer Joe Louis worked with the US government and gave charity benefit fights for the war effort. Hollywood and Roosevelt's administration co-operated closely through the Bureau of Motion Pictures. In the UK, the performer Gracie Fields gave considerably to the war effort, both in time and money. Vera Lynn (a singer) won fame as 'the forces sweetheart' in the UK.

For thirty years after World War II, development and humanitarianism were dominated by the Cold War, and by government actions and imperatives. The US government worked with jazz musicians in a cultural battle with the Soviet Union to proclaim the virtues and freedoms of its capitalist democracies.[44] The irony was that African-American jazz musicians were celebrating the 'freedom' of a country still steeped in racist segregation policies, North and South.[45]

In the poorer parts of the world, renown belonged to leaders championing contested ideals of what development and progress should be (Ghandi, Fidel Castro, Che Guevera, Pinochet). But there was little fame associated with development and humanitarian organisations per se. The only world famous figure to emerge was Mother Teresa, who was awarded a peace prize in 1979 for her work with the poor of Calcutta.[46] There are some small exceptions. Black notes that Oxfam's leader, Leslie Kirkley, who visited the Congo during a famine in 1961, 'was, fleetingly, a celebrity on whom British hopes of saving lives were visibly pinned'.[47] The flamboyant co-founder of Médecins Sans Frontières, Bernard Kouchner, was also adept at getting in the news.[48] John Pilger's (a journalist) hard-hitting films came to public prominence and provoked strong public reactions during the crisis in Kampuchea (now called Cambodia) in the late 1970s. But these are marginalia to the general absence of public figures.

There were interactions between famous people and international development causes, but these were the relatively shallow and fleeting sort that occurred when NGOs worked with famous people to raise money. In the UK Oxfam teamed up with the Beatles (a band) to raise a million pounds in their Christmas appeal in 1963.[49] UNICEF also got famous painters to paint their Christmas cards.[50] Lynskey claims that the benefit concerts were 'kick-started' in 1971 when musicians, including Eric Clapton and Bob Dylan, led by George Harrison, teamed up to support famine relief in Bangladesh.[51] Amnesty International enjoyed astute collaborations with classical musicians in the 1970s and with comedians in the same period, most successfully with the Secret Policeman's Ball in 1979.[52]

These activities could be important for the financial health of the organisations involved, but they did not lead to sustained relationships between a cause and a public figure. This point is best demonstrated by the exception to it. Danny Kaye's (a comedian) highly committed work as a UNICEF ambassador began (at his initiative) in 1954.[53] But it brings into sharp relief the fact that this initiative was not replicated in the entertainment industry.[54] Kaye remained UNICEF's *sole* celebrity ambassador for many years. Peter Ustinov did not join him until 1968; Liv Ullmann followed in 1979. A formal ambassador programme, with a large number of ambassadors, was not set in motion until the early 1980s, and not replicated by other NGOs until the 1990s. Similarly, the Entertainment Industry Foundation, founded in 1942, existed to facilitate philanthropy in the US by wealthy entertainers.

If celebrities were not getting involved in development causes, they were increasingly fighting domestic issues. This was particularly so in the US with the civil rights campaign and the protests against the Vietnam War. The leftist leaning of such protest (following the politics of Woody Guthrie and Pete Seeger's folk songs) made it increasingly difficult for politically orientated artists to speak out in the early years after World War II.[55] However, as McCarthyism subsided, and the civil rights movement gathered steam, speaking out became easier. After May 1963, when dogs and fire hoses were turned on peaceful demonstrators in Birmingham, Alabama, it became hard not to. Lynskey writes that 'every black performer had to decide which side they were on'.[56] Similarly, a host of artists (Phil Ochs, Joan Baez, Edwin Star, Neil Young, Joe MacDonald) protested against the Vietnam War, which began in earnest in 1965. John Lennon's (a musician) opposition to the war earned him the attention of the FBI and attempts to deport him.[57] Jane Fonda (an actress) gained notoriety in the US for her opposition to the war, particularly after her visit to Hanoi in 1972.

The relationship between fame and protest was not easy, and not just because some stars suffered for their convictions. When protest becomes fashionable, it can fall apart under the weight of its contradictions. Tom Wolfe wrote his brilliant semi-fictional essay *Radical Chic* to capture the paradoxes involved when protest, and potentially violence, became fashionable among the privileged literati. Conflicts that had so much of their roots in economic inequality and disadvantage were being celebrated in fancy Manhattan apartments.[58]

60 A brief history of celebrity advocacy

But more than that, the business of being famous, and creating famous protest leaders could cut those leaders off from the roots of their movement, and leave those leaders circulating in a repetitive, empty world of media events, as Todd Gitlin described: 'They floated in a kind of artificial space, surrounded by haloes of processed personality; the media became their constituency.'[59] Stephen Tuck, in his history of the black freedom struggle in America argues that mediagenic leaders like Martin Luther King, and media focus on him, provide a distorted picture of the struggle. He also notes that in the 1970s the absence of (male) charismatic leaders was 'no bad thing' for many activists.[60]

Nevertheless, the 1960s were years of a general mood of protest and change in which musicians seemed at the fore. It is difficult to recapture the giddiness of the times. 'For a while', notes Lynskey, 'in the dizzying rush of the 1960s it was thought that pop music would change the world'.[61] Doggett observes the same moment: '[a]nyone . . . who was attracted by the seductive power of rock, and the flamboyance of its emotional and political rhetoric, found themselves swept into what appeared to be a life-or-death struggle for survival and freedom'.[62] The rapid social changes and much of the social protest of the 1960s found its voice among musicians.

The reasons for musicians' prominence in protest lie in the structural changes to the music industry that occurred after World War II. By the late 1960s the major record companies had learned that they could not determine what the radical new tastes were to be. They were happy to cede that role to independent labels and the artists themselves, buying up the more successful ones.[63] This gave considerable freedom to the individual stars who wished to make more political statements. The political activism of the music industry could be led from below.[64] In due course the growing commercial power of African-American, and later Hispanic, consumers in the US gave more freedom to artists (James Brown, Stevie Wonder, Gil Scott-Heron) who wished to sing about the causes of oppressed North Americans. Or, put another way, if the consumers were prepared to buy protest songs, then the major companies were happy to provide them, and if not, there was no need to provide any.[65]

Commerce and protest, then, can live together in music.[66] Iconic events such as Woodstock were underwritten by the music industry which bought the rights to film and record it.[67] Free entry was possible because the organisers of this most disorganised of gatherings failed to make adequate arrangements to sell tickets, or keep out the crowd. Commerce and oppositional politics made space for each other.[68] Moreover, with vigorous debates about what development might actually mean – black power, self-determination, decolonisation, communism, feminism and much more – there was much to sing about.

By 1972 this revolutionary moment had virtually vanished, to the shock of many involved.[69] However, while the revolutionary fervour died, the blooming of the music industry and its concentration of controlling the rights and distribution of the products, gave it two excellent means of responding quickly to the charitable needs of the hour, albeit in a much more staid fashion. As one figure high up in the music industry observed:

We've got ... the two perfect mechanisms, one putting out a record ... just bunging together a compilation ... which we do all the time anyway ... get everybody to pay over their proceeds and you stick the Japanese tsunami on the front of it and you are off to the races ... it's an easy thing to do. Or you put on a concert, same thing. If you look at the other industries its much much harder for them, you cannot make a film in a week.[70]

Even if musicians and music became less radical immediately after the 1960s, the music industry was well placed to appear to act for social change and to appeal to its tradition of doing so.

Overseas development returns to fame

From the 1980s onwards the associations between fame and development and humanitarian causes comes to life again. But it is a mistake to think that the concerts of the 1980s and other activities of the decade initiate a gradual rise in celebrity advocacy that culminates in the present time. Instead, we need to see three stages in the development of current relations. There is the flurry of activity of the 1980s, this then dies off in the early 1990s before returning with a vengeance in the form of Princess Diana's advocacy and the Jubilee 2000 campaign. The most recent years are different from earlier periods, in part because these are the years when post-democratic politics come to dominate, in part because of the systematically organised and intensive relations that now characterise interactions between celebrities and charities in general, and between development and humanitarian NGOs in particular.

UNICEF, through its ambassadors Danny Kaye and Peter Ustinov, probably enjoyed the highest profile of all the charitable organisations working overseas, and, with their New York base, were well placed to interact with the jet set. In 1976, they appointed their first full-time special events manager, who handled interactions with public figures, because of the demand for work. Note that at this stage it was as much the public figures coming to the cause as the other way around.[71] There was not yet a deliberate policy to engage the entertainment industry even in UNICEF. It was not until later in the 1980s that UNICEF ambassadors became considerably more numerous.[72]

The 1980s saw the growth of a number of media-savvy causes. The Nicaraguan Solidarity Campaign in the UK worked with musicians, comedians and actors to raise funds and awareness and to enthuse and support its grassroots supporters. There was no particular celebrity strategy involved, instead 'part of our basic idea was that people being active on the Nicaragua campaign ought to be quite fun'.[73] More sustained interactions between deserving causes and public figures, in particular in the entertainment industry, became more prominent in the anti-apartheid movement, with Nelson Mandela birthday concerts in 1983 and 1988 and the anti-apartheid Sun City album in 1985.

62 A brief history of celebrity advocacy

Perhaps the most major single event of the decade with respect to celebrity and humanitarianism was the response to the Ethiopian famine of 1984. On 24 October 1984, the British Broadcasting Corporation (BBC) broadcast a devastating newsreel created by Michael Buerk and Mohamed Amin in refugee camps in Korem, Ethiopia. The broadcast caused a huge outpouring of grief, sympathy and money internationally, producing a significant surge in NGO revenues (Figure 2.1). The broadcast also prompted Bob Geldof and Midge Ure (another musician) to put together Band Aid (with nearly forty UK artists), releasing its best-selling record in November 1984. Their success prompted Harry Belafonte (an actor) and Ken Kragen (a music manager) to form the group USA for Africa (with nearly forty US artists) releasing *We Are the World* in 1985. The subsequent Live Aid concerts in July 1985, organised by Geldof and Goldsmith, involved unprecedented numbers of musicians (over fifty acts) and viewers (nearly two billion) and raised over £60 million to support famine relief.[74]

The famine also provoked a collection of British comics led by Richard Curtis (a writer) to come together to try to raise money for the African poor through their comedy. Comic Relief was first broadcast in December 1985, with record releases and other entertainment events in 1986 and 1987 and the first 'Red Nose Day' in 1988. The latter cast comedians and other celebrities in sketches, field-trips and short films in poor countries in a single 'telethon' (a fundraising genre first attempted in the UK by the BBC with its Children in Need appeal of 1980). Comic Relief is crucial to the subsequent interactions of celebrity and development in the UK because it has been continually present and growing more prominent ever since its inception. After the first telethon, subsequent Red Nose Days were held in 1989 and biannually since.[75]

The mid to late 1980s are also significant for the rise of HIV/AIDS. The disease had a particularly strong effect on the entertainment industry. AIDS came to prominence in Los Angeles (it was first reported there in 1981) and some of the early victims were part of the entertainment community. The Elizabeth Glaser Paediatric Aids Foundation was set up in 1988, and the musician Elton John set up his Aids Foundation in 1992. As HIV/AIDS later morphed into an illness of the African poor, so the focus of these organisations, and the public figures supporting them, became more development orientated.

The late 1980s saw further large-scale musical events supporting good causes.[76] The Nelson Mandela Birthday Tribute in 1988 resulted in an 11-hour broadcast which was shown in 72 countries and reached 200 million viewers.[77] Greenpeace launched the album *Rainbow Warriors* in 1989.[78] In the same year Amnesty International launched its Human Rights Now world tour. This built on a smaller 'Conspiracy of Hope' tour in 1986 in the US, but was much larger, with bigger names (the highlight was the rock star Bruce Springsteen), and it covered 15 countries in 6 weeks, with the documentary of the tour being seen by over 1 billion people in 67 countries.[79] The fact that the musician Sting (who featured in all the events in this paragraph) also set up the Rainforest Foundation in 1989 and supported it with concerts, now seems a relatively minor event in comparison.

These musical extravaganzas, however, did not initiate a period of even growth or gradually increasing engagement and intensification of relationships between musicians and good causes in the 1990s. In some respects things went backwards. Among musicians at the height of Britpop and grunge it was an important part of their brand and image *not* to get involved in charitable activity.[80] Collaboration between celebrity and good causes overseas came in fits and starts, focusing around key events. One significant moment came with the conflict in Yugoslavia.[81] It prompted film makers Bill Leeson and David Wilson to start the NGO War Child in 1993. The charity enjoyed good links with the music and entertainment industry in the UK and, following the massacre at Srebrenica, War Child released the album *Help* in 1995, which was notable for enrolling the support of bands like Blur, Oasis and Massive Attack that had hitherto avoided supporting charitable activity.[82]

The last years of Princess Diana's life are also significant in this history, not just for what she did for different causes, but for the fact that her charitable activities were so beneficial for her public reputation and popular support. Other celebrities and their managers were quick to notice that. After she died, some charities for whom she had played a prominent role were besieged with offers from public figures to take her place: 'We didn't really want anyone to take over from Diana but of course we had offers coming in from everywhere . . . because it was good for a celebrity . . . to take over from [her].'[83] Certainly, when agents were approached by charities looking for people to take Diana's place they were quick to recognise the value of this opportunity. One agent told me that he was favourably impressed by a request to make one of his clients a patron of a charity in succession to Princess Diana because it would do a lot to her profile 'because of course she was seen in the same . . . peer group as Diana'.[84]

The most significant episode of this period with respect to development issues was the Jubilee 2000 campaign of 1996–2000.[85] This international coalition of NGOs and campaigners sought to reduce the debt repayments by poor countries to the wealthy that were constraining these countries and dwarfing aid payments made by the rich to the poor. The campaign deliberately sought to enrol the music industry to support Jubilee 2000 and engaged consultants to advise how to interest them. A particularly successful coup was Muhammad Ali's appearance at the Brit Awards to receive an award from Bono for the Jubilee 2000 campaign. This had particular impacts within the music industry as well as in the press.[86]

Jubilee 2000 is significant for three reasons. First, it was remarkably successful: $27 billion in new debt reduction was agreed in 1999 and further promises were made to write off debt amounting to $100 billion owed by 35 of the world's poorest countries.[87] Cox observes that '[m]any of those in government, both then and now, identify Jubilee 2000 as one of the most effective campaigns'.[88] He admits that much of this debt had already been written off, and the deals announced merely formalised those write-offs, but the important point is that '[i]n a matter of three years, the world's attitude to debt had been turned on its head'.[89]

Second, it highlights a new political order in which celebrities are listened to keenly, and where being famous meant having access to political power, just as

64 A brief history of celebrity advocacy

having political power gave access to the famous.[90] The Clinton and Blair governments (which came to power in 1993 and 1997 respectively) were well known for their leaders' and members' eagerness to be seen next to celebrities.[91] Kofi Annan's appointment as UN Secretary-General in 1997 strengthened the zeitgeist.[92] The UN was already well advanced in the establishment of goodwill ambassador programmes before Annan's appointment (Figure 5.1). Annan further intensified the use of celebrity within the UN agencies, appointing his own 'Messengers of Peace' as well as overseeing a doubling of ambassador programmes within UN agencies during his tenure.

Third, it also illustrates well the extent to which working for good causes, and taking a stand on difficult issues, could now constitute a significant element of the public persona of public figures. Geldof and Bono, in particular, won renown for their grasp of the issues, the ability to gain access to key public figures and persuade them to join their cause.[93] Their interest, moreover, has been sustained. They both played prominent roles in (or in tandem with) Make Poverty History in 2005. Geldof served on Blair's African Commission in 2005. Bono went on to found DATA in 2002, which later merged into ONE in 2008 and he launched (Product) Red in 2006 which has raised over $170 million for the global fund to fight AIDS in Africa.[94]

Geldof and Bono are not unique. In terms of personal devotion to causes, precedents include Paul Robeson, Jane Fonda and Vanessa Redgrave. But few have enjoyed their access to the powerful (which is partly a product of the celebrity-orientated politics of the time), powers of persuasion, or the widespread popular appeal for their actions (we will examine them in more detail in Chapter 7). They are also marked, along with figures like Angelina Jolie, by the extent to which development activities have become part of their personal brand. This is best illustrated in Bono and Jolie's appearance in Louis Vuitton advertisements, which try to capture celebrities in natural conditions, with Louis Vuitton bags as part of their normal life. Bono is pictured with his wife leaving a place somewhere in Africa (the caption states, 'Every Journey Begins in Africa'). Jolie is photographed in Cambodia.[95] Similarly, Geldof's role as chairman of the recently launched 8 Miles private equity fund has credibility and appeal because the fund seeks to invest in African business opportunities.[96]

In the 2000s celebrity was becoming integrated into NGO practices. One CEO of a small charity recalled that it was 'the established orthodoxy' that to get media attention and major funders one had to have a celebrity.[97] 'Celebrities . . . had become a kind of received wisdom in the little international NGO-Aid industry in London where we were based.'[98] Celebrity was even becoming part of the academic development community. Prominent public intellectuals in the development sector such as Jeffrey Sachs, Joe Stiglitz, Paul Farmer and Paul Collier began either mixing socially and professionally with celebrities and/or producing commercially valuable products (books, TV programmes) which can be promoted with, or in the manner of, celebrities. Sachs has been best at this. His popular book about development has a Foreword written by Bono, and he and Jolie toured Africa together in 2005 for an MTV show.

Make Poverty History and the Save Darfur Coalition

The changes that I am documenting were brought to a spectacular conclusion in two celebrity-dominated campaigns in 2004–6. Indeed, 2005 saw so much celebrity activity for good causes that *Time* magazine called it the 'Year of Charitainment'.[99] One of these was the Make Poverty History campaign in the UK and its sister ONE campaign in the US. Make Poverty History was a concerted attempt by a coalition of NGOs to seize the opportunity of Britain's chairing of the G8 and EU to push wealthy countries to support poorer countries through debt cancellation, fairer trade and more and better aid.[100] The campaign peaked in July 2005 when the G8 summit was held at Gleneagles in Scotland. Thereafter it lost momentum, and was able to exert little pressure on subsequent trade negotiations. However, Make Poverty History's work with celebrity is an enduring part of the story that unfolds in this book and we must examine it in some detail.

The campaign was steeped in celebrity messaging from the start. It enjoyed substantial logistical and creative support from Richard Curtis who, with Comic Relief, then marshalled a large body of celebrities in a variety of advertisements and public service announcements. Make Poverty History's other association with celebrity arises from its rather fraught association with Geldof. The Live 8 concerts (11 venues, over 1 billion viewers) which Geldof organised independently from Make Poverty History, clashed directly with the activist marches Make Poverty History promoted, and came to dominate coverage of the G8 and Make Poverty History's own campaign.[101] Focus group research after the summit revealed that some people thought that Make Poverty History was merely the slogan of the Live 8 concerts.[102] This confusion of Live 8 and Make Poverty History was frustrating for activists for whom the concerts were merely a poorly timed distraction from the real campaign.

Make Poverty History was a tense alliance of NGOs because of the campaign's proximity to power. It enjoyed a close relationship with the British government. Nicky Sireau observed that the alliance tried to marry 'radical outsiders' who felt most comfortable lobbying oppositionally with 'moderate insiders' who wanted a more intimate relationship with authority.[103] The prominence of celebrities, the simplicity of some of their messages, and the lack of control that some members of the campaign felt over them, became a flashpoint for the underlying conflict.[104]

These tensions boiled over at the (now infamous in NGO circles) post-summit press conference in July. In public Geldof humiliated the Make Poverty History campaigners by welcoming the measures the G8 adopted in response to the campaign, and berated Make Poverty History's own response which complained of the inadequacy of the measures adopted.[105] Behind the scenes there was a physical altercation between a leading member of the UK government team and a leader of the Make Poverty History group. The conflicts have had a lasting influence. They were still visible in my interviews (six years after the events). They flared up spectacularly when the documentary *Starsuckers* was shown in the UK on Channel 4 in April 2010, which attacked the role and power of celebrity in the Make Poverty History group.[106]

66 A brief history of celebrity advocacy

Amid all this furore it remains important to consider what Make Poverty History achieved. The campaign had three goals: more and better aid, reduction of debt and fairer trade. We have to assess what was pledged by the G8 countries, what they delivered and what lasting impact the campaign has had on public awareness of development. With respect to aid, the G8 pledged $25 billion to double their budgets for specific countries in Africa by 2010.[107] On debt they announced an agreement to forgive the debts of eighteen countries (mainly African) that had already been agreed a month earlier. On trade there was 'little movement'.[108] Cox observes that, at the time, these agreements were greeted with derision by more radical groups who competed to outdo each other in angry rhetoric.[109] This probably reflects the fact that the most important goal for them was structural reform to trade relations which are so damaging to poorer countries and on which so little was agreed. Nevertheless, Cox observes, these same organisations are now complaining that their leaders have not lived up to these apparently inadequate promises – and in the main, they have not. They have delivered only about half of the promised extra aid by the 2010 deadline.[110]

With respect to public awareness, Make Poverty History achieved extraordinary brand recognition in the first half of 2005, with 87 per cent of the public reporting that it knew about the campaign. People who reported themselves to be very concerned about levels of international poverty increased from 25 per cent (which it is routinely) to 33 per cent. There were high levels of involvement: 15 per cent of the public responded to a request for action (such as sending texts, or wearing the wristband) with many of those new to campaigning.[111]

However, that awareness rapidly tailed off, and six months later most of those who had acted had forgotten that they had. People who were very concerned about levels of international poverty fell to below 25 per cent.[112] Behind these unimpressive numbers is a deeper problem. As Graham Harrison has observed, Make Poverty History produced, effectively, an 'Africanisation' of poverty which reflects, and contributed to, a popular British perception that equates poverty with Africa and vice versa. It also reflects the influence of Geldof, for whom the goals of Make Poverty History came to implement the findings of Blair's Commission for Africa, which he had helped to set in motion.[113] Harrison's analysis demonstrates that a campaign for justice and systemic change globally was transformed into a charitable cause raising money for Africa 2010. Darnton concluded that '[t]he charity not justice message was not understood by the audience',[114] and that 'the overall conclusion is that a vast amount of effort was required to deliver relatively small shifts in public perceptions (and) . . . the positive impacts very soon disappear'.[115] It was partly in response to this disappointing development that a number of NGOs collaborated on the work that became *Finding Frames* (discussed on p. 28).[116]

Kate Nash's analysis of the campaign suggests further problems with this public awareness.[117] Nash acknowledges that it was 'hugely successful in constructing public space for its claims', but the public space did not include a sufficiently powerful 'cosmopolitan solidarity' to support its radical agenda. There was little space for African voices in the publicity or the concerts; and the campaign for the needs of the global South did not consider how those needs might conflict with those of the North, of the campaigners themselves. Hence there was a political mandate for rather minor, harmless or unenforceable promises about debt and aid, but nothing more substantial like trade relations. What was missing, and what cosmopolitanism requires, is 'the working through and incorporation of different perspectives from positions of . . . inequality and conflicting socio-economic interests to reach consensus on how "we" nevertheless belong together, sharing mutually recognized belonging to a community of fate.'[118]

In parallel to Make Poverty History the other force for celebrity involvement in overseas causes in the mid-noughties was the US-based Save Darfur Coalition. This brought together a wide range of activist groups united by the conviction that the Sudanese government's brutal repression of a nascent rebellion in Darfur in 2003–4 amounted to genocide. Between 2004 and 2006, actors including George Clooney, Mia Farrow and Don Cheadle helped to fuel media attention in what became 'the biggest social movement in the United States since the campaign against apartheid'.[119] At its peak, the movement involved hundreds of thousands of activists, a broad range of celebrities, wealthy philanthropists such as Pam Omidyar and highly effective lobbying of Washington, corporations and even Beijing.[120]

The Save Darfur Coalition was effective because it achieved its lobbying goals, perhaps most notably when it exploited China's hosting of the Olympics (labelled the 'Genocide' Olympics) to push China into adopting a more neutral position, less obstructive to putting pressure on Sudan and when it encouraged the International Criminal Court to issue an arrest warrant against President al-Bashir of Sudan. Whether those goals were effective in seeking peace in Darfur is another issue. Experts and journalists argue that the NGOs in the Save Darfur Coalition did not have an adequate grasp of the nature and progress of the conflict.[121] They were wrong to label the horrendous violence as genocide – it did not amount to that. Moreover, they exaggerated the violence and did not have a good grasp of the facts on the ground. George Clooney, speaking to the UN Security Council, insisted that without a replacement to the African peace-keeping force then in place, there would be widespread massacres. In fact, there were about 4,000 reported deaths that year in the conflict (half of them government forces). De Waal observes that

> [i]n private, US officials concede that this pressure forced the US government into an over-hasty attempt to impose UN peacekeepers on Sudan's government. This, in turn, inflamed Khartoum's suspicions, emboldened its enemies, and undermined slow-maturing efforts to find a compromise that would end the war.[122]

It may be a principled pursuit of justice (insisting that criminals are brought to court) but those pursuing it are largely living in the US and they do not directly experience the greater suffering resulting in the Sudan.

68 A brief history of celebrity advocacy

Conclusion

There are other elements to this outline history which I have not covered. The Live Earth concerts, organised by Al Gore (a former US Vice-President) in 2007, played on all seven continents and enrolled over 150 musicians.[123] In the UK in 2009 the actress Joanna Lumley prominently fronted a successful campaign to get the British government to allow former Gurkha soldiers to settle in the UK. Major disasters such as the Indian Ocean tsunami of 2004 embroiled more public figures,[124] as did the Haitian earthquake of January 2010.[125] But these are relatively minor details in a broader history which should now be plain.

It should be clear that celebrity has been prominent in the contests over what 'development' might mean. This is particularly visible in the third quarter of the twentieth century when different possible development paths were being vigorously contested in the public domain, and when different celebrities, particularly musicians, were joining those contests. In the last decades of the century, as the Cold War ended and apartheid was abandoned, there is somehow a loss of oppositional verve. We have entered a period of market triumphalism.[126] Protest may be possible, but what constructive cause could it espouse?

Related to that is the rise of post-democratic politics embedded, as Crouch has detailed (see p. 36), in social and economic transformations in the North which made the old oppositions between capital and labour hard to sustain. Celebrity is not a necessary part of the new post-democratic politics which have arisen. There was nothing particularly celebrity-friendly about the political policies of Blair or Clinton, but the fact that these leaders, as individuals, combined their post-democratic politics with a penchant for celebrity certainly made it easier for celebrities to join the new policy-making elites who were coming to dominate politics.

We can see the transformations in political space that post-democratic politics afford in changes to musical protest. At the close of his book on a history of protest song after World War II, Lynskey tells the story of how, in 2009, the subversive pop group Rage Against the Machine re-released their revolutionary 1992 single *Killing in the Name* as a form of 'grassroots resistance against a perceived tyrant'. The catch, Lynskey observes, was that the tyrant was Simon Cowell (a reality TV mogul), and thus 'a song conceived as a missile to be launched at the institutional racism of the US Army and LAPD was reduced to a water pistol, squirting at a TV talent show'. For Lynskey, the problem lies with the listeners. We, the audiences, do not have the tolerance for musical protest any more, instead 'the discourse around politics and pop has become absurdly unforgiving'.[127] As Crouch says, 'boredom, frustration and disillusion have settled in', and this gives much less space for oppositional politics musicians might want to promote.[128]

My point here is not that celebrity advocacy must somehow become anodyne and politically neutral, but rather that it will find it difficult to find a broader overarching narrative with which it can engage, and hard to find a sympathetic public looking for that narrative. It might 'work', in the sense of achieving policy change – indeed, I will show that it can work most effectively in post-democratic ways. But circumstances of contemporary celebrity advocacy now are far removed from the popular protests of the 1960s.

We have reviewed the main events of the recent history of celebrity advocacy. We have not, however, examined the changes within the NGO sector which underlie these events. In the next chapter we examine how these relationships have become organised and systematised.

Notes

1   Lomax *et al.*, 1999 (1967): xxi. Guthrie was a famous radical folk musician.
2   This paragraph is based on Dorian Lynskey's work (2010). Geldof's reference to clowns and wankers is in Lewis, 2010.
3   Other overviews and perspectives are available in West, 2008; Anonymous, 2009; Trope, 2012; Marks and Fischer, 2002 and Wheeler, 2013.
4   Gitlin, 1980; Tuck, 2010 and cf. Wolfe, 1970.
5   This periodisation matches Barnett's division of the history of humanitarianism (2011). He identifies an 'imperial humanitarianism' which extends from the early nineteenth century to World War II, a 'neo-humanitarianism' extending up to the end of the Cold War, and a 'liberal humanitarianism' since then.
6   Morgan, 2010, 2011.
7   Kleinberg, 2011.
8   Jacques de Vitry cited in Kleinberg, 2011: 393–4. Halpern reports celebrities in the US in the 1940s having their clothes torn off by souvenir hunters (Halpern, 2007: 191).
9   cf. Inglis, 2010. Cashmore (2011) argues for a shorter history of celebrity.
10 Rojek, 2001. Rojek also notes that it is one of the paradoxes of democracy that while it celebrates the possibilities of anyone doing anything, the condition of capitalist democracy is that most people do not reach high status. Celebrity, ironically, celebrates the possibility of universal achievement, at the same time as it emphasises its scarcity.
11 Mole, 2008: 347.
12 Mole, 2008.
13 Boorstin, 1992 [1961]. See also Marshall, 1997.
14 Marshall, 1997; Schickel, 2000 (1985).
15 Dyer, 1979; Marshall, 1997; Schickel, 2000 (1985).
16 Ewen, 1988.
17 Horkheimer and Adorno, 1972.
18 Even though, in the latter case, some of the people on the list have died and are yet to be removed, it still remains a large number of famous people.
19 It is not mentioned in Beer and Penfold-Mounce's review of celebrity studies in academia (Beer and Penfold-Mounce, 2010).
20 Note that in the process, programmes like *Dr Phil* celebrate and promote a particular form of authenticity which is about finding and expressing one's true inner-self. As Guignon notes, this is at best a partial route to happiness (2004). It is difficult to find solace looking within oneself for problems derived from without. cf. Peck's work on Oprah for a similar argument (Peck, 2010).
21 Goldman, 1994.
22 Barnett, 2011.
23 Douzinas, 2007: 8.
24 Hettne, 2009.
25 Rist, 2008 (1996).
26 Ross, 1998; Mitlin *et al.*, 2007; Rist, 2008 (1996).
27 Ross, 1998; Rist, 2008 (1996).
28 Ekbladh, 2010: 77.

70 A brief history of celebrity advocacy

29 Ross, 1998.
30 Edwards and Hulme, 1992.
31 Edwards and Hulme, 1995; Hulme and Edwards, 1997.
32 Sklair, 2001.
33 Cooper, 2007, 2008b; Wheeler, 2011a.
34 Hochschild's excellent history of Morel's work provides wonderful insights into the work of the famous at this time (Hochschild, 2006 [1998]).
35 Cowen and Shenton, 1996.
36 Source 36.
37 This is Ian Hislop's (the editor of *Private Eye*) term, from a three-part documentary of that title shown in Britain in 2011.
38 Schweiger, 2009.
39 Hochschild, 2006 [1998].
40 Lynskey, 2010: 24.
41 Lynskey, 2010: 25. Joe Hill was questionably convicted of murder and executed in 1915. 30,000 people attended his funeral.
42 Tuck, 2010: 103–12.
43 Chambers, 2006. On Robeson, see also Dyer, 2004 [1986]) and Heble, 2003.
44 Davenport, 2009.
45 Many Americans challenged their country's claims to represent the free world and drew on independence struggles overseas to support domestic battles. Tuck reports a commonly told tale 'of Vice President Richard Nixon, attending Ghana's independence celebration, [and] asking a black man what it felt like to be free. "I wouldn't know," he replied. "I'm from Alabama"' (Tuck, 2010: 285).
46 Note also that Mother Teresa's work has been criticised for not providing adequate support for the poor and sick in the film *Hell's Angel* and subsequent book *The Missionary Position* (Hitchens, 1995).
47 Black, 1992: 63. My thanks to Cheryl Lousely for pointing that out to me.
48 Cooper, 2008: 98–9.
49 Black, 1992: 82–3.
50 Source 16.
51 Chambers, 2006: 20; Lynskey, 2010: 226.
52 Available at: www.amnesty.org/en/for-media/press-packs/AI50-press-kit#celebrity engagement (viewed 17 September 2013).
53 Sources 16 and 88. Kaye's work provides a popular origin myth to the current entanglements of development with celebrity. This story locates the start of the relationship in the cabin of a passenger plane that was flying from New York to Ireland in 1953. On board were Maurice Pate (the Secretary-General of UNICEF) and Danny Kaye. One of the propellers of the plane caught fire and it had to return with no certainty of a safe arrival. When a second propeller failed Kaye promised Pate that he would make UNICEF famous if they got back (Black, 1992; Source 88). He kept his promise. Among the initial activities Panasonic offered to underwrite the production of a film showing Danny Kaye's encounters with children overseas, to release that film commercially and to donate the profits of the film to charity.
54 Not replicated in international development affairs, that is. Danny Tomas played a highly significant role in the funding and promoting of St Jude's Children Research Hospital, but note also that his was a highly individual initiative, not an institutional affair, which, like Kaye's, followed a promise he made (Weberling, 2010).
55 Lynskey quotes Lomax who reports that after Seeger met Guthrie in New York on 3 March 1940 that 'You can date the renaissance of American folk song from that night' (2010: 28).
56 Lynskey, 2010. A few musicians did not join in. Fats Domino said he would continue to play at segregated venues and Nat 'King' Cole thought celebrity activism 'idiotic', but for most other musicians, such as Nina Simone, Sam Cooke, Louis Armstrong, Lena Horne, James Brown, Duke Ellington and Sammy Davis Jnr, with bitter experiences of racism behind them, this was not such a difficult decision.

A brief history of celebrity advocacy **71**

57 My source for all these names is Lynskey, 2010.
58 'Radical Chic', wrote Wolfe, 'after all, is only radical in style; in its heart it is part of Society and its traditions. Politics, like Rock, Pop and Camp, has its uses; but to put one's whole status on the line for *nostalgie de la boue* in any of its forms would be unprincipled' (Wolfe, 1970: 79).
59 Gitlin, 1980: 154–5.
60 Tuck, 2010: 354.
61 Lynskey, 2010: xiv.
62 Doggett, 2007: 4.
63 Garofalo, 1992b: 20–1.
64 For useful accounts, see Street, 1986, 2003; Fischlin and Heble, 2003; Doggett, 2007; Lynskey, 2010; and for some of the songs themselves, Lomax *et al.*, 1999 [1967].
65 The musical revolution was not completely laissez-faire. Doggett notes that the CIA was so alarmed at the 'almost treasonous anti-establishment propaganda' that was rife in the underground press that it persuaded Columbia records to stop advertising in them, predicting, with some accuracy, that 80 per cent would fail without the advertising revenues. This happened at about the same time as Columbia tried to proclaim its support for revolutionary music and produced a much derided advertisement for its ware, claiming 'But The Man Can't Bust Our Music' (Doggett, 2007: 220–1).
66 Street, 1986: 23. Street reports that Electrical and Musical Industries (EMI) in Allende's Chile was quite content to release anti-capitalist music (and then drop those artists when Pinochet took power). Its priority was not opposing Allende (or Pinochet) but making money.
67 Woodstock was a three-day open-air rock concert held in 1969 and attended by 500,000, ten times the number expected by town officials (see Lynskey, 2010 and Doggett, 2007). In some ways it marked the high point and end point of the (music-led) radicalism of the sixties. The high point was its verve, excitement and the possibilities; the low-point was its actual politics. When one of the activists tried to make a political speech from the stage he was told to 'fuck off' by an angry musician named Pete Townsend.
68 Street, 1986: 74; Doggett, 2007: 266. Woodstock also demonstrates an astute use of brand power, for it was named after a small town where Dylan lived and where the event was originally to be held. It retained that name, and hence the associations with Dylan, after Woodstock refused to host Woodstock and the event was moved to Bethel, some 40 miles away.
69 Frith and Street, 1992. Nevertheless, in the UK, musicians continued to be active later in the 1970s in service of Rock Against Racism, which was prompted by musician Eric Clapton's (a musician's) drunken on-stage call to 'Keep Britain White' and which brought together bands like the Clash, the Tom Robinson Band and Steel Pulse. Multiracial groups like the Specials and UB40 formed and wrote a variety of issue rich songs and Linton Kwesi Johnson launched his career with anti-racist poetry; see Street *et al.*, 2008.
70 Source 81.
71 Source 88. The more significant events were when Don King (a boxing promoter) and Muhammad Ali (a boxer) suggested a 1976 boxing event in Madison Square; Robert Stigwood (manager of the musical group the Bee Gees) and David Frost (a journalist) suggested a concert in the UN General Assembly in January 1979; and Harvey Goldsmith (a UK music promoter) promoted the 'Concerts for Kampuchea' in December that year in London.
72 The first three ambassadors were appointed over a twenty-five-year span (1954–79). The next seven joined in seven years: Tetsuko Kuroyanagi (1984), Harry Belafonte and Richard Attenborough (both 1987), Audrey Hepburn (1989), Roger Moore and Youssou N'Dour (both 1991). cf. Alleyne, 2005; Wheeler, 2011a, b; Wilson, 2011.
73 Source 89.

72 A brief history of celebrity advocacy

74 Lynskey, 2010. The spending of the money raised then has caused some controversy with allegations that it might have prolonged the war and supported inept policies that fuelled famine, see Franks, 2010b.

75 Note, however, that for the first few years each event was organised as if it were the last. Only in 1995 did the trustees on the board of Comic Relief agree to a five-year plan that committed to future fund-raising events, and only in 2000 did the BBC agree to a spring telethon, which was to benefit Comic Relief and Sport Relief on alternate years (Source 71).

76 By the mid-1980s Geldof's account suggests that musicians are being pressed so often to support causes that it is hard for them to spare their time (Geldof, 1986: 362–3). Garofalo reports '[t]here is scarcely a social issue in the eighties and early nineties which has not been associated in a highly visible way with popular music and musicians. Hunger and starvation in Africa, apartheid, racism, black-on-black violence, AIDS, Central America, industrial plant closings, and homelessness have all been themes for fundraising concerts, popular songs, or both' (Garofalo, 1992b: 16).

77 The event was so large that it overshadowed other benefit concerts planned for the time. Garofalo reports that an AIDS benefit concert planned for 1987 and featuring George Michael (a musician) had to be cancelled, and an Amnesty International concert that went ahead that year lost $200,000 (Garofalo, 1992a: 64).

78 Lahusen, 1996.

79 Lahusen, 1996.

80 In part, theirs was a reaction against the earnestness and moral tone that had characterised the recent concerts (such as Sting's, cf. Alan Jones of *Melody Maker* to Christian Lahusen in 1992), but with *Help* it became cool again to work for charity (Source 5, 80). Michka Assayas notes a similar tone of 'self-disgust' afflicting music in the early 1990s that he suspected might have led to a decline in U2's activism at the time (Assayas, 2005: 267).

81 The fracturing of the country prompted the actress Vanessa Redgrave to tour the region for weeks with UNICEF (UK), promoting unity among the entertainment and artistic community there. Source 69.

82 Sources 5, 6, 80.

83 Source 48.

84 Source 23.

85 Collins *et al.*, 2001; Pettifor, 2006; Barrett, 2000.

86 Source 46. Bono was presented an award at the Brits for his work for charity, but he instantly ran into the audience to present it to Muhammad Ali on behalf of the Jubilee 2000 campaign.

87 Cox, 2011: 17.

88 Cox, 2011: 18.

89 Cox, 2011: 19. The new Poverty Reduction Strategy Papers developed by the World Bank and the International Monetary Fund (IMF) helped to channel those resources into social spending with mixed success (Hulme, 2010: 132–5).

90 cf. Street, 2004.

91 Alastair Campbell describes the tone of the time when he reports Blair unwillingly going to a meeting on African development, but choosing Geldof and Bono from that throng to come back with him to Downing Street (Campbell, 2007: 592).

92 cf. Alleyne, 2005; Fall and Tang, 2006.

93 Cooper, 2008b. For the Jubilee Campaign this involved both getting US President Clinton to support debt relief, and then Congress to support it (Jackson, N., 2008).

94 Richey and Ponte, 2011.

95 See www.dailymail.co.uk/femail/article-1308429/Stuck-Louis-Vuitton-moment-Bono-Ali-Hewson-pose-French-megabrand-clothes-ethical-label.html (viewed 2 June 2012) and http://fashion.telegraph.co.uk/Article.aspx?Id= TMG8572326 (viewed 2 June 2012). The photographs of Jolie and Bono were taken by Annie Leibovitz who is herself a celebrity photographer of celebrities and who has built her reputation partly

on development-focused pictures including the cover of the 'Africa Issue' of *Vanity Fair* in July 2007, which featured twenty-one famous faces in an issue guest edited by Bono and dedicated to African development issues. Available at: www.vanityfair.com/politics/features/2007/07/onthecover_slideshow200707#intro (viewed 2 June 2012).

96   Available at: www.guardian.co.uk/world/2012/mar/01/bob-geldof-africa-private-equity (viewed 2 June 2012).

97   Source 119.

98   Source 119.

99   Poniewozik, 2005.

100   Sireau, 2008.

101   Available at: www.guardian.co.uk/music/2005/jul/05/live8 (viewed 15 August 2011); Harrison, 2010.

102   Darnton, 2006; Darnton and Fenyoe, 2007.

103   Sireau, 2008.

104   Sources 24, 39, 46, 47. As the campaign progressed, some of the more radical members of the coalition began briefing against it, complaining of too moderate a stance (Hodkinson, 2005b).

105   The Make Poverty History response was 'The people have roared, the G8 have whispered'. Geldof, who spoke after them, said 'There are no equivocations. Africa and the poor of that continent have got more from the last three days than they have ever got at any previous summit . . . On aid, ten out of ten. On debt, eight out of ten. On trade . . . it is quite clear that this summit, uniquely, decided that enforced liberalisation must no longer take place' (Hodkinson, 2005a). Geldof's humiliation of the Make Poverty History communiqué is best described by Tony Blair, in part because it communicates the lack of purchase the Make Poverty History critique had on him. He writes in his memoires: 'I did the press conference in the garden of the hotel. There was the usual nonsense from some NGO bloke about how we had all let Africa down, and the unusual riposte from Bob who basically tore the bloke's head off for being so negative and followed him down the path from the press area, shouting abuse as only an irate Irishman can' (Blair, 2010: Kindle location 10,937, quoted in Browne, 2013).

106   Invited to respond to the film before it was aired on UK television, Geldof wrote a 6,000 word letter of complaint to the makers, defending his work and criticising the more activist campaigners. This letter was made public – www.starsuckersmovie.com/bob-geldof-letter (viewed August 2011). When a summary of that letter appeared in the *Guardian* (generating 126 comments; Lewis, 2010), John Hilary, of War on Want and a radical outsider in Sireau's terminology, wrote an article in response criticising Geldof's position (and generating 389 comments; Hilary, 2010). The day after the film Adrian Lovett, a moderate insider who now works with ONE, and who had been the main coordinator between the Make Poverty History group and the publicity team working with Comic Relief, wrote a passionate blog in defence of Make Poverty History. Available at: www.savethechildren.org.uk/blogs/2010/04/make-poverty-history-and-live-8-what-really-happened (viewed August 2011).

107   David Hulme observes that 'This was a cleverly packaged commitment. First, it was laudable: this was a lot of money and by focusing the pledge on the poorest countries, where need was greatest, it could draw on the public support and direct resources towards Africa. Second, by focusing the increase only on the poorest countries (and not on all recipient countries) it meant that aid could be "doubled" without doubling the size of aid budgets' (Hulme, 2010: 125).

108   Sireau, 2008: 24.

109   Statements complaining of the measures were numerous. Cox wrote: 'For example, "the people roared the G8 whispered" (Global Campaign for Action on Poverty), "G8 Turn Their Backs on the World's Poor" (War on Want), "a disaster for the poor" (World Development Movement) and "a sad day for poor people in Africa and all over the world"(Christian Aid)' Cox, 2011: 48.

74 A brief history of celebrity advocacy

110 $27 billion of the promised $50 billion of aid was delivered by 2010. African countries received $13.7 billion of a promised $25 billion (Cox, 2011: 15).
111 Darnton, 2006.
112 Darnton, 2009: 7.
113 Geldof wrote that 'At the launch of Our Common Interest [the popular version of the African Commission report] Blair was asked by a journalist, whom I had put up to ask the question, would the report be UK policy for the upcoming UK G8 summit in Gleneagles. Blair had privately been resisting because he feared a failure. He was worried that the other leaders would not accept a deal of this magnitude or radical nature. He therefore had no desire for a domestic and international political disaster. Having asked the question and Blair hesitating in a stumbling response I, who shared the platform with the PM and Gordon Brown, jumped in and said "Yes he will. Won't you prime minister?" Everyone laughs and Blair says something like "oh well if Bob says so I'd better". All very jolly but now it's on record and he's anxious because the Sherpas are saying there's no possibility of this happening. Fellow commissioners asked me what I intend to do that will allow him to carry this through the G8. I begin to think of Live 8.' Available at: www.starsuckersmovie.com/bob-geldof-letter/ (viewed August 2011). Sherpas are civil servants who negotiate the texts which their leaders will sign at a summit.
114 Darnton, 2006: 10.
115 Darnton, 2006: 10–11.
116 Darnton, 2011; Darnton and Kirk, 2011.
117 Nash, 2008.
118 Nash, 2008: 177.
119 Hamilton, 2011: xvi
120 Off-shoots include the Enough Project, co-founded by John Prendergast and Gayle Smith (both activists) in 2007, which draws attention to atrocities in Africa, and Not on Our Watch founded in the same year by Clooney, Cheadle and fellow actors Brad Pitt and Matt Damon, David Pressman (a lawyer) and Jerry Weintraub (a producer), which campaigns on issues in Burma, Sudan and Zimbabwe. See also Hawkins (2011).
121 Flint and De Waal, 2008; Crilly, 2010.
122 De Waal, 2008.
123 Audiences, however, appear to have been quite small. Thrall *et al.* report that the Live Earth audience was 8 million (2008: 378), two orders of magnitude smaller than the 400 million who watched Live Aid (Lynskey, 2010: 484).
124 Such as the model Petra Nemcova who survived it and set up a foundation in response.
125 It prompted significant interventions from the singer Wycliffe Jean and the actor Sean Penn.
126 Biccum (2011) sees parallels between liberal subjectivity and empire building in the nineteenth century and neoliberal subjectivity (and hence empire building) that they read in celebrity interventions with development. It is an intriguing thesis, especially given the prominence of celebrity advocates for good causes overseas at that time, but I lack the historical skills to explore it.
127 Lynskey, 2010: 681–4.
128 Crouch, 2004: 19.

5

THE CURRENT STATE OF CELEBRITY ADVOCACY

After the Japan quake . . . people were blasting me . . . Why aren't you doing anything about Japan, where are the celebrities?[1]

Ashton Kutcher

When I began this research I assumed that, since Live Aid in the mid-1980s, there would have been a gradual reorganisation of celebrity-NGO interactions. But, as we have seen, the history of these relationships is not smooth. Advocacy became unfashionable for some musicians in the early 1990s. The NGO movement itself was still growing rapidly in the early 1990s and it had not then learned, or professionalised its learning of, how to deal with celebrity. It was still developing skills in working with the media. The surprise for me was how late the interactions between these two sectors have become professional, systematic and well organised. These changes date, approximately, from the late 1990s.[2] They are a recent phenomenon.

As a result of these new practices, relations between NGOs and the celebrity industries are now systematically organised as never before. As Ashton Kutcher suggests above, celebrity involvement is expected in important world affairs. Part of the purpose of this chapter is to demonstrate that fact. We can understand better how NGO-celebrity relations fit into current forms of capitalism and politics by understanding how they are organised. Its other purpose is to describe how well engrained they are in development NGOs, what tasks they undertake and what specifically they try to achieve.

I will first describe the system of intensive celebrity-NGO relations that has developed. I then try to map out the current state of celebrity advocacy, using some of the sources this intensification has produced. This demonstrates the idiosyncrasies of the more committed celebrities and shows that development and humanitarian causes make up a considerable proportion of celebrity advocacy work. I also examine attempts to evaluate aspects of its impact. This last topic highlights the importance of personal encounters with celebrity, rather than mediated encounters, which will become particularly important when we consider how celebrity works with elites.

Systematic celebrity–NGO relations

Perhaps the most important change in NGO workings with celebrity has been the increase in the number of full-time, dedicated liaison officers working for NGOs (Figure 5.1). This was led internationally by the (often US-based) UN organisations, but has been followed in the last decade or so by British-based NGOS. Many of the celebrity liaison officers I was interviewing were the first or second full-time appointees of their organisation.[3]

BBC research found that three-quarters of the largest thirty charities now have full-time celebrity liaison officers.[4] The liaison officers, moreover, have become more organised. They meet monthly in London at the celebrity liaison officers' forum (which began in 2004) and train other charities to work effectively with celebrity in workshops run, since 2003, by the Media Trust.[5] A blog set up by one of the more experienced liaison officers in 2010 had over 1,000 readers less than a year later; it now has over 500 Twitter followers and forms an occasional

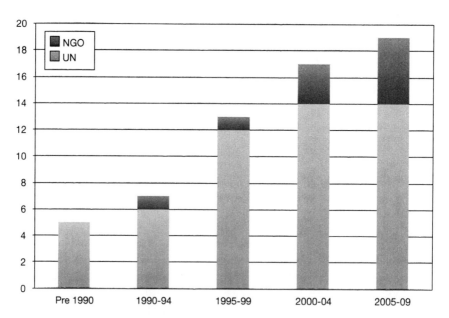

FIGURE 5.1 The cumulative growth of NGO celebrity liaison officers and UN Goodwill Ambassador programmes

Source: Fall and Tang (2006) and author's own survey data.

column in the *Guardian*'s Voluntary Sector Network.[6] Occasionally, celebrity liaison officers will co-ordinate their activities, their approaches to celebrities and their management of them for particularly complicated events. Similarly, the UN celebrity liaison officers meet every quarter to co-ordinate their requests, approaches and activities.[7]

These heightened standards of professionalism and expertise when dealing with celebrity are matched by developments in the celebrity industries. Three of the four major talent agencies in Hollywood have set up foundations to promote charitable activities to their clients and as a vehicle of these companies' corporate social responsibility: William Morris in 2000, the Creative Artists Agency in 2001 and the United Talent Agency in 2004. Dedicated staff at these foundations facilitate their clients' expression of their charitable interests, providing them with contacts, reading and information on the causes that they wish to pursue. As Rene Jones, who performs that role for the United Talent Agency, explained to Jonathan Foreman:

> It's mostly counselling advice. You meet, get to know one another, and then you act as a matchmaker and bring credible organisations to their attention. It's not always an instant process, but the ones that last longest are those with an organic connection.[8]

These organisations now play a major role in brokering relationships between major international NGOs searching for talent at functions, parties and meetings where they can plan new charitable roles for their clients and where the NGOs can learn with whom they can start to build relationships.[9] Apart from these large organisations, other agents frequently advise their clients to choose three to four charities to support. This will allow them to build up credible relationships with these charities, and it will make it easier for the agent to deflect the hundreds of other requests that can come in.[10]

It is a measure of the professionalisation of work between NGOs and celebrity that corporate and charitable endorsement interests are thoroughly merged. The merging is visible in several ways. NGOs sign up to professional celebrity contact databases, which keep updated lists of how to contact different public figures – and these databases advertise their more important NGO clients to signify the value of their services. The Red Pages, for example, announces its services to Oxfam and the British Red Cross on its front page. They are listed alongside other commercial clients such as M&C Saatchi and Vivienne Westwood.[11] A competitor of Red Pages, Celebrities Worldwide, advertises the services of a celebrity booking consultancy, Upfront, which offers to 'arrange celebrities for . . . Corporate and Charity Events' – an interesting couplet.[12] Another development, in about 2004, was that the Red Pages began listing celebrity ailments systematically, thus helping health charities to target the right people. And then there are the biweekly bulletins themselves that the Red Pages provide, which contain a blend of corporate endorsements, celebrity industry news and charity support. I have provided a sample in Box 5.1.

78 The current state of celebrity advocacy

BOX 5.1 Samples of Red Pages bulletins

13 December 2012

Sophie Ellis-Bextor signs as new Nioxin Ambassador
Louis Smith donates leotard to charity auction
Blind Veterans UK launches new campaign with Waterloo Road star
Rick Parfitt lends support to the BHF's Rock Up In Red campaign
Celebrity hairstylist launches LUXHAIR collection

16 May 2012

Stars customise items for Christian Aid auction
Teyana Taylor signs to Kanye West's label
WME inks deal with Adrianne Palicki
Jodie Kidd fronts search for Ultimate British Sandwich
Freedom to Marry enlists Audra McDonald's support
Nina Dobrev parts ways with agent
Jake T Austin named charity spokesperson
Stars design for Kiehl's charity initiative
Christine Taylor named Ambassador for organic skincare company

21 October 2011

Twilight actress inks deal with DKNY and DKNY Jeans
Paula Patton unveiled as new CoverGirl Ambassador
Celebs design Christmas cards for charity
Christina Hendricks stars in video game
Film director teams up with Jessops and The Mob Film Company
Caroline Monk inks with Handmade UK
Tamara Ecclestone signs to Money Management
Footballer joins UNAIDS programme
Delia Smith appointed Patron of Sir Bobby Robson Foundation
High Maintenance Agency represents Charley McEwen
Howard and Beth Stern create charity calendar
KISS team up with Fan Mosaics
Horror writer takes over Scholastic's social media

Source: Red Pages bulletins.
Each headline listed here would be accompanied by a short story explaining its content. I regret that on this occasion I have not tried to find out what all the people listed here are famous for. I do hope that you are able to recognise some of them.

The current state of celebrity advocacy **79**

There has also been a growth in companies that specialise in liaising between celebrities and charities. The Global Philanthropy Group, begun in 2007 and based in Los Angeles, advises the philanthropy of high net worth and high-profile individuals.[13] The Cause Effect Agency also mediates between public figures and NGOs in the USA; it first began trading in 2005.[14]

Then there are the increasing efforts to document and keep track of all these activities. The Look to the Stars website, which documents the work of celebrities for good causes, was set up in 2006. It has grown in size and reputation such that by 2009 Look to the Stars was sponsoring Oscar Night parties and being sought out by NGOs, agents and publicists as a means of promoting their public figures' activities.[15] The Ecorazzi website, documenting celebrity support for the environment, was also set up in 2006 and expanded its remit to cover more general good works by celebrities a few years later. MTV established a website aimed at its activist viewers in 2008. *Third Sector's* (the trade journal for non-profits and NGOs in the UK) dedicated column to the work of celebrity in NGOs in the UK first appeared in 2002; it became weekly in 2007. The Red Page's weekly newsletter detailing deals between celebrities and corporate brands, and celebrities and charities (or all three) first came out in 2007 and went biweekly two years later.

Celebrity and charitable activities are now part of the mainstream by which the celebrity industries operate. Celebrity-orientated magazines deliberately make use of the opportunities that charities, and especially charity-orientated field-trips, provide. When I asked an editor of one of these magazines if they ever tried to get access to talent through charities, the answer was unequivocal:

> Yes definitely, all the time . . . If we have a target list for celebrities for example . . . if we are looking for an interview . . . we definitely might go through a charity if we know that there is something coming up in a campaign. For example Christmas is a great time to target the charity side of things to get the celebs . . . We are often approached by charities about certain [tasks] and we might use that as an excuse to try and get a particular celebrity so we will look for them to chase a certain celebrity for us for a specific [task].[16]

Indeed, their importance is such that magazines will co-operate to divide up the stories resulting. The same person told me that:

> Nowadays . . . there seems to be quite a few different publications that will be allowed to do one trip, whereas perhaps in the olden days it would be like . . . an exclusive whereas nowadays we sort of split it between non-rival publications or we split the celebrities and we try to organise it with more than one celebrity on the trip.[17]

Celebrity liaison officers can also act as sources of talent for game shows in which celebrities compete in order to win prizes for their chosen charities. The companies arranging these shows will approach the celebrity liaison officers directly in order

80 The current state of celebrity advocacy

for them to approach their ambassadors and patrons to appear on the show.[18] Performing such services for entertainment companies can lubricate subsequent corporate sponsorship: 'we were helping bring in someone else that makes their programme interesting . . . so they want to collaborate with us.'[19]

The intertwining of celebrity and charity is not so great that celebrities are paid by charities. Across all the collective years and organisations' experience that I encountered charities only reported paying for celebrities' presence twice (see p. 114 for details). Only one celebrity told me that their commitments to a charity were so extensive that it required a commercial contract.

Also, associations with charities are generally *not* such an important part of the celebrity industries now that celebrities require charities in order to get publicity. As one of the more experienced interviewees told me: 'I guarantee that if they wanted to get publicity for themselves they could; they don't need the charity to do it.'[20] The point here is that most celebrities are part of industries that are too practised in creating publicity (and most charities are equally inexperienced) for charities to provide extra publicity opportunities. But we must still qualify this general truth in ways that illustrate well the role that the charitable sector can perform for the celebrity industries. Some public association with charities can be useful to some sorts of celebrities. Waning stars' agents might ring up charities to remind them that they could use their clients.[21] New, and potentially fleeting, celebrities may also welcome the publicity that charitable events can afford. Reality TV stars, for example, 'actually kind of needed the push in their career, they had a 4–6 month window after Big Brother where they could . . . make a killing and really work on raising their profile.'[22]

Agents of these fleeting celebrities have approached NGOs in the hope that they might be able to design events that catered for them.[23] Some liaison officers refused because the connections were too weak. Others recognised that this was part of cultivating the relationship: 'we kind of did them a favour as much as them doing us a favour'.[24] One NGO was able to build a good relationship with an agency representing those celebrities because they ran 'shopping events . . . where there was the right fit' between the character and quality of the celebrities and the task required of them.[25] Another strategy of providing events for such people was to make them a spokesperson for generic tasks such as fundraising weeks, which are fun, not heavy and the messages are quite light.[26]

More established celebrities will not need such publicity opportunities, but they may welcome those opportunities that fit well with their brand. Some NGOs (UNICEF, Oxfam, the Red Cross, World Wide Fund for Nature among others) have very strong brands, and associations with them are valued highly.[27] The reason why three of the leading four Hollywood agencies meet regularly with leading charities is because the agencies want their (major) stars to be associated with such organisations.

Indeed, for the larger NGOs the risks of association with public figures were 'all about the brand', which meant what these figures might do to the NGO brand.[28]

The current state of celebrity advocacy **81**

For 'that is the other side of celebrity ... if you screw up you screw up in the headlights'.[29] So, for example, when Salman Khan (an actor) shot a protected antelope in India shortly after appearing in a calendar for the WWF, or when Ralph Fiennes (an actor) was reported to have had casual sex with an air hostess en route to India to promote HIV/AIDS awareness for UNICEF, then this just brings in the normal routines of damage control.[30] Some NGOs undertake careful due diligence on the public figures with whom they build relationships, before they get serious, to prevent any embarrassment.[31]

The celebrity industries face similar considerations. Good agents will have their clients' long-term interests at stake; they will be carefully building their clients' brand and assessing the connections between their clients' brands and those of the NGOs who work with them accordingly.[32] Successful collaborations are a mixture of balancing the commercial considerations of the celebrity industry with the brand of the NGOs:

> It works well because it works with everyone's schedule and it works with our branding and their personal branding, it stays in their voice and therefore is more authentic and therefore resonates more with the audiences whom we are trying to reach and influence.[33]

It helps that there is a mutual interest in these relationships working for all sides. As one liaison officer said:

> my goal is not to have anything to be approved by a publicist ... because quite honestly I don't want you to look bad either ... The ideal is for when they have their [organisation M] hat on for me to be their [organisation M] publicist and for that to be enough.[34]

Finally, in addition to brand considerations, there are other minor perks that charities can offer. Some of my sources were adamant that there had to be some quid pro quo:

> Charities might not pay them in money but they definitely do pay them with something. Whether it's lots of exposure that they wouldn't otherwise get or whether it's in goods that they have exchanged as a free goodwill gesture etc etc there aren't many celebrities who are doing something for nothing.[35]

Some organisations blagged gifts from corporate partners that they could give to celebrity supporters as tokens of thanks.[36]

In summary, there has been a sea change in the way in which celebrity interactions with NGOs are conducted. What had been ad hoc relationships are now being seized and organised by NGOs themselves with the co-operation of

82 The current state of celebrity advocacy

the celebrity industries. From creating new celebrity liaison roles to the formation of new institutions, and companies lubricating interactions between talent and charities, NGOs are learning to interact effectively with celebrity.

Mapping celebrity advocacy

In the public domain, and for the media, the results of the professionalising and intensifying of relationships between celebrities and NGOs are visible in the richness and variety of celebrity advocacy activities. They are undertaking field-trips, donating clothes, possessions, photographs and meetings with other celebrities, designing handbags and recipes, donating rights to songs and performing concerts. They are adorning meetings of key decision-makers, undertaking negotiations themselves, facilitating access to political leaders and undertaking public-facing campaigns on the streets. They are setting up their own foundations and organisations, or forming strategic and bespoke alliances with established charities. They are sending messages to supporters, launching campaigns and appearing in public service videos.

They are doing, therefore, a lot. I can hint at some of the variety of celebrity advocacy, but I would prefer to describe it more systematically. That, however, is hard because there is so much going on that it is difficult to map out.[37] Given that there are tens of thousands of celebrities, this should not be surprising. Indeed, keeping track of celebrity advocacy is not a job for any lone researcher. It has become part of the commercial life of the celebrity industries. Just as one keeps up to date with celebrity contacts using commercially sold address lists, so similar devices exist to help one choose celebrity advocates.

We can identify some patterns in celebrity support in the records of the Look to the Stars website (for 2011). This is by far the most comprehensive of the three sources and has helpfully categorised the causes supported according to their sector. From these records it is clear that some of the most popular charities are, predictably, the safer, apparently non-political causes. Children's charities are by far the most popular (with 515 charities supported for this cause alone). There are 845 charities receiving support across several diverse health issues. But it is also plain that the difficult and complicated humanitarian and development charities overseas are receiving a good deal of attention – 498 such NGOs were receiving celebrity support. Indeed, the charities with the most celebrity supporters, according to Look to the Stars, are UNICEF and the Red Cross. Moreover, there are nine other development and humanitarian organisations in the top fifteen most celebrity-supported charities on Look to the Stars' lists.[38] Celebrities are not shying away from these issues. Or, equally possible, humanitarian and development NGOs have become adept at recruiting them. Another possibility is that celebrity supporters are endorsing politically neutralised messages about development.

Look to the Stars also shows how idiosyncratic celebrity support could be. Some stars are involved in supporting dozens of causes, not the three to four that agents

The current state of celebrity advocacy **83**

commonly advise. Despite the commercial pressures and organisation of charity-celebrity relations, some celebrities are clearly involved in a different way and to a different level from others. Put another way, the reasons why, for example, Joanna Lumley, Annie Lennox (a musician) or Jon Snow (a presenter) are so active in different charitable affairs seems to be largely due to their own personal decisions, desires and consciences.

We can see the effectiveness and vigour with which development and humanitarian NGOs have pursued celebrity in Britain by examining the leading British NGOs' use of celebrity – and by the quality and prestige of the talent with which they work. I have chosen eleven NGOs identified by Atkinson and colleagues' analysis to be the most significant fundraisers in the UK, and added to them UNICEF (UK) and UNICEF International, because of UNICEF's well-known and long history of work with celebrity ambassadors.[39] I have presented in Table 5.1 information available about work with celebrity sponsors and ambassadors that was visible on these organisation's websites in February 2013 and from their most recent annual reports.

The table shows clearly how extensive some of these associations can be. Most of the leading development NGOs in the UK have recruited a large number of celebrity ambassadors, some of them extremely famous. These organisations have often devoted space on their websites to their ambassadors to promote (and possibly deepen) these relationships. Other organisations still have full-time celebrity-liaison staff, even if they have not yet promoted their work clearly on their websites.

Evaluating celebrity advocacy

It is not only hard to describe the work of celebrity advocates; it is also hard to explain what they have achieved. In part, this reflects the fact that monitoring and evaluation were often rudimentary. It was virtually non-existent in the early days of working with celebrity. Some of the organisations most involved in celebrity advocacy reported that evaluations was 'definitely a weak point'[40] and that 'we are working on it to be honest'.[41] Measures of success could include simply 'the atmosphere on the day' or 'the opinions of the people who organised the event'.[42]

Others kept a track of the resulting press coverage and were able to turn that coverage into an equivalence of how much similar advertising space would have cost, in footfall at shop openings or in donations received.[43] But the more intelligent answers to my questions about evaluation queried even those measures. After all, how do you know that any story appears because of the celebrity in it?[44] How can one tell what difference celebrity actually makes to fundraisers?[45] How do you quantify the value of being on the front cover of a nationally circulated magazine?[46] The impact of field-trips is certainly dramatic, as we shall see in the next chapter, but not in ways that are measurable.[47]

It is hard to determine precisely what celebrity advocacy achieves. As we have seen, even with events as powerful as Diana's advocacy of landmines we cannot

TABLE 5.1 Celebrity ambassadors and supporters of major development and humanitarian NGOs

NGO	No. of Supporters	Names of celebrity supporters include	Activities of celebrity supporters include (but are not limited to)	Web page for celebrity supporters	Comments
UNICEF International	32	Amitabh Bachchan; Angélique Kidjo; Berliner Philharmoniker; Danny Glover; David Beckham; Femi Kuti; Harry Belafonte; HM Queen Rania; Ishmael Beah; Jackie Chan; Judy Collins; Lang Lang; Leo Messi; Leon Lai; Liam Neeson; Lord Richard Attenborough; Maria Guleghina; Maxim Vengerov; Mia Farrow; Myung-Whun Chung; Nana Mouskouri; Orlando Bloom; Ricky Martin; Sebastião Salgado; Serena Williams; Shakira Mebarak; Sir Roger Moore; Susan Sarandon; Tetsuko Kuroyanagi; Vanessa Redgrave; Whoopi Goldberg; Yuna Kim	Field visits; campaign support; fundraising; international advocacy; public speaking and lecturing; high-level government advocacy	www.unicef.org/ people/people_ ambassadors.html	UNICEF International's ambassadors listed here only include the 'Goodwill Ambassadors'. The website also lists 14 regional ambassadors, over 300 (!) national ambassadors (which include the UNICEF UK ambassadors listed below) and 6 'alumni'.

Christian Aid	17	Alex James; Beverley Knight; Damian Lewis; Diarmuid Gavin; Greta Scacchi; Hayley Atwell; Jill Halfpenny; Kara Tointon; Kris Marshall; Kwame Kwei-Armah; Lemar; Lily Cole; Nicholas Hoult; Pearl and Daisy Lowe; Ronan Keating; Suranne Jones	Field visits; performances; media interviews; project visits; headlining rallies; campaign launches; political lobbying in public events and ministerial meetings; fundraising; awareness raising; promoting eco-gardening	www. christianaid. org.uk/ aboutus/ celebrity- supporters/ index.aspx	N/A
Oxfam (Interna-tional)	17	Angélique Kidjo; Annie Lennox; Archbishop Emeritus Desmond Tutu; Baaba Maal; Bill Nighy; Coldplay; Colin Firth; Djimon Hounsou; Gael García Bernal; Helena Christensen; Helen Mirren; Kristin Davis; Livia Firth; Miguel Bosé; Minnie Driver; Rahul Bose	Elite lobbying; field visits; public campaigning; public service announcements and adverts; public speaking; musical performances and conference attendance; organising and running shopping events; designing fashion accessories; donating items and premiere tickets for sale in fundraisers and money; appearing on reality TV shows; publicity stunts and awareness raising; working with progressive coffee shops; work with corporate partners	www.oxfam. org/en/ ambassadors	Oxfam are one of the most experienced of the British NGOs with dedicated liaison staff since 1994 and an office in Los Angeles to work with talent there.

Note these are Oxfam global ambassadors who work across different country offices. I could not find information about ambassadors specific to Oxfam (GB). |

continued . . .

TABLE 5.1 *Continued*

British Red Cross	16	Chris Parker; Chris Terry; Christopher Eccleston; Dr David Bull; Dougray Scott; Escala; James McAvoy; Jemma Redgrave; Josie Darby; Konnie Huq; Michael Buerk; Nancy Dell'Olio; Nicholas Owen; Nigel Havers; Richard Bacon; Stephen K Amos	Awareness raising; hosting events; work with corporate partners; field visits; private visits to projects; attending first aid courses; international appeals	www.redcross.org.uk/About-us/Celebrity-support/Entertainment-and-Artists-Supporters-Network	I could find no celebrity supporters page on the International Red Cross website.
UNICEF UK	16	Sir Alex Ferguson; Andrew O'Hagan; Cat Deeley; Charley Boorman; Claudia Schiffer; Lord David Puttnam; Duncan Bannatyne; Ewen McGregor; James Nesbitt; Jemima Khan; Martin Bell; Matt Dawson; Paul Clark; Robbie Williams; Ryan Giggs; Trudie Styler	Public, private and corporate fundraising; field visits; awareness raising; campaign launches and support; recording audio stories; making and participating in TV programmes and films; making Public Service Announcements; work with corporate partners; public performances; fronting appeals	www.unicef.org.uk/UNICEFs-Work/Our-supporters/Celebrities	Not included here are the 'High Profile Supporters', who are Björk; Elle MacPherson; James Callum; Michael Palin and Sophie Okenodo.
Sightsavers	13	Amadou and Mariam; Ben Quilter; Debra Winger; Haydn Gwynne; Himesh Patel; James Corden; Joanna Lumley; Lorraine Kelly;	Visiting clinics in the field to see the benefits of Sightsavers' work and meeting families helped by their operations. Fundraising and awareness raising	www.sightsavers.org/about_us/media_centre/	This list omits nine celebrities who took part in 'The Big Red Nose Desert Trek' (Craig David; Dermot O'Leary; Kara Tointon; Lorraine Kelly; Nadia Sawalha; Olly Murs;

		Nina Wadia; Rankin; Sunetra Sarker		celebrities/ default.html	Peter White; Roni Ancona and Scott Mills). Also listed on the 'Vision India' page are Bally and Sita Sagoo; Hema Malini; Lord Dholakia; Shay Grewal and the Family and Natasha Patel.
Save the Children (UK)	9	Ashley Jensen; Erin O'Connor; Mario Testino; Mary Portas; Michael Morpurgo; Myleene Klass; Natasha Kaplinsky; Paul O'Grady; Samantha Cameron	Supporting, launching and fronting campaigns; field visits; awareness raising; participating in appeal films; fundraising; retail advice and endorsements; promoting shopping events; donating items for sale.	www.save thechildren. org.uk/about- us/who-we- work-with/ artists-and- ambassadors	These appear to be the celebrities who work with STC (UK) only. I could find no celebrity page on the STC International site, or that of STC (US).
Water Aid	7	Rachel Stevens; Camilla Dallerup; Cyrille Regis; Ringo Starr; Helen Lederer; Adam Hart Davies; Tamzin Outhwaite	Field visits; raising awareness; speaking assignments; writing articles; designing clothes for auction.	www. wateraid.org/ uk/about_us/ media_centre/ 6090.asp	Water Aid had a famous misadventure with celebrity when a visit with Martine McCutcheon (an actresss) went wrong. It was listed by Ann McFerran in her catalogue of problematic celebrity trips (McFerran, 2000). This made the organisation cautious about working with celebrity and it appointed its first ambassadors only in 2012. WaterAid also includes a list of other celebrities who have lent their support, but are not fully fledged celebrity ambassadors. They include JLS, Miranda Hart and Christine Bleakley.

continued . . .

TABLE 5.1 *Continued*

Action Aid	Not clear	Emma Thompson	Field visits and blogs	No dedicated web page	Action Aid has full-time celebrity liaison staff.
Amnesty International	Not clear	No bespoke celebrity supporters listed but hundreds of names mentioned in the six different press releases which celebrate 50 years of working with celebrity in a variety of fields.	Designing clothes; supporting campaigns; setting up art exhibits and sculptures; performing concerts; releasing albums and singles in support of Amnesty; writing letters; publishing and promoting books and making films.	No dedicated web page	Amnesty International has full-time celebrity liaison staff.
CAFOD	Not clear	Dermot O'Leary; David Harewood	Writing newspaper articles; giving interviews; field visits; endorsing and supporting campaigns.	No dedicated web page	CAFOD has full-time dedicated celebrity liaison staff.
Islamic Relief	Not clear	None visible (and no search function on their website); celebrity not mentioned in the 2012 annual report.	Not clear	No dedicated web page	Islamic relief has full-time dedicated celebrity liaison staff.
Tear Fund	Not clear	None visible	N/A	No dedicated web page	Tear Fund has just started full-time celebrity liaison.
Médecins Sans Frontières	0	None mentioned on the website or in the annual reports.	N/A	No dedicated web page	The Head of MSF (UK) appeared on a podcast in 2009 to state that her organisation did not work with celebrity but that there was a lot of public interest in their doctors. That podcast is still one of the leading hits for the word celebrity on the organisation's website.

Source: Author's survey, February 2013.

Note: I do not have the space to say who all these people are and why you might have heard of them, but then part of the point of this table is to see how many you recognise without any prompting. Note also that these lists can be subject to change.

The current state of celebrity advocacy **89**

tell what that did to negotiations. Even organisations like Comic Relief, which can tell to the second who is pledging what, cannot necessarily attribute donations to the celebrity who is on TV at the time. After all, are the donations coming in response to what is currently on, to what has just been shown, to the celebrity of the person talking, or their script?

Occasionally, it is possible to know with certainty what difference a celebrity intervention has made. My favourite, and I believe the clearest example, is Katie Couric's live on-air colonoscopy.[48] Couric is a well-known television presenter of the *Today Show* in the US, and she beamed her colonoscopy to millions of viewers during her programme (she did so after being widowed by colon cancer). The results were unambiguous. Researchers studying colonoscopy rates in the months before and after the performance recorded a remarkable and sustained jump in colonoscopies (of at least 20 per cent) across the US that occurred exactly after Couric's intervention.[49]

Other examples exist that are more germane to development. Jamie Drummond (CEO of Bono's ONE) reports that when Brad Pitt (an actor) travelled with the organisation ONE in Africa he recruited over one million new followers for the organisation.[50] But, more often, ambiguity reigns. In this respect there is a paradox to celebrity engagement. We have always known it works, but we have never known how we know. Celebrity, as one experienced campaigner told me, 'is tried and true but like anything that is tried and true, it is not that innovative and so how effective is it really, I don't know'.[51]

One of the ironies of celebrity advocacy is that, years after it has become thoroughly entrenched, technologies that can more precisely monitor the reach of celebrity advocacy are now being developed. Web 2.0 technology allows hits to be measured in response to specific stories and the sources to be traced. Twitter, Facebook and other social media allow fan communities to be cultivated and counted and their participation monitored directly.

However, even this precision may miss the point. The problem of evaluating impact is not peculiar to celebrity, but general to media engagement, or indeed any attempt to change the world.[52] What, after all, does a newspaper article achieve, or a television show? The bigger problem here is how you know that anything at all that you are doing is having an effect anywhere.

> I don't think we have any very accurate or sophisticated way of [gauging impact] . . . in that sense it is a bit hit and miss because . . . it is not clear how you measure whether that change has actually taken place. And this is a bigger challenge with monitoring and evaluation of campaigns generally . . . you are working on a model of change that has some reasonable set of assumptions and you are using proxy indicators . . . so if you believe greater levels of public awareness will shift behaviourally some people . . . then you equate greater public awareness with media reach. We also have to have the humility to realise that we do not change the world on our own, we are

90 The current state of celebrity advocacy

> contributing to a larger process of societal change. . . . What you need is some
> kind of model of change.[53]

For some organisations, therefore, the key measures were not so much what buzz is created by a story but what sort of change they can see in the way people are thinking, or the high-profile stakeholders who they are trying to influence. Their ultimate measures of success are determined by their own high-profile stakeholder surveys or public surveys.[54] Needless to say, determining the cause of the change, and specifically the role of celebrity in it will be virtually impossible.

There is one aspect of celebrity advocacy that rarely makes the news, but whose consequences are relatively clear: their impact on the supporters of the organisations. This was mentioned several times by my interviewees. One observed that celebrity advocacy is 'also about feeding your supporter base, . . . it's good for your supporters to see solid smart advocates for your own quite complicated issue who are able to amplify the message.'[55]

But a much more common theme was the value to supporters of personal encounters with celebrities, of the *unmediated* presence of celebrities. This instantly touches otherwise 'ordinary' events with the magic and glamour of the 'media world'.[56] These sorts of encounters are obviously good for volunteers, especially in public-facing work: 'It's exciting . . . for volunteers . . . going out talking to people on the street with your favourite local artists.' [57] Celebrities working for charities and with supporters report something similar, in that their fans love meeting them, and other people, even if not fans, enjoy encounters with residents of the media world.

These interactions are clearly powerful too for professional staff. One spoke of the 'affirmation' he felt when a famous person attends an event supporting your work.[58] Another noticed the benefit for his colleagues when 'you get a big name local celebrity and people are excited to be working with them and it affirms our work . . . I've seen that as a big benefit that it brings that . . . sense of excitement and affirmation to the staff'.[59]

In fact, some of the most powerful effects of celebrity advocacy on NGOs could be specifically where events are aimed not at the media but keeping up the local activists' energy.[60] One activist described a meeting of the development movement in Westminster in the mid-2000s in which various celebrities took part in either planned, or impromptu ways, including the musician Thom Yorke who delivered an unexpected performance:

> This was the movement gathering itself. [It was] incredibly moving, incredibly reinforcing and part of the joy of being part of this thing . . . The movement renewed itself spiritually . . . [Specifically on Yorke's contribution] It was fucking exciting, it was great. Do I want to monitor and evaluate that? Should I really care about it? It was just great, he was one of us.[61]

We will return to the importance of unmediated access to celebrity advocates when we look how it works with elites.

Conclusion

Celebrity advocacy is currently increasingly well organised. It displays a vibrancy that makes patterns in celebrity advocacy hard to discern. It is an important niche element of the celebrity industries, useful for building brand image and fulfilling the reporting needs of some of the celebrity media. Development and humanitarian causes are popular within this busy field. At the same time as it has grown in importance, the reasons why NGOs should seek stronger relationships with celebrity advocates remain curiously unarticulated in terms of their evaluation of what celebrity advocates can achieve. The received wisdom is that it 'works', and so it is pursued.

In terms of the broader argument of the book, this chapter has demonstrated the nature and extent of celebrity advocacy that now flourishes in the post-democratic environment the UK affords. Celebrities do not just have more opportunity to mix with political and policy elites. They are being actively cultivated and marshalled to do so by media-savvy and politically savvy NGOs.

We cannot, however, leave the story there. We know that organised relations exist between the NGO sector and celebrity industries, but what do they do? What are they like in practice? How are celebrities cultivated and marshalled?

Similarly, it is unsatisfactory simply to say that celebrities who want to serve charities do so. How are they able to? How do they identify their causes – and how do their causes identify them? It might be relatively straightforward to turn up at a children's hospital in Los Angeles, or donate cast-off clothes to 'Clothes off our Back', but many of these causes, and especially international development and humanitarian causes, are complex and difficult affairs. How do celebrities get to the point where they are able to speak at all on these difficult issues in public?

You might well object that they do not, and that is why columnists like Marina Hyde are able to supply us with a steady stream of gaffes and ludicrous interventions.[62] But the point of these examples for me is that they are so few. Amid the thousands of endorsements, field-trips and other celebrity interventions, most do not ring so hollow and false. They have been carefully and thoughtfully constructed and brought together. We must learn how it is done – and that is the task of the next chapter.

Notes

1 Available at: www.usatoday.com/life/people/2011-04-11-demiashton11_cv_N.htm (viewed 30 July 2011). Ashton Kutcher is an actor.
2 In the late 1990s Marshall wrote briefly that 'a whole political consulting business has developed in Hollywood to aid celebrities in choosing issues with which to become involved' (Marshall, 1997: 110). The British NGO response to that celebrity industry, and increasing aptitude, seems to have developed later than in the US.
3 Few of them, though, used the title 'celebrity liaison'. 'Celebrity' has poor connotations, and the people I met were working in 'high-profile personality liaison', 'artist liaison', 'talent liaison', etc. Nevertheless, they were all working on the same set of tasks.
4 Source: BBC programme, Radio 4, February 2011.

92 The current state of celebrity advocacy

5 The Media Trust is a charity whose mandate is to help other charities make better use of the news and media.

6 Available at: http://charitycelebrity.blogspot.com/see entry for 10 May 2011 (viewed 18 February 2012).

7 Source 85.

8 Foreman, 2009.

9 Sources 3, 85; Foreman, 2009.

10 Sources 23, 35.

11 Source: www.theredpages.co.uk (viewed 25 August 2012).

12 Available at: www.celebritiesworldwide.com (viewed 25 August 2012).

13 It worked, for example, with Demi Moore (actress) and Ashton Kutcher's campaign against sexual trafficking when these actors were a couple, and was behind the report condemning Madonna's educational interventions in Malawi. Madonna subsequently became one of their clients – available at: www.rollingstone.com/music/news/madonnas-charity-organization-drops-plan-to-build-school-in-malawi-20110325 (viewed 8 January 2013); www.newyorker.com/reporting/2012/03/26/120326fa_fact_colapinto (viewed 8 January 2013).

14 Sources 21, 55 and 69. This kind of organisation has existed before but their earlier iterations were not always sustainable. In the UK Cause Celeb has met less success, since starting up in 2004. Another, Celebrity Outreach Inc, began as a non-profit in 1988 connecting public figures to other non-profits in the US. In the late 1990s it morphed into a company that acquired signed celebrity memorabilia wholesale for auction by charities. It is struggling now because, as part of the intensification of relations between charities and sports companies, the latter are now themselves selling this sort of memorabilia directly to the NGOs for auction (Source 10).

15 Source 11. Sought out means that they receive briefings and updates on celebrities' advocacy from publicists, agents and press officers which have been written in a format that suits the website.

16 Source 90.

17 Source 90.

18 Source 96.

19 Source 104.

20 Source 35.

21 Sources 9, 14, 85.

22 Source 76.

23 Sources 51, 76.

24 Source 76.

25 Source 76. A shopping event is when a charity takes over a major store (or part of it) for a short time; staffs it and is rewarded with a share of the proceeds of the takings for that period. They use celebrities as shop assistants, to drum up interest, footfall and sales.

26 Source 51.

27 Source 23. One former agent said he would have advised his clients to switch support from the existing charities they work with to UNICEF or Oxfam if they were asked to work with them.

28 Source 14.

29 Source 80.

30 Khan's escapade is detailed in Brockington, 2009; Fiennes' extra-curricular activities are reported here: www.dailymail.co.uk/femail/article-436846/Air-stewardess-secrets-mile-high-sex-romp-Ralph-Fiennes.html (viewed 3 June 2012).

31 Sources 14, 34, 53, 99, 104.

32 Source 26.

33 Source 93. 'Voice' is defined to note 89 in the next chapter.

34 Source 85.

35 Source 98.

36 Source 71.

The current state of celebrity advocacy **93**

37 I had planned to use three of these sources to describe the exuberance and busyness of celebrity advocacy. I recorded the Red Pages biweekly bulletins, the weekly reports of the Third Sector, and I was given access to the records of the Look to the Stars website. These are different sorts of records. Third Sector's weekly report is brief and designed to give NGOs a flavour of what is going on. The Red Pages biweekly newsletters are a means of showing how up-to-date and on top of the game it is, and they try to be more comprehensive. Look to the Stars is by far the most detailed and they have become the leading authority (with a US bias) on celebrity advocacy and are well supplied with information from a network of enthusiastic volunteers around the world, as well as with a deluge of publicity briefings sent to them unasked. They cannot post all the material they receive, but in the words of one close to the inner workings of the site, their objective is to 'out-nice everyone', so they never refuse to post news, they are just not able to keep up with all that is sent in and have a growing backlog of material to put up.

I have six months of overlapping data from these three sources (November 2010–April 2011). But the first thing that became apparent from these three separate sources is that *there is no pattern to report*. By that I mean that there is hardly any overlap across these three sources. There is no core of activity going on which they are all capturing in slightly different ways. Rather, there is so much happening, and they can hear about it in so many different ways, that each can produce an (almost) entirely separate record. In these six months these sources mention 1,800 different people getting involved in various forms of advocacy and support of charities. Note that the Look to the Stars website is by far the most comprehensive source of the three, with over 1,300 of these names mentioned by it, and over 1,000 mentioned only by it. Third Sector is the Cinderella of the group, reporting only 156 names in this period. At least half of the people mentioned in each source are only mentioned by one source, and not by the others. Only sixty-nine people are mentioned in all three sources; moreover, there is no overlap in the ten people mentioned most frequently in each source. But far more striking than the lack of common figures frequenting the social worlds of these databases is the fact that *they are not reporting the same events*. So, even if they do mention the same people, they are not likely to mention them for the same reasons.

38 They are Oxfam, Comic Relief, Save the Children, Amnesty International, Elton John Aids Foundation, One Campaign, Heifer International and Habitat for Humanity.

39 Atkinson *et al.*, 2012. Note also that this method of selecting NGOs will miss smaller organisations like War Child and the Elton John Aids Foundation, which have excellent links with the music and entertainment industries and work closely with many celebrities.

40 Source 55.

41 Source 85.

42 Source 99.

43 Sources 9, 14, 32, 53, 76, 96.

44 Sources 23, 35, 75, 116.

45 Sources 37, 68, 117.

46 Sources 45, 49.

47 Sources 37, 68, 117.

48 It is my favourite only for its clarity and pedagogic value, and not for any reason pertaining to Katie Couric or the procedure performed. It proved such a popular intervention that soon other celebrities were having publicly screened colonoscopies as well. Even Homer Simpson joined in. All these are viewable here: www.youtube.com/user/SU2C?feature= watch (viewed 8 January 2013). Please note that there is also a dissenting view as to how useful an intervention this was. Robin Larson and colleagues note that 'it is not known whether celebrity endorsements increase screening utilization among individuals who stand to benefit the most from the promoted screening test' (Larson *et al.*, 2005: 695). For other similar incidences, see Boudioni *et al.*, 1998; Chapman and Leask, 2001.

49 Cram *et al.*, 2003. Note that the sample size here is 95,000 procedures. The researchers tracked rates for twenty months prior to the show and ten months afterwards.

94 The current state of celebrity advocacy

50 Available at: www.guardian.co.uk/world/audio/2010/dec/17/focus-podcast-celebrity-aid-development (viewed 5 February 2013).
51 Source 73.
52 Sources 39, 94, 104.
53 Source 104.
54 Sources 61, 64, 67.
55 Source 74. The 1989 Amnesty International Human Rights Tour, for example, boosted the morale of Amnesty International's country groups as it came through (Jim Hanke to Christian Lahusen, 1992).
56 Couldry, 2001.
57 Source 104.
58 Source 120.
59 Source 104.
60 Source 89.
61 Source 40.
62 Some of these deserve to be widely known. Jude Law (an actor) has visited Afghanistan in 2007 on a mission to 'bring peace' and reported that, while he could not meet with the Taliban personally, he was 'led to believe that the effects of our conversations with the right people have filtered through to them'. When Geri Haliwell (a singer) visited Nepal with the UN's population fund, she said that she felt that the prime minister had benefited from 'a western presence'. Hyde had fumed in response: 'A "western presence"? Time was a western presence meant Madeleine Albright, or at least the US ambassador. Now it's the *soi-disant* author of Ugenia Lavender and the Burning Pants' (Hyde, 2010: 12; www.guardian.co.uk lifeandstyle/lostinshowbiz/2009/sep/25/geri-halliwell-united-nations-nepal (viewed 17 December 2012).

6

'GETTING IT'

Producing authentic celebrity advocacy

> 'Don't you remember the rules I taught you?' he said. 'Hmmm? Friends of the famous? You have to recognize the boundaries. You must accept the inequality without drawing attention to it. Don't behave like a member of the public. Don't stare, don't look around the room for the famous ones and make a beeline, don't put them on the spot, don't demand famous-person favours, reassure, don't lecture . . . you're an old friend now, so you make them feel loyal. You do something non-media so you make them feel deep'
>
> Helen Fielding: *Cause Celeb*[1]

We know that relations between charities and the celebrity industries are more systematic than ever before. What allows them to blossom? A succinct answer to this query was presented by an employee of a talent agency in Hollywood. I was told that not all NGOs can work with talent but the ones that do are distinguished by a key attribute: 'They get it'.[2] This was intriguing, but not enlightening. What could it mean? I reached out to a couple of celebrity liaison officers to see if they could explain the secret – what made for effective interactions between talent and NGOs? Again, they had ready answers, but not ones I found particularly helpful. The first one told me 'I get it, I get the relationship'.[3] The second clarified that for those involved, 'by and large everybody . . . gets it'.[4]

Not everybody. They may have been getting it, but I was not. My lack of intuition and interviewing skills were frustrating my ability to understand how, in practical terms, this flourishing of interactions between the celebrity sector and different NGOs had been worked out on the ground. I had a new quest: I wanted to 'get it'.

There were no written accounts to assist me here. The closest, reproduced above, about how to behave around the famous when asking favours of them is fictional. It comes from Helen Fielding's first novel, *Cause Celeb*. It has some authority in

96 Producing authentic celebrity advocacy

that it is about celebrity support for famine relief and is based on her experience working and filming with public figures for Comic Relief in the early 1990s. Nevertheless, this conversation probably did not take place. The more significant issue, however, is that while these sorts of rather servile interactions may occur among individuals, such interpersonal behaviour is not actually that important. It will not help me 'get it'. What matters instead is how the demands and needs of the organisations, as well as the people, are professionally handled on both sides of the relationship.

In this chapter I explain what I think 'getting it' entails and how the relationships between NGOs and public figures are formed and managed, and how they are reported and represented. This is based on my interviews with people who certainly did 'get it', and on their feedback to me when I first tried to write up what I thought it meant.

The chapter has several purposes. It is partly, I admit, an attempt to claim some authority, some way of showing that despite the fact that I have never worked with celebrity advocacy I do have some idea of what is going on 'behind the scenes' (for the experts' verdict on that quest, see the feedback I received from my interviews on an early draft of this paper, Box A1.1 on p. 171). I feel this is needed because previous accounts of celebrity advocacy, particularly critical accounts, have lacked an intimacy with its workings. They condemn from without, which is a weak position.

And from the more intimate view I develop here, I hope two points will become clear. First, we shall see the inequality that characterises relationships between NGOs and the celebrity industries. The two interact closely, but it is very much on the celebrity industries' terms. We have had some hint of this in the previous chapter when I explained the relatively marginal contributions that most NGOs make to most celebrities' publicity needs. But the nature of the inequality becomes much clearer when we listen to accounts of how relationships between celebrities and NGOs are pursued and constructed.

Second, we can explore the nature of the authenticity of celebrity advocacy. The defining goal of celebrity liaison officers is to create opportunities for celebrities to build long-lasting relationships with their organisations. These relationships, and the process of constructing them, provide the basis for the most reliable performances of authenticity. However, I also show that some of the mechanisms that exist for reporting on and representing the relationships, especially in the field of development, can do away with the need for strong, authentic relationships altogether. This is because they can present the appearance of understanding when there has been none or very little. Weak relationships with causes can be portrayed in the same way as strong ones. The public presentation of celebrity field-trips can thus conceal some of the skills, abilities and experience gained on them.

The character of authentic celebrity advocacy has important implications for the work of celebrity advocates in post-democracies. Its construction creates resources for political elites to demonstrate their grasp of the popular (by being seen with celebrities) and for celebrity advocates to demonstrate their authority (by being seen with politicians). Moreover, the fact that some celebrity advocates can build up skills that are only poorly captured in some of the reporting of their work makes it even more likely for celebrity advocacy to work more effectively with elite lobbies than it does with the public.

The chapter proceeds as follows. First, I describe the processes by which relationships between celebrities and NGOs are initiated and then strengthened. I emphasise in particular the work of field-trips in strengthening and building relationships between celebrities, and development and humanitarian NGOs. I then examine some of the constraints that limit the work of celebrity liaison, in particular the unrealistic expectations of colleagues within NGOs, and the demands of the celebrity industries themselves. Next I explore in detail how celebrity field-trips are represented, looking at the journalistic practices that report on celebrity work for development organisations. At this point we will have established what it takes to build authentic relationships between celebrities and NGOs. We can then consider what that authenticity might mean.

Developing authentic relationships

The first task facing a liaison officer is to establish a good reason for forming a relationship between a celebrity and a charity. There has 'got to be a relevance when you approach someone'.[5] Relevance is not given. By this I mean that authentic connections between a celebrity and an NGO do not exist, awaiting discovery. They have to be recognised and then realised (i.e. brought into effect) by the NGOs, the celebrities and those surrounding them. This requires knowing the field and exploring people's backgrounds and interests, deciding when it would be best to make the approach.[6] It requires careful designing of the letter asking for assistance. Agents insist that a well-crafted letter which is clearly designed specifically for their client alone, and is not part of a mass mailing, is vital in attracting notice.[7]

Once a public figure has offered some form of support to NGOs it becomes possible to build closer, lasting relationships with them. This is the hallmark of NGOs' new professional approach to working with talent, and often the key change newly appointed liaison officers seek to make in their organisations.[8] The common goal

> is to avoid having . . . ad-hoc celebrities doing bits and pieces for you which doesn't really form any longevity of work together and is not coming from an authentic place because it is all a bit on the surface. People sense that and there is no genuine feel about it.[9]

Successful relationship-building hinges on treating public figures as human beings. The fact that they donate their time, and often cover their own costs to boot, makes them effectively major donors-in-kind and they need to be treated like other donors and engaged personally by the causes they support.[10] 'I personally . . . see them as human beings and valued supporters . . . To me our celebrity supporters are very, very valued individuals'.[11] Many celebrities want relationships with NGOs that matter and that can be nurtured over time. The associations have to

98 Producing authentic celebrity advocacy

feel authentic for the public figures too.[12] Just asking for things without adequate involvement in the causes could leave public figures feeling 'prostituted out'.[13]

To maintain that involvement the liaison officer's role is to 'stay in their lives'.[14] There are a number of common ways across the NGO sector of staying in people's lives. Liaison officers are writing bespoke newsletters, sending thank you cards, birthday cards, flowers and sometimes small gifts. They report back the outcome of fundraising ventures or what the funds had been spent on. They provide updates on the welfare of people or projects encountered in the field.[15]

The 'asks' themselves can constitute one of the means of maintaining and developing relationships where they allow more personal contact, interaction time and all the other things healthy relationships require. Some organisations deliberately designed publicity events as opportunities to initiate or develop relationships with public figures. One liaison officer said, 'I'll create situations where talent can come to learn about something'.[16] Another was 'working to invent' more domestic events to develop their relationships with public figures rather than waiting for the right sort of international trip to become possible.[17] Others designed gradations of events specifically to initiate and then deepen relationships.[18] Sometimes the only value of lighter 'asks' is the longer term engagements they can lead to: 'the only use of the photo-and-a-quote is as part of a . . . planned engagement programme with an individual celebrity.'[19]

A difficulty for smaller NGOs is that they are not big enough to generate sufficient meetings that celebrities will want to attend and where associations can be nurtured:

> It is difficult when you work for a small charity to provide the range of things to . . . keep people's interests up . . . It was easy at [a large charity] . . . there were always events going on . . . you wanted someone to keep their involvement . . . and therefore you could invite them to open something or come to something . . . at a smaller agency that is much more difficult, you don't have those kind of on-going things . . . so you are working much harder . . . to find things which allow you to maintain that relationship with people which is really important as otherwise they forget you and move on.[20]

Where organisations manage larger stables of celebrities, part of the challenge was thinking up the right sort of events that would keep them all busy and involved.[21] Interviewees among numerous development NGOs insisted that the field-trip was an essential part of the work of producing credible, genuinely passionate and informed celebrity spokespeople, who can survive the media scrutiny that their efforts must undergo.

> It's part and parcel of working with an NGO that has work in the field. If you want someone to talk about . . . your work and inspire people to give, get involved, campaign etc . . . they need to have met the right people . . . in the field . . . to know what they're talking about and to be able to answer

Producing authentic celebrity advocacy **99**

questions from specialist journalists . . . about sustainability and foreign aid and all those sorts of tricky subjects.[22]

There are several reasons why field-trips are such an essential element of celebrity advocacy for development. Probably the most important element of field-trips was the powerful effect it could have on the celebrities themselves. The trips can be 'life changing'[23] where the public figures on them 'get converted'[24] or 'get the religion':[25] 'If we can get someone to the field and work around their interests and availability, without a doubt most people find it's a really moving, engaging and inspiring experience.'[26] They are so powerful partly because celebrities experience the culture shock of being in a poor country and their own reduced circumstances while there:[27] 'you are not staying in the Four Seasons and waking at noon and what not, you're up at the crack of dawn [and] you might not have . . . electricity or a pot to piss in'.[28]

They also meet people personally who live with poverty, inequality and disadvantage, not merely the statistics: 'It enables the people that we work with to speak from personal experience versus trying to memorise a bunch of facts and figures.'[29] It brings home vividly the messages of pre-trip briefings:

> when you go and talk to someone in a paddy field in Ghana and they can tell you about the IMF and World Bank it becomes clear to you where the buck stops – so everything they learn in the briefings is reinforced in a black and white way when you go on a field trip.[30]

Moreover, celebrities plainly enjoy the competence and credibility that field contacts NGOs afford:

> Celebrities are very conscious of how they are perceived in the world . . . [T]hey don't want to be misperceived as dilettantes who are indulging in some sort of a cause-of-the-weak flirtation, but they really want to really learn about an issue, often go to the country themselves on one or more trips to talk to people directly and speak in a very personal way. They also like to tag team with . . . field researchers who can ground them and lend their advocacy some gravitas and make sure that what they are saying is accurate, timely, comprehensive and helpful [and] effective.[31]

All this concentrated and dramatic experience can then be turned into stronger relationships between the celebrities and the NGOs. Field-trips allow for quality time between the liaison officers and celebrities at a time when the latter may be rapidly changing their world view:[32] 'there are just so many examples that I could give you of the difference that a trip like that makes to a celebrity and just in terms of really engaging them and really cementing the relationship.'[33]

The power of the field-trip as a personal experience is probably best illustrated, ironically, by one of the rare known failures. It occurred when Rupert Everett

100 Producing authentic celebrity advocacy

(an actor) visited Kenya and Ethiopia with Oxfam. This is probably unique in that it was not a good trip, and because both the journalist covering the trip, and Everett himself, were able to write frank accounts about its failings. Collectively, they give good insights into the demands such trips exert.

According to Everett, his publicist had arranged the trip because she thought he was 'becoming a tiny bit selfish'.[34] She may have been right because the journalist's account describes a rather badly behaved, at times 'extraordinarily childish', Everett whose conversation and demeanour made 'scorching wrecks' of his Western companions' egos.[35] It is not a flattering portrait.

However, the significance of this trip is not what is shows about Everett's character; it is the shock of what he saw and had to cope with. From his point of view, it was just too much. On arriving at a desolate feeding station in the Ethiopian desert he recounts:

> at first my brain froze. It was impossible to take in and there wasn't any time because now my job began. The TV crew and Brian the photographer were going to walk with me to the feeding station to meet a woman who had just arrived, and accompany her back to their hut. It was an excruciating experience. The woman's husband was dead. She had walked a hundred miles to get to the feeding station. On the journey one of her children had died. The other was a little barely breathing bundle of bones in a sling around her neck. She recounted all this through an interpreter, in a listless voice with vacant dilated eyes . . . when we got to her tent, she and I went in, followed by Brian . . . Obviously it had to be done. The photo-op is all. The world only responds when they see the living proof in pictures, at which point it is often too late but I was amazed and horrified by the photographer, by the whole world around this tragic scene, myself included.[36]

Everett found it, initially, difficult to perform the role demanded of him – i.e. to listen and learn from the NGO accounts, get on well with their staff and connect with the people he was meeting in a way that could be favourably depicted in the media. The gulf was too great. Although things improved later, he describes himself as a 'lost cause' on the trip, and that the trip itself as 'disastrous'.[37]

The failings of Everett's trip illustrate well the strains, alienations and physical difficulties of celebrity field-trips. They are such powerful experiences because they take people to the edge of what they can endure – or beyond. They can become cathartic moments of realisation and commitment.

Coping with constraints

There are three significant constraints that have to be negotiated when developing strong relationships between celebrities and NGOs. The first is so important that I will devote much of the next chapter to it. It concerns the relationships with corporate partners that have helped to produce and shape the current performance of celebrity work with charities.

The second is that this work requires an understanding of the instability and uncertainty that defines the lifestyles of many public figures' professions. They often cannot say for whom they will be working, or where, next week. A job may become suddenly available that can ruin the most carefully laid plans of NGOs:[38] 'Especially at the higher echelons of talent their agents are continually juggling competing demands of work which might fall through, making them available, only for something else to come up making them unavailable.'[39] This also means that it does not make sense to lose interest in celebrities who appear to be on the wane, for you never know what might happen next: 'half the trick is always maintaining relationships with everyone as if they are at the height of their career because you never know what these people are going . . . to do'.[40]

Third, it requires coping with the demands and expectations of colleagues in NGOs who 'do not know what we do or understand our world'.[41] The celebrity liaison managers' forum began partly as a refuge for employees who needed empathetic professional friends. While the liaison officers may 'get' the relationships, many other people within NGOs clearly do not.[42] They are keen to use public figures, do not know how to, but think they do. One person found it 'maddening . . . half of my job, half of my week, is about managing the expectations of my colleagues.'[43] This came out repeatedly in interviews: 'Quite often the teams themselves will just say "Hi there we need a celebrity"; they don't really know why or what they will use them for or what they will gain from it'.[44] The popular belief in the power of celebrity which motivates these interventions makes for a poor guide as to how to use it.

Part of the skill of the celebrity liaison officer is to promote events when celebrity is *not* used. They only have limited access to the celebrities who do want to work with them and have to use those chances wisely. This might mean pointing out to colleagues that some stories might better be conveyed by a member of staff who would be 'better than a celebrity who actually doesn't know the work that well and wouldn't be that inspiring'.[45] It also means insisting that adding celebrity because it is part of some magic formula creating attention and publicity will not work: 'it still has to come back down to being a good story either to get the celebrity or to get the coverage'.[46]

The advantages of not using celebrity were clearest with two different types of organisations: those who deliberately eschewed it and those who worked with the most famous names possible. For the former I was told that a press officer with a good story based on solid research, and who knows how to work the media (knowing editors and having good contacts), will get material prominently into the press.[47] You did not need a celebrity. For the latter, their publicity was striking for the frequency with which celebrity did not appear. The famous names were used sparingly.[48] Other NGOs avoided the news coverage that celebrity could have provided because it was not helpful to have the celebrity storylines (celebrity adoption, Geldof's rants) dominating their news coverage.[49]

102 Producing authentic celebrity advocacy

A related misconception is that work with celebrities must involve extremely famous people: 'There is this myth that you need an A-lister for everything. You don't, you need the right person.'[50] Rather, people trust their own local talent, 'their local weather men' and you do not need international superstars to make an impact.[51] This misunderstanding was not restricted to the NGO domain. Some celebrities make the mistake of thinking that they are not sufficiently famous to serve charities' needs:

> when I was first asked to be an ambassador for [Charity P] I was totally flattered . . . and I was actually very surprised . . . and a little bit embarrassed because I was thinking well . . . I'm not as high profile as, you know, as some of these top footballers or celebrities that you see on TV.[52]

Working with the celebrity industries

The relationships that develop between celebrities and the NGOs they support cannot be understood without reference to the personal assistants, agents, publicists and managers who surround celebrities. There are two central facts that govern these relationships. The first is that NGOs refuse, almost all the time, to pay any form of fees for the time of public figures who work with them.[53] There is little variation here – relationships with the celebrity industry cannot be understood except in the context that NGOs generally demand that their public figures work for them for free.[54] The second is that, because NGOs do not pay, they are always asking for favours. The condition of being a celebrity liaison officer is that one's requests are always at the bottom of the pile, if they have made it there at all.[55]

These facts mean that the defining characteristic of the relationship between the celebrity industry and the NGO sector is its inequality. The latter depends almost entirely on the charity of the former. In many respects, as we discussed in the previous chapter, most NGOs need celebrities far more than any given celebrity needs a particular NGO. Few celebrities have to cultivate a special relationship with any one particular organisation in order to support a cause. There will be many other NGOs doing remarkably similar work who will also be asking for their favours. As a result, most NGOs are dependent on the largesse of celebrities for their interactions to happen. Their requests have to be fitted into whatever commercial work is being undertaken and can be dropped if new commercial opportunities come along. Even important events like field-trips have to be fitted in 'around their interests and availability'.[56]

Some of my interviewees accept this weak position: 'you have to just be grateful for whatever inch they give you, whatever dime they give you'.[57] Others resented this inequality, comparing the sensation to waiting for 'crumbs from the table' of privilege.

> It is interesting how resentful you do feel . . . as far as we were concerned we were working with the people in the world who probably have the rawest,

rawest deal . . . you couldn't find a group of people who deserved some decent treatment [more], and yet the difficulty of getting a celebrity to commit an evening was painful . . . It was a jading experience.[58]

Part of 'getting it' is to accept the inequalities and all the symbolic violence they entail, and ensure that the experience of working with your organisation is pleasurable for the celebrity so that they will want to work with you again and not the competition (hence the perks and gifts blagged from corporate partners). The advice given out at a Media Trust workshop on working with celebrity included making sure that the celebrity was greeted and hosted properly and that, 'however well the event had gone', they received good feedback from it.

Good relationships with celebrities' agents were particularly important because they could control schedules and shut down potential events. One interviewee insisted that all contact must be through representatives as it would be 'wildly inappropriate' and 'unprofessional' to call public figures directly even if you are friends.[59] This is because 'celebrities never want to say no to anything because they always want to be viewed as nice easy going people' so you must never put them on the spot with things and risk making them feel uncomfortable.[60] Indeed, it was the agents' job to take that pressure: 'my whole job is to make my clients look good and it is embarrassing to turn down charity work'.[61]

Whether they were the gatekeepers or not, agents were vital. Some liaison officers therefore 'treat the agent as well as I treat the celebrity'.[62] The NGOs who 'get it' know how to reassure the people managing public figures' lives that they can be trusted, that they will be consulted on quotes and pictures if necessary and that their clients will be looked after well.[63] In the best relationships an agent who is on board will actively look out for opportunities for their client to promote particular campaigns.[64] In the long term it is not just the individual relationships surrounding particular public figures which matter but also the reputation of the NGOs themselves among the celebrity industries, which are at stake:

> I want to present [my organisation] amongst the talent industry as . . . we'll only use their artists [where it will have] value for their time, its going to have huge impact . . . or useful impact, and they're going to get a good experience out of it. Its going to make a difference to us so their time is not going to be wasted.[65]

After all, in the long term the celebrities come and go, but the agents remain.[66]

Representing celebrity advocacy

Given that field-trips are essential in forging relationships between celebrities and development NGOs, let us examine in more detail how they are represented. There are several ways of reporting on field-trips. The most common is to have some sort of press coverage of the trip itself, preferably with photographs, which features

104 Producing authentic celebrity advocacy

in a magazine. Here I draw in particular on interviews with journalists who have been involved in these trips.

It was clear from my interviews that creating stories from the trips suffered from two constraints that impede the nature of the messages they are able to communicate and connections they are able to establish with the audience. First, everything has to be viewed 'through the prism of the individual celebrity's experience'.[67] The photographs have to feature the celebrity, as well as the images and issues they are there to highlight. The text of the interview and the resulting story has to cover the celebrity themselves, their personal life and professional engagements: 'when you go on these trips you are basically covering the celebrity highlighting the issue that they are going to cover'.[68]

The effect is most visible by comparing trips with celebrities to trips without them. When covering development and humanitarian issues without celebrity:

> you are not dictated by having to focus on a celebrity with perhaps what is going on in the background . . . It makes your job a lot easier . . . You photograph it very differently. You are not looking for the best light . . . You are there to document it as it is . . . You are not putting a celebrity on the right hand side of your frame and making sure that that stuff in the background isn't too gratuitous and [thinking] . . . I can't get that because I've got a celebrity in it.[69]

Several interviewees expressed dissatisfaction with celebrity field-trips as a means of practising their profession, and a couple had even stopped doing them because they no longer found them fulfilling.[70] As one put it, 'I just felt that the issue . . . was being clouded because of the concentration on the celebrity'.[71]

The second constraint is that whatever is said and shown must show the celebrity in a good light. This is a general property of news coverage requested by and for celebrity.

> You photograph the whole package in a very positive light . . . there are no shadows in the world of celebrity; everyone looks beautiful. It is not about creating an interesting photograph with moody lighting, it is about creating the happy world.[72]

Celebrities can be reduced to tears on these trips because they are so hard hitting. But, I was told, those images unfortunately do not get shown. Crumpled faces do not make for good pictures.[73]

The pressure to produce such impressions comes from several quarters, from the editors who commissioned the pieces in the first place and, more indirectly, from the organisations the celebrity visit is serving.[74] Journalists can feel an obligation to the charities who have taken so much trouble to arrange these visits and contacts.[75] Moreover, they are often more than happy to write well of organisations of which they think highly: 'The organisation want you to portray a positive image of what they are doing and all these organisations . . . are doing great works . . . Their work to me is not questionable.' [76]

Then there is the influence of the celebrity industries themselves, who want their clients to be seen in the best possible light.

> You do get some really great celebrities who really get involved and get their hands dirty and really want to take in what they are seeing. And I would say that that is a huge majority of them . . . [But] it's not always what the PR wants . . . A celebrity has a PR. The celebrity to that PR is a product. They do not want their product viewed that way.[77]

And it can come from the celebrity themselves:

> *Author:* 'Has any figure said "great photograph . . . but I don't like that because it points too much to me rather than the issue"?'
> [Pause and interviewee stares at author, surprised.]
> *Interviewee:* 'God. That would be nice wouldn't it? I don't want to say any more on that. [Laughs] Wouldn't that be nice?'[78]

It is important to note that this attention to surface and appearance is not universal. One interviewee described interactions with a famous figure who

> works in the make-up industry but didn't wear a jot of make-up, wasn't interested in how she was going to look, didn't say 'No not that one, not that one' in the photographs, didn't want to edit it . . . she didn't want to be seen all dressed up and glossy and that is so refreshing. So refreshing and so rare.[79]

Other interviewees reported that some celebrities were reluctant to talk too much about themselves on these trips, but did so because they knew they had to 'play the game'.[80]

The limitations inherent in reporting on these trips could make communicating an interesting account hard. The end story was almost already written before the trip had happened. 'The celebrity thing restricted you in so many ways', in how and what you could write, it was formulaic.[81] The way these constraints operate are best visible in the (rare) accounts of trips I was told about where people either did very little in the field, or just behaved badly there. Behaving badly included walking away from people who are in the middle of telling tragic stories of their personal experiences of a disaster in one instance and not wanting to be touched by any of the people the celebrity was meeting in another.[82] But, in the mediated representation of these visits, all those aspects were erased. Instead, both for failed and successful visits, the celebrity's thoughts and understandings of the lives and circumstances of the impoverished people they 'met' are reported in depth. One NGO interviewee who had hosted a visit recalled that her visitors 'were disgusted

106 Producing authentic celebrity advocacy

[with what they saw] . . . they did not connect with people' but then in the TV interviews afterwards saw that 'they had just like copy-pasted my phrases and sentences. Which I don't mind but it just told me they didn't understand what was going on.' [83] Another happy write-up reports the celebrity's own sense of humility when faced with other people's poverty which they apparently endure so happily – this for a trip which is still remembered widely within development circles for its artifice and failure.

Performing authentic advocacy

Authenticity, and the credibility it provides, are perhaps the most important goals for the people negotiating relationships between public figures and NGOs. As I hope the preceding material makes clear, authenticity in this instance is the product of much hard work recognising, enabling, creating, managing and producing authentic relationships between celebrity advocates and their causes, and negotiating significant hurdles in order to do so.

Yet despite the constant appearance of authenticity as a theme in the interviews, and the myriad processes that contribute to the construction of authentic relationships, *the nature of the authenticity was not defined* by almost all the people I was talking to. The concept was invoked as being self-evidently important, but what it constituted was not explained.

What it might mean was eventually spelled out in one interview:

> Authenticity. . . can mean several things. Have you seen the problem? Have you been there, do you go there regularly? Do you have empathy with the issue and with the audience – e.g. if it's a story about children, are you a mum or dad? Are you concerned with issues of injustice?[84]

We can name these sources of authenticity:

1 Expert or Experiential Authority: an intellectual knowledge or practical life experience that provides special insights into other people's condition.
2 Affinity: some sort of structural similarity with others (being a parent, living on the wrong side of unequal power structures).
3 Empathy: the shared emotions one has with others as a result of some shared experience or affinity.
4 Sympathy: the emotions provoked in you by another's fate which you do not share.

We can see these different sources of authenticity in action in the field. Consider this statement:

> There was one actress . . . [who] had never been to the developing world before and ok you could say that well that was a risk . . . but it actually gave

Producing authentic celebrity advocacy **107**

a real freshness to it because she gave a very honest fresh open account about what she had experienced out there. [She] conveyed what she had experienced really well. She was an engaging person anyway who went out with a friend and their collective experience was informative and honest – about their uncertainties, shock and hesitancies.[85]

Evidently the authenticity that the advocate offers in this case is an empathetic connection with the audience. The desire for that sort of authenticity was common in reporting on celebrity advocacy. Some journalists and magazine editors are convinced that they need the celebrity interest to make difficult issues interesting for the reader. From the magazine's point of view they see it 'as a good way to promote worthwhile causes' and of broadening the issues covered: '[I]t can be the most depressing story in the world but if the celeb is there and covering it then we've got a way to spin it to make it suitable that the reader can identify with it.'[86] From the journalist's point of view, it makes writing the story to connect with the audience easier. It gives you 'an instant way in'.[87]

However, there is also evidence that celebrity advocacy is not just about seeking empathy with Northern audiences. Instead, it can be more ambiguous and confused. Consider this statement:

> *Author:* 'So what works well?'
> *Interviewee:* 'Somebody having a genuine connection with the issue we are trying to put through . . . like here, where they have visited and seen for themselves and they can speak really passionately and really care . . . because I think it also gives them the confidence to talk about an area that otherwise . . . they are not a specialist in. What would they know about that particular strand of development or that particular type of work? But if they feel . . . some emotional connection with it they suddenly feel qualified to talk about it and more comfortable to talk about their experience because they can relate it directly to [that experience].'[88]

The interviewee suggested that emotional connection makes public figures feel 'qualified' to speak. That verb could imply an expert authority. I am not sure that this is what the speaker intended. I think they meant an empathetic connection (it is not clear with whom), but its ambiguity makes my point.

The variety of forms of authenticity also points to another central aspect of the authenticity of celebrity advocacy. It is forged in the public domain. It is *performed* to publics and represented by the media.[89] This form of authenticity, as I mentioned in the Introduction (pp. 10–12), is in keeping with current tropes. The varieties of forms of authenticity can be seen as resources upon which celebrity advocates can draw in their performances.

My emphasis on performance and representation in celebrity advocacy is likely to offend two groups of people on each side of the debate about the legitimacy of celebrity interventions. For critics of celebrity, what matters is not appearance but substance. Any claim to authenticity which is based on representation is therefore illegitimate. To such critics I would reply that the paradox of working with celebrity and good causes is that it is only as a result of extensive representation and mediation that the authenticity of these associations can be recognised at all. Authenticity here is not some outpouring of a true inner-self. Rather, as I argued in the Introduction, authenticity can only be recognised as such by virtue of its being effectively *performed*.[90]

On the other hand, the people producing celebrity interventions already know how real and substantial the concerns of their famous colleagues are. They may object to any account that focuses on the representation of that concern rather than its reality. Again, I would reply that my account of how the relationships are constructed and negotiated between NGOs and celebrities is no denial of the reality of the motivations, energy and enthusiasms that animate both groups. Rather, and this is the key, I have sought to clarify what authenticity means, what forms of authenticity are desired and how claims to authenticity can, practically speaking, be made in the public realm. This chapter can be seen as mapping out how the problems of artifice and superficiality are combatted by protagonists deeply embedded in the construction of representations.

Note, however, that there is a hierarchy of performances at work among celebrity advocates, as a comparison of the journalists' accounts of celebrity field-trips (above) and Chouliaraki's analysis of Hepburn and Jolie (see p. 22) makes clear. Chouliaraki considered how Hepburn and Jolie's performances to the media after field-trips communicated the needs of distant strangers. These were performances given in addition to any coverage by journalists in magazines that derived from their strong commitments to these causes.[91] However, if we turn from these extra performances to the reports that appear in newspapers and magazines, then Chouliaraki's question – 'How do celebrities authentically perform the aspirational discourse of humanitarianism?' – disappears. Instead, we have a system that produces aspirational discourse, voiced by celebrities, without the need for any special personal techniques to produce a convincing performance. The techniques of reporting celebrity field-trips that I encountered seem designed to ensure that *irrespective of the personal behaviour, a robust public performance appears*. They are able to erase the problems and personal deficiencies. The joys of a good trip, and miseries of a bad one, are confined to the journey itself. What comes out in the media is the 'world without shadows'.

As Everett demonstrates, behaviour in the field matters. A good trip was clearly easier to represent well than a bad one.[92] But the system of representation of which trips are part means that authenticity (the credible representation of effective engagement in humanitarian issues) does not hinge on personal performance on an individual trip. Instead, the celebrity field-trip provides a useful proving ground to develop and train talent that aspires to the convincing aspirational discourse of leading celebrity humanitarians, and allows NGOs quietly to discard, with no harm to anyone's image (theirs or the celebrity's), those who cannot perform.

Thus, at the lower levels of the hierarchy, in the early stages of relationships, the performance is relatively scripted. However, as relationships between the advocates and the NGOs prosper (as they did with Hepburn and have done with Jolie) so the performances become more important, personalised and significant. They become a more central part of the celebrity's voice, and brand. They enable new possibilities of personal advocacy in more specialised and expert settings.

Conclusion

The work of celebrity liaison officers, the task of 'getting it', is characterised by an abiding set of tensions that attend their attempts to establish authentic relationships between public figures and NGOs. They will seek to establish enduring relationships with public figures and be rebuffed by their agents, or they will set up meetings and events that public figures' fickle commitments then undo, all while negotiating with colleagues' occasionally unreasonable demands. The events and interactions they arrange must both demonstrate an authentic relationship with a cause and at the same time be a means of deepening and extending that relationship, making it more authentic. Sometimes, when the celebrity liaison officer is helping the celebrity to establish 'a reason to be there' to the press, they are also establishing a reason to be there with the NGO. And even when everything goes well, authenticity still has to be performed and enacted before publics who may well demand a different variety of authenticity than that the celebrity can deliver. These are not problems that are solvable; they are issues that liaison officers have to become skilled in dealing with every day.

There is evidence that these forms of celebrity advocacy can be superficial encounters that are more about linking Northern audiences to celebrities than they are about encouraging cosmopolitan sensibilities (i.e. a deep and rigorous concern for others). There is evidence, too, that these forms of advocacy can merely be an appendage to the brand-building of the celebrity industries. However, it is not just that. In the hands of the more experienced celebrity liaison officers, and more committed celebrities, there is considerable potential for more meaningful relationships to be established.

However, it is also clear that the means of conveying commitment and understanding are limited. In part, this is because of the reporting practices that present field-trips, in part, because of the post-humanitarian tropes governing the mediation of distant others' needs (see Chapter 2). Celebrity humanitarianism as portrayed in the media is not necessarily the same as celebrity humanitarianism on the ground. This means that different groups of people will have different experiences of this advocacy. The public experience the mediated representations of authentic relations. These show everything as authentic, and for that reason are not good at capturing the variation in levels of commitment that different celebrity supporters can demonstrate. Corporate and political elites, however, will often be able to interact more personally with these celebrities, not least because NGOs will try to arrange events where this is possible. These unmediated interactions

110 Producing authentic celebrity advocacy

allow for a much richer encounter with people who can diverge considerably in their grasp of the issues. Mediated representations of celebrity advocacy are rather flat. Unmediated interactions with effective celebrity advocates can be quite a different experience.

This point sets the stage for the next part of the argument. We need to see how different groups of people respond to celebrity advocacy. The power of celebrity advocacy rests partly on belief in it, and we must now examine the nature of that belief. We will examine first the response of corporate and government elites, for these are not only interesting and important in themselves, but they are also instrumental in shaping the practices of 'getting it' among NGOs. We will then examine the more general public responses to celebrity advocacy in Chapter 8.

Notes

1 Fielding, 1994: 210.
2 Source 3.
3 Source 35.
4 Source 37.
5 Source 35. When NGOs approach agents or managers for support (and it is almost always that way round), they have to have worked out how 'their artists [are] going to have credibility and relevance' (Source 51). When agents approach NGOs asking them to take on public figures as patrons or supporters (which happens rarely) then, if the connection is not there, these relationships have been discouraged or refused by the NGOs. They turn away talent if it is not suited (Sources 9, 27, 34, 45, 51, 53).
6 Sources 26, 35, 37, 74, 81. As one celebrity liaison officer put it: 'my job is to read everything' (Source 9). Tracking people before making an 'ask' (a request for action or assistance) can take longer than a year (Source 45).
7 Sources 94, 108. Celebrities, their agents and contacts, can receive hundreds of requests weekly to work for free for good causes, and they turn down or ignore the vast majority. The increasing numbers of NGOs jostling for the attention of public figures has made successful first requests harder to get (Sources 23, 53, 73, 75, 78).
8 Sources 65, 71, 77.
9 Source 69.
10 Sources 35, 70, 71.
11 Source 53.
12 Source 51.
13 Source 21.
14 Source 45.
15 Sources 14, 23, 37, 67, 70, 71, 77, 86.
16 Source 61.
17 Source 37.
18 Source 26.
19 Source 35.
20 Source 48.
21 This is especially true when celebrities they work with are becoming decreasingly famous (Source 34). Agents representing struggling famous supporters have been known to remind liaison officers that their client has not been approached to do anything for a while (Sources 9, 14).
22 Source 99.
23 Source 37.
24 Source 34.
25 Source 8.

Producing authentic celebrity advocacy **111**

26 Source 85.
27 Sources 26, 76, 85.
28 Source 85.
29 Source 85.
30 Source 74
31 Source 93.
32 Sources 37, 85. Conversely, NGOs who did not 'get it' would entrust field-trips to staff who were not particularly interested in, or unable to relate to the celebrities sympathetically, thus losing the opportunity the visit could have afforded (Source 105).
33 Source 53
34 Everett, 2006: 335.
35 Cantacuzino, 2000.
36 Everett, 2006: 338.
37 Everett, 2006: 340.
38 Sources 14, 21, 35, 37, 45, 49.
39 Source 86.
40 Source 76.
41 Source 51.
42 Source 35.
43 Source 54.
44 Source 77.
45 Source 99.
46 Source 48.
47 Source 24.
48 Sources 64, 93.
49 Sources 32, 39.
50 Source 35. The right person being someone who is a public figure, who has relevance and authenticity, and who has sufficient prominence to capture the attention required in the media or from funders.
51 Source 85.
52 Source 91.
53 Sources 5, 6, 9, 14, 26, 35, 37, 51, 53, 54, 71.
54 Despite this strong line against payment, agents (who are paid according to the work they bring in for their clients) will still try their luck, asking for, and being refused, payment (Sources 23, 51, 53). There are also some grey areas. NGOs do not expect public figures to pay for their own travel expenses (Sources 5, 6, 9, 14, 26, 35, 37, 51, 53, 54). This generosity does not extend to any entourage, at least I have not encountered an organisation which would pay for it. They would also pay for people who are doing their job (Sources 27, 51). If a musician or comedian is to be reliably booked to perform for an important event which is scheduled months in advance, then it is reasonable to pay them. The uncertainties in their schedules means that such a commitment could incur considerable opportunity costs for them.
55 Source 76.
56 Source 85.
57 Source 55.
58 Source 119.
59 Source 54.
60 Source 54. Compare these sentiments to Michael Ahearn's about artists and charity in a book about Bill Graham's life. Graham produced the Live Aid concert in Philadephia in 1985, organised the Conspiracy of Hope tour with Amnesty in 1986 and worked on the Human Rights Now, also for Amnesty, tour in 1989. Ahearn worked with him at the Fillmore in San Francisco and then later as an independent production manager. He said 'The artist is not and certainly never wants to be the person to sit there and say no to *anything*. The artist will say yes to *everything*, go behind the door and say "Miles, *listen*. I'm a nice guy. I'm doing this because I love peace, light, freedom, and all that kind of

112 Producing authentic celebrity advocacy

stuff. Would you please go tell these people the answer is *no*? It can't be me saying because how can I be an asshole?' (Graham and Greenfield, 2004 [1990]: 485). Miles refers to Miles Copeland, the manager of Sting and his former band The Police, who was causing the Human Rights Now tour organisers some difficulties.

61 Source 41.
62 Source 51.
63 Sources 35, 37, 71, 76.
64 Source 48.
65 Source 51.
66 Source 35.
67 Source 25.
68 Source 56.
69 Source 118.
70 Sources 29, 31, 56.
71 Source 56.
72 Source 118.
73 Source 118.
74 Sources 25, 29. cf. Clark's writings on how photographers of famine experience pressure to perpetrate stereotypes (Clark, 2004).
75 Source 29.
76 Source 118.
77 Source 118.
78 Source 118.
79 Source 118.
80 Source 29.
81 Source 29.
82 Sources 31, 118.
83 Source 114.
84 Source 64.
85 Source 59.
86 Source 90.
87 Source 59. As Chouliaraki has made clear (p. 23), seeing oneself in the celebrity, which this form of authenticity entails, is a form of narcissism that bodes ill for the possibilities of connection with distant strangers, and cosmopolitanism that development and humanitarianism require.
88 Source 37.
89 This is sometimes expressed as the need to keep the work that celebrities do with NGOs as 'staying in their voice' (Source 93). Voice, I was told 'has to do with personal branding' (Source 93). It means finding issues, and messages about those issues, that the celebrity can say with comfort and authority because it fits the rest of their public persona. cf. Rae McGrath on Princess Diana's 'voice' on p. 6 above.
90 This is what Chouliaraki refers to as 'the paradox of authenticity' inherent in the theatricality of humanitarianism (Chouliaraki, 2013).
91 My interviewees hoped for this sort of additional outcome from their work with celebrities. I was told it was great if celebrities 'are genuinely interested in an issue [because] they are going to keep on talking about it' (Source 104), but for most this was an added, unexpected extra.
92 As one public relations worker explained to me, PR is easier, and one feels better about it, if you are representing something with some truth behind it. It feels better for the PR officer if it is well grounded and for the client themselves they can speak with more honesty and conviction if speaking with knowledge and background. 'It's easier because its real.' The source added that it is possible that without that sort of grounding, one can brief clients 'to the hilt', but it could still feel fake (Source 94).

7

ELITES AND CELEBRITY ADVOCACY

A radical reconfiguration of development studies would ... recognise the importance of policy-makers, the wealthy and others with power ... For they are the biggest blind spot in development studies. If we are serious about poverty we have to be serious about powerful people.

Robert Chambers[1]

Celebrities are, by definition, privileged. They have access to places, events and people that most of us do not. And if, according to the agents I spoke to, not all are wealthy, then at least the way they earn their money appears more interesting, varied, and with less drudgery and more freebies than most of us enjoy.

Celebrities, then, are part of the elite. But what does that mean in terms of post-democratic politics, and the work of celebrity advocacy for international development in such regimes? How does their access, their convening power and their influence work for the NGO sector? If part of the business of 'getting' celebrity advocacy for NGOs is to know how to wield its influence among corporate and government elites, then what do NGOs have to do to work it effectively? As Chambers reminds us above, these are important questions.

There are three issues that have to be covered to answer these questions and I will explore each in this chapter. The first concerns the importance of celebrity contacts for corporate sponsors and partners of NGOs. Working with NGOs' celebrity advocates can makes good economic sense for corporate sponsors. The rise of celebrity within the NGO movement reflects also the broader influence of trends in corporate social responsibility.

More than that, many elites enjoy meeting and interacting with celebrities; it is pleasurable for them personally. This is the second aspect. Celebrity encounters reinforce their own elite status and, especially for politicians, it is good for their public image.

114 Elites and celebrity advocacy

But perhaps the over-riding point here is that elites believe in the popularity of celebrities. Celebrity represents to many elites the affective will of the people. They value it because they believe it has such popular traction. In times when increasing inequality and political disengagement can render publics far and distant, celebrity brings them up close and personal.

The argument of the chapter is that celebrity advocacy wielded and guided by NGOs has become a part of the mechanism of elite governance that characterises post-democracy. Celebrity makes it easier for NGOs to gain access to corporate and political leaders in post-democratic times. But, in typically post-democratic fashion, it encourages particular forms of popular participation in politics that are not especially empowering. This is partly because the mechanisms offered for participation can require only a rather passive involvement. But it is also because celebrity signifies the public in the minds of decision-makers. Celebrity involvement can disempower citizens because it suffices to persuade elites that the public are behind a campaign – whether they are or not.

Celebrity, then, can displace public engagement. And this effect will be redoubled should celebrity not signal the broader public support it is widely believed to capture. We will consider that issue in the next chapter. Let us first examine the nature and texture of celebrity advocates' role in elite governance.

The corporate interest in celebrity advocates

Across the interviews I conducted the corporate fascination with celebrity, and especially the celebrities that NGOs could provide, proved a constant theme. Corporates, I was told, are 'star struck',[2] they 'really liked having celebrities involved'.[3] The corporate teams within NGOs can be those who make the most requests for celebrity involvement.[4] Indeed, the only two occasions where I have come across NGOs paying celebrities to attend events had arisen because corporate partners had so strongly insisted on celebrities being there.

Celebrity has long been a significant aspect of corporate advertising. Matching the celebrity with corporate brand is a matter of keen investigation by a number of researchers, for some associations have been astonishingly successful and lucrative.[5] However,

> it's very expensive for a corporation to get a celebrity spokesperson, so they love it when by doing good works they also get to grab a few photos . . . or do a joint press conference with a celebrity. It's a big added benefit . . . They love getting that opportunity to be associated with a celebrity for free.[6]

The result is that 'corporate partners, a lot of the time they use charities as a free celebrity agency'.[7]

One of the attractions to companies of working with charities with good celebrity contacts is that it provides the opportunity for celebrities to become associated with these companies' products and brand. This presents an additional source of tension that is par for the course in celebrity liaison work. More than one organisation has drawn up written guidelines for celebrity liaison officers to follow so that they do not cross the line beyond a legitimate partnership between celebrity, charity and corporation.[8]

We need to see this move towards supporting celebrity-sponsored charities as part of a broader shift within corporate social responsibility. As Sam King has described, corporate philanthropy (including corporate social responsibility) has become increasingly strategic.[9] This means that donations to charities are frequently part of a broader marketing strategy and brand-building exercise. When companies seek associations with NGOs, they are seeking also to improve their profile. Therefore, links to (the right sort of) celebrities that NGOs offer can be particularly advantageous.

For some companies it is not just the potential marketing opportunities; it is also that the resulting access to the celebrities is integral to their business model, as was the case for Virgin's sponsorship of Amnesty International's Secret Policeman's Balls in the late 1980s.

> It's a good thing to be associated with. It is the biggest human rights organisation in Great Britain. It would be good for our image to be associated with and supporting that, because that was the way that Virgin wanted to project itself: a youth orientated company . . . and it suited our agenda to get involved with some of the artists that they could pull in because although we could always ring them up and talk to them it is much better to be working on a project.[10]

Sometimes companies will pay for and arrange celebrity endorsement themselves, and join with strong NGO brands as a means of emphasising the social/environmental value and altruism of their work. One example of this is singer Lily Allen's promotion of rainforest conservation for the satellite television company BSkyB in conjunction with the WWF. The company acted thus because such charitable activities are good for its brand; the consumers like it. The trip is covered by newspapers that are also owned (as is BSkyB) by Rupert Murdoch, whose journalists were flown out, at Sky's expense, to write the story.[11]

But events arranged by NGOs can still make excellent marketing and brand-building opportunities. The obvious examples of these are the NGOs that can host prestigious and plush events, with celebrity attendees, which are good business to be associated with. The scale of these events is remarkable. Journalists from the *Daily Mirror* have recently compiled a league table of the most expensive and luxurious occasions which bears summarising, for the costs are eye-watering (Table 7.1). It is not surprising, therefore, that some corporate sponsors are so keen to be associated with them:

> in the first instance the draw is going to be that to have [public figure E] associated with their product is highly desirable and to sponsor an event that we do at [location F] which is very elite which an awful lot of very rich or famous people come to is perfect to their brand.[12]

116 Elites and celebrity advocacy

TABLE 7.1 Costly charitable occasions

Event	Year	Cost (£)	Money raised (£)	Costs as a proportion of money raised (%)
Sunseeker Charitable Trust Ball	2009	400,000	550,000	72
Raisa Gorbachev Foundation Gala	2007	400,000	1,200,000	33
Prince's Trust Berkeley Square Ball	2008	420,000	450,000	93
Caudwell Children Annual Ball	2009	818,000	2,520,000	32
Grant and Anthea's Summer Ball	2007	829,000	942,000	88
Elton John's White Tie and Tiara Ball	2007	972,000	8,010,000	12
ARK Gala Dinner★	2007	3,900,000	26,000,000	15

★ The large sums here are accurate. The dinner is hosted by a billionaire financier who insists that the party must be 'mind-boggling' for his guests who pay £10,000 for a ticket. The organisation has also tried to curb the expenses of subsequent galas, frugally keeping them to below £2 million for an evening.

Source: Sommerlad, 2009.

But more generally, apart from such elite affairs, the possibilities of celebrity associations lubricating corporate sponsorship of NGOs are becoming ever more normal. Application forms for corporate sponsorship designed by firms increasingly include questions about celebrity supporters.[13] Numerous charities advertise the possibilities of association with their celebrity spokespeople on webpages aimed at corporate sponsors.

Some NGOs can get part of a virtuous circle where their supporters coincide with the target market for particular companies. If the market is in luxury goods, which also appeal to certain celebrities, then both they and the corporate brands may attract more supporters to the NGO. As one charity's celebrity liaison officer explained:

> We were seen as quite a good keyholder to targeting that group of individuals who have high disposable income, no kids and like the nicer things in life ... That benefited us in terms of high profile supporters because we had ties with very luxury brands.[14]

Corporate sponsorship can be so important that it determines, more than anything else, the level of celebrity engagement. One charitable campaign reviewed its activities and questioned whether they should continue working with celebrities or instead use 'real' women in their public announcements. They realised that fewer celebrities might be better for some of the consumers of their advertisements and messaging but,

> we came to the conclusion that actually the corporates like to be associated with the campaign because of the kudos it holds and because of the level of

celebrities it has supporting it. Because the majority of the income is raised through corporate partners . . . we do actually need to have celebrity support to keep them engaged.[15]

And, as is well known, relying excessively on corporate sponsorship can restrain the possibilities of NGOs' protest. Some of the most mainstream and inoffensive organisations can find it hard to get corporate sponsorship for events that are perceived to be putting pressure on governments. '[W]e found it very difficult to get sponsorship because the big brands did not want to be associated with attacking or putting pressure on prime ministers and presidents . . . It was actually a very real problem for us.'[16]

A subtler constraint are the risks that celebrities could pose to NGO brands through their associations with the wrong sorts of companies. Celebrities might, for example, subsequently develop relationships with companies who are doing things the NGOs oppose. This happened to Oxfam when two different ambassadors, Kristin Davis and Scarlett Johansson (both actresses), on separate occasions endorsed products made in occupied Palestinian territories by an Israeli firm while Oxfam does not support trade in goods made in those territories.[17] Hence the extensive checks that NGOs run on celebrities' backgrounds to ensure there is no risk to their organisation's brand.

Conversely, however, some celebrity associations with good causes can become so powerful that they protect commercial interests from popular protest. One vigorous public campaigner described shying away from taking on a particular company because of their celebrity endorser:

> Why was I going to try and use [public figure X] to go against [company Y] . . . to do something that it wasn't going to do? . . . I didn't want to ruffle the feathers of [public figure X]. I didn't want to make trouble for him because he is so good. I do not need to score some publicity points by making him look bad, plus that would be impossible. No one could make [him] look bad, they [the critic] would always look bad . . . It wasn't strategic to do it.[18]

The celebrity's brand, and association with the cause, were so strong that they precluded campaigning against a company whose business opposed the campaign's objectives.

Celebrity and elites

Corporate fascination with celebrity sponsors at charitable events is not just about dismal economics and the bottom line. Business leaders can be personally interested in celebrities and in meeting them. When Jolie and Pitt turned up at the World Economic Forum (WEF) at Davos in 2006 'everyone from chief executives to WEF staff started to behave like love-struck teenagers, mobbing them and disrupting proceedings'.[19] Cooper describes numerous instances also at Davos, where the presence of celebrities, amid some extremely powerful and wealthy people,

118 Elites and celebrity advocacy

generated a great deal of excitement.[20] One of the pleasures and privileges of success in business is that one meets in person the famous people who everyone else only hears about in the media. Celebrity liaison officers learn to use this to their advantage: 'I have learnt in that job never to underestimate the vanity of anyone in the world to associate with someone well known. It gave them a shine, a glamour – look who I am and look who I associate with.'[21]

Meeting each other is one of the things that members of elites do. It is part of reinforcing their collective status and individual self-esteem. Elite insiders made this plain: 'Well known people are very keen to get to know other well-known people. They want to know as many as they can.'[22]

One of the ways in which celebrity works really well for NGO advocacy, therefore, is in providing the sort of access to the unmediated company of celebrities that other elites feel they have earned and enjoy so much, and which will reflect well on them socially. It is one of the ways in which distinction is maintained.

Politicians are most aware of the beneficial publicity that can result from being seen to be associated with popular public figures. They are keen to meet them and to be seen to meet with them. They respond well to invitations to talk to NGOs if there is a celebrity present.

> You might be able to meet with someone lower down in the office but suddenly you are meeting with the chief of staff or with the principal instead of a staff member two or three levels below because you are accompanied by a celebrity. You also might be able to get a hearing on Capitol Hill because one of those testifying would be a celebrity . . . That happens all the time.[23]

Celebrity is also as a means of gaining the attention of important decision-makers at public gatherings: 'If you find a Bono politicians will meet them . . . at the end of the day they all love to meet celebrities, they really do, it's incredible. Their faces light up when they see [public figure D] coming at them.'[24] This reflects not just the pleasure of the company of the celebrities, but its potential impact on electorates. Some informants found that celebrities were useful for gaining access because 'politicians were very interested in being seen with celebrities'.[25]

Sometimes, however, there is little rationale and calculating about such meetings. An element of the draw is the sex appeal of people who are famous (in part) for being attractive (young or old). One interviewee with many years of experience attending such gatherings observed that:

> A lot of middle-aged men melt at the idea . . . A lot of middle-aged business men, and young ones and older ones actually just kind of fawn at the idea of somebody reasonably well known and reasonably attractive. I'm sure that there are equally a number of business women [who are similar].[26]

A specific example came from another source:

[Company G] absolutely loved [public figure H] . . . she's very special to a group of men of a certain age . . . She's . . . lovely and charming and articulate . . . she delivers both emotionally and rationally and . . . appeals to the softer side of them'.[27]

Celebrity, then, is not just a pawn in negotiating arrangements between charities and corporations, nor is it just a vehicle for getting into the news. It is also a lubricant in the negotiation machinery; it helps bring people to meetings, facilitates the negotiation of deals and enables a large number of policy and financial discussions to take place at a speed and with a conviviality that would not otherwise be possible.

One of the most interesting manifestations of the contemporary elite power of celebrity is 'the Elders' which is a fascinating conjunction of corporate, celebrity and political power. Founded in 2007 and convened, at least symbolically, by the late Nelson Mandela, this group of ten statesmen and women, are internationally respected (sometimes adored) figures. They act as an independent lobby group on some of the most pressing issues of the day (Sudan, Nuclear Weapons, the Middle East, Zimbabwe, Women's Rights).[28]

But the Elders is not just a diplomatic initiative. It was thought up by Richard Branson and Peter Gabriel (a musician). Its sponsors include some of the leading philanthropists of our era: the Skoll Foundation, Pam Omyidar and Humanity United as well as media mogul Ted Turner's United Nations Foundation.[29] Clearly, a great deal of symbolic and social capital was leveraged by their creation. The website abounds with symbolic images of the world's great people gathered together to express concern, concentrate cameras and draw attention to ills afflicting the world.

The Elders also demonstrate some of the problems that make people wary of such elite groupings. As of January 2013 the Elders' website did not describe its governance structure; it contained no annual or financial reports, and while it described its activities, it did not describe its achievements. Nor could I see any physical address or telephone number – contact arrangements are by 800 character messages sent via the website. This organisation exemplifies the symbolic power of the current elite, yet also its inaccessibility and lack of accountability. It may well be championing the causes of righteousness, but it is doing so in ways that the beneficiaries may not be able easily to direct.[30]

It should be clear, therefore, what this high-level networking produces. It strengthens the patterns of governance by elites that Crouch observed constituted one of the defining features of post-democracies. NGOs are using celebrity to allow them better access to these elite circles. They do not, as Crouch observed, have many other practical options. If post-democracies work through lobbies, then NGOs have to join them; they will be weaker if they stay out of them.[31] Nevertheless, the point is that celebrity is part of the social and political functioning of these elites. It extends, shapes and characterises the nature of governance by elites which occurs in post-democracy.

NGOs respond in different ways to the opportunities this presents. Some do not work with celebrities when working behind the scenes on policy matters –

120 Elites and celebrity advocacy

'you use serious people for that'.[32] Some did not need to because they already have the access to the meetings they want to get into.[33] Others deliberately and carefully train up selected celebrities so that they can help them both to obtain access to the right people and then be an effective part of the negotiation team.

We have already seen that the efforts of development and humanitarian NGOs is producing a cadre of committed celebrities whose field experience, briefings and long-term relationship with particular NGOs may be enhancing their skills such that they are able to cope with the sorts of negotiations that elite level interactions require. From this body there are emerging a number of people who are acquiring the experience, and have the desire, to work and engage with politicians and policy-makers. Or, as Geldof puts it:

> Whether they like it or not the agents of change in our world are the politicians. Otherwise you're always outside the tent pissing in. They stay inside their tent pissing back out at you. This is futile. My solution is to get inside the tent and piss in there.[34]

These negotiations (or 'pissing', if you will) require considerable skill. One senior and experienced interviewee listed the qualities required:

1   You need to be famous.
2   You need to remain famous (not X-factor).
3   You need to be articulate . . .
4   You need to be able to understand the issues.
5   You need to be able to synthesise the issues.
6   You need to be willing to engage and dedicate yourself to them.[35]

Perhaps the most successful celebrities in development and humanitarian activities who have demonstrated these qualities have been Geldof and Bono. There is ample evidence that their grasp of the issues was sufficient to impress the leading politicians with whom they were negotiating. Alastair Campbell (then Tony Blair's press officer) reports a meeting with Bono and Geldof about Jubilee 2000 in which their acumen and abilities were impressive – 'there was no way this was just a spray-on cause to help their rock star image'. The Canadian prime minister described Bono as a 'policy wonk' because he was so 'interested in the minutiae and mechanics of international aid'.[36] Nathan Jackson lists numerous public accolades to Bono from politicians who met him and were impressed by his grasp of the detail and substance of aid and development policies.[37]

They, or at least Bono, combined that grasp with effective diplomatic skills. When Tony Blair complained that the Jubilee 2000 tasks were like climbing Everest, Bono replied 'When you see Everest Tony, you don't look at it, you fucking climb it'.[38] Alastair Campbell said 'it was impossible not to like them'.[39] Bono used a different style, and presumably language, when praying with US President George

Bush to persuade him to attend the Monterrey aid summit in 2002. This, and World Bank pressure, helped to persuade Bush to attend the summit, and announce an increase in aid of $5 billion per year. Bono's other famous success was persuading right-wing senator Jesse Helms to reverse his position on international aid and, it is alleged, made him cry in the process.[40] Alex de Waal observed both Geldof and Bono in Downing Street effectively coercing Tony Blair to follow their plans for more proactive aid to Africa. They had attended a breakfast function with other aid leaders, and then after the prime minister had left, waited in the corridors for him to appear and pressured him to appear with them in front of the cameras. De Waal observes that this 'breakfast-time prime ministerial hijacking was a crucial step in the project that culminated in Blair's "Commission for Africa"'.[41]

Part of their diplomatic power is that these individuals are prepared to use the threat of their popularity against powerful leaders. Blair presumably agreed to the impromptu press conference because if he did not attend Geldof and Bono would have embarrassed him in his absence. Similarly, Bono promised Paul Martin that he would be a 'pain in the butt' if Canada did not agree to increase their aid to 0.7 per cent at the G8 summit in Gleneagles, and, Martin records, Bono lived up to his promise.[42] Wikileaks have showed that the Italian President Sylvio Berlusconi considered increasing Italian aid to avoid a 'tongue-lashing' from Bono.[43] What these threats achieve is a different question. The point is that they mattered in the minds of the politicians.

For those comfortable with the power that such celebrities can wield, the results of this influence are only beneficial:

> I can argue as passionately as is possible about the fantastically positive role that celebrity has played in all of this . . . I think it's been a clever dynamic which has been a win–win for the charity sector, for the politicians and for the celebrities who wanted to deliver for the charities . . . When G8 was taking place in Gleneagles Bob and Bono had access to the G8 leaders in a way you just couldn't believe imaginable because nobody gets into those unless they are part of the inner teams . . . they had parity in discussions and lobbying opportunity that came through their celebrity and not just through their celebrity but what they delivered credibly with their celebrity.[44]

Another high-level advocate of this process welcomed the efficiency and ease of getting things done this way, as opposed to working with larger public lobbies. 'The fewer [people involved] the better. If we could do all that without the bother of reaching out to millions of people we would do so. It's cheaper and easier.'[45]

This is not to say that seasoned campaigners are eschewing the power of popular voice. Bono may well have pursued an elite-based lobbying strategy when advancing the Jubilee 2000 goals.[46] However, his organisation DATA used a mixture of elite lobbying *and* constituency pressure to achieve its goals.[47] When politicians proved obstructive, DATA would ask members in a politician's marginal constituencies to write in protesting. They also took out radio advertisements and

122 Elites and celebrity advocacy

lobbied through Church networks.[48] But note the direction of this 'grassroots' campaigning. These are objectives that are decided by NGO leaders, in an organisation funded by elite philanthropists and foundations, which mobilises grassroots members in support of predefined goals. It is a top-down model of participation.

My point is not that this is inappropriate or ineffective. It may well achieve more than something which is membership lead. These are, after all, complex issues and working out which is the priority, and what strategy is needed to achieve it, can require elite leadership. Nevertheless, in describing this situation we have also to recognise that, from a Crouchian perspective, it reinforces governance by elites. We will return to these arguments in the conclusion of the book.

Belief in celebrity power

In addition to the pleasures of personal interactions, and to the effectiveness of individual celebrities there is another force at work here. Consider again the penultimate quotation above. My interviewee who argued passionately in favour of celebrity lobbying spoke of 'lobbying opportunities that came *through their celebrity*' and that they 'delivered credibly *with their celebrity*'. The word 'celebrity' in those statements means those people who are believed to convey popular opinion, and do so in a popular way.

There are two forces at work here. On the one hand celebrities can fill gaps in the political process where elected representatives are failing to meet popular needs and celebrities can both understand these and voice them. This is John Street's argument, which I discussed on pp. 38–9. Classic examples include the long struggle for black freedom in the USA and opposition to the Vietnam War.

The second is the belief of elites that celebrities speak for the people. In this case celebrity matters to elites because of the way they think celebrity functions and the power that they think celebrities convey. This can be the case whether or not any popular connection, and popular representation, actually exist. Even if there is little or no public connection, what matters is that elites believe it to be the case.

The evidence for this comes from several sources. First, there is the corporate world's belief in the power of celebrity advertising. Stock prices tend to rise for firms who announce endorsement campaigns featuring celebrities, even before these campaigns can take effect.[49] The stock market responds positively to anticipated profits, betting on the favourable outcome of these campaigns. The important point here is not that these stockbrokers were wrong in their belief, but that it is impossible to tell whether they are right or not.[50] Despite the lack of hard evidence as to the precise consequences of celebrity advertising, they are still prepared to bet on it.

The importance of belief in celebrity, without hard evidence of its power, is also apparent in a rather misleading, but large and influential body of research on the effectiveness of celebrity endorsers. This work has been undertaken in business schools and marketing colleges for decades. But it is misleading because it has been dominated by research on US citizens, and in particular US college students for much of its history. Indeed, before 1998 it was *only* conducted on US citizens, 76 per cent of whom were college students. This matters because US college students are particularly receptive and responsive towards advertising, in ways in which other people, who are not US citizens or US college students, will not be.[51] An edifice of work demonstrating the effectiveness of celebrity has been built on selective foundations. Those who follow this work will have good reason to believe that celebrity is persuasive, but may risk extrapolating inappropriately from the opinions of US college students to dissimilar populations.[52]

Corporate belief in celebrity endorsement leaks into the development and humanitarian sector. Consider, for example, Matthew Bishop and Michael Green's book *Philanthrocapitalism*, which was written in praise of the current generation of super-rich philanthropists and on the basis of interviews with the most prominent among them. They are full of compliments for 'celanthropists' – the celebrity philanthropists – and claim that:

> Celanthropists are becoming an integral part of philanthrocapitalism – mirroring the growing importance of brands and famous personalities as a source of wealth creation in capitalism. As well as often donating large amounts of their own fortunes . . . and being particularly effective at raising funds from others, the best celanthropists bring a mastery of branding, mass communication skills, and high-level access that can be invaluable to any cause. As Angelina Jolie, perhaps the most famous of all celanthropists, put it 'People take my calls.'[53]

More detailed insights into the views of development and humanitarian elites are available from a gathering of the Brookings Blum Roundtable in 2007, which brought together a number of famous faces, and people close to famous faces in the development and environmental fields. Attendees at the three-day event included former US Vice-President Al Gore, former Irish President Mary Robinson, Madeleine Albright (former US Secretary of State), Bobby Shriver (co-founder of (Product) RED and Ngozi Okonjo-Iweala, then a Managing Director of the World Bank. It was, in other words, a high-level gathering. Its purpose was to look at the new actors in development, including celebrities, philanthropists and the private sector.[54]

The overwhelming tone when celebrity is mentioned is of approval and commendation. Celebrities are 'maximizing the power of their public appeal to champion global poverty awareness and activism' and 'injecting a dose of credibility and charisma into the foreign assistance and development debate'.[55] They 'have focused public attention on humanitarian crises such as HIV/AIDS and the conflict in Darfur' and helped to raise billions of dollars in development funds.[56] Perhaps most of all they are infusing some passion, joie de vivre, anger and excitement into topics that can be dull to Western minds:

124 Elites and celebrity advocacy

> Whether rock stars, movie stars, moral leaders, or political icons, these 'celanthropists' are infusing antipoverty campaigns with their own charisma and brand allure. Some are adept at crystallizing complex issues in catchy slogans like 'Drop the Debt' and 'Make Poverty History.' Others have made energetic use of the popular media to attract new development audiences: witness MTV's Diary of Angelina Jolie and Dr. Jeffrey Sachs in Africa. Seasoned performers on the global stage, these development champions are eloquent and impassioned in their appeals on behalf of the impoverished – invoking emotional language and images designed to anger, engage, and inspire action.[57]

The report even finds a way of welcoming the fact that these new activists are inexperienced but still believe they can make a huge difference. Normally called 'arrogance', this trait is welcomed thus: 'Many of the new development players are entering the field unburdened by the weight of conventional wisdom and are blessed with confidence in their own ability to achieve outsized results.'[58]

These representations are interesting partly because of what is missing. For example, the role of celebrities in the Make Poverty History campaign is only painted in a positive light, even though it caused the most intense controversies at the time in the British NGO community.[59] The achievements of celebrity interventions in Darfur, again reported favourably, are also hotly disputed.[60] The report does mention problems of simplification of messages, and refers to the uneasy relations that can exist between the celebrity industries and NGOs, but these occupy just three paragraphs in a long document.

The report is also interesting because one of the strongest characteristics of elite approaches to celebrity, at least as identified in this report, is their faith in the power of celebrity, particularly with respect to converting the public to their causes. This is stated in the baldest terms: 'It works. The public is answering their call in unprecedented numbers.'[61] Al Gore is quoted as saying that 'Rock stars proved instrumental in supercharging a new generation of climate crusaders during 2007's Live Earth.'[62]

But what sort of public voice, produced by these celebrity interventions, is being welcomed by these elites? This is one of the most significant aspects of the report. This elite gathering celebrated these examples of the public voice:

> the hundreds of thousands who attended the ten 'Live 8' concerts in the run-up to the Gleneagles summit, the more than 2.4 million signatures for the ONE Campaign, and the 63.5 million-strong audience for the 2007 U.S. television special American Idol: Idol Gives Back.[63]

In other words, this elite gathering celebrated rather passive audiences expressing themselves through concert attendance, texted donations, switching on televisions and signing on-line petitions. The signs of democratic disillusion which so worry post-democratic commentators are welcomed here as evidence of success.[64]

The reasoning behind this sort of enthusiasm was clearly expressed to me by Brendan Cox, who is both an experienced campaigner and an analyst of campaigns.[65] He expressed the role of celebrity in campaigns in ways that captured not just their leverage on elites, but also the gap that can exist between what those celebrities are perceived to deliver and what they actually represent. The purpose of celebrity in a campaign, he said, 'is to *simulate* [note not 'stimulate'] mass engagement and concern'.[66] This reflects the sentiments in his report on development NGOs' campaigns: 'Engaging celebrities is particularly valuable in short-term campaigns that want to simulate mass public support but do not have the time to build it in key countries.'[67] And, as he clarified to me later, 'Celebrity is a proxy for public engagement even though in pretty much all cases they, the public, were not engaged initially.'[68] Simulating public concern is important, first to influence policy decision makers – 'the ultimate group they are trying to influence' – and second the media who needed convincing that the public would be interested in the topic if a celebrity were on board. Third and fourth came the public themselves, and supporters who could be encouraged by celebrity endorsements.[69]

Some campaigning, particularly in the early stages, is 'smoke and mirrors' in which you try to show that a campaign is bigger and more popular than he or she really is. Celebrity is a good way of doing that, particularly in the early stages.[70] It provides an indicator, 'a totem . . . of mass audience engagement'.[71] Celebrity signifies the public.

Make Poverty History is particularly fascinating for the insights it affords into the way that celebrity power, and belief in celebrity power, can work in elite circles. Cox reports that the campaign, and the prospect of the Live 8 concerts, made the UK government less flexible in the negotiations leading up to the G8:

> Those outside the United Kingdom put the inflexibility of the British government down to it being hemmed in by MPH, while those inside the U.K. system say MPH helped the government hold its nerve, especially knowing the Live 8 concerts were still to come.[72]

Geldof, writing to the makers of the film *Starsuckers*, expressed a similar view:

> The negotiations were endless. We met most of the leaders in Gleneagles. They wouldn't budge and uniquely Blair insisted, despite the bombs in London, in refusing to bend an inch. That is true. I was there. Rather than massive public failure and the public expectation raised by the concert and MPH, they succumbed.[73]

It is not clear what precisely the concerts portended to the British government that proved so effective in maintaining its position. Cox explained to me that, for the negotiators working with the British government, the prospect of Live 8 strengthened their hand in that they knew that there was a big event coming up which would have a large number of the world's greatest musicians present, with

126 Elites and celebrity advocacy

tremendous press coverage and that this would go on to create domestic pressure within each country where a concert was held that would make it easier for each government to concede to British demands (for more aid).[74] For that reason they did not concede to the demands of the other governments' teams (much to those teams' annoyance) and held on until the last minute. The US government negotiating team only reached agreement when they were on the plane en route to Scotland for the summit itself.

Cox emphasised that we cannot 'put too much sophistication' into the UK negotiator's analysis.[75] They did not have a precise understanding of what the concerts would do to whom and how it would exert pressure, but they knew it was playing into their hands. Ultimately, however, the important point is not how the concerts had that effect, *but that they did so*. Large-scale concerts, with mass, superficial participation and run by celebrities, provided the sort of spectacle to which governments could listen.[76]

Conclusion

The rise of celebrity in the NGO sector has been fuelled by corporate interest in getting access to celebrity as part of larger brand management and marketing activities. Corporate sponsors seek the added benefit of celebrity associations and NGOs advertise them. Celebrity has lubricated the increasing proximity of NGOs to the corporate sector. The merging of NGOs with corporate interests which has characterised the changing nature of civil society in the last two decades has been accompanied by, and encouraged, the rise of celebrity within NGOs.

In addition to the financial benefits of these associations, celebrity ambassadors of NGOs help to construct the governance elites that Crouch described as operating so powerfully in current democracies. They provide an opportunity for NGOs to host gatherings and meetings which corporate and political leaders will want to attend because of the pleasures of meeting, and being seen to meet, the celebrities present. One of the reasons why celebrities have the unearned and unauthorised power for which their interventions arouse such hostility is because elites are so willing to welcome them into their ranks and give them the platform they desire. The nature of elite governance in post-democracy is shaped by the presence, style and personal politics of celebrity as a result.

Powering all this is the strong belief in the power of celebrity to speak for the people and to mobilise large numbers of people to speak with them. Celebrity begets popular voice, begets legitimacy. Celebrity motivates governments to act because of the connection they are perceived to have with their populace.[77]

This, however, is manifest in a tendency to look for forms of political participation which involve relatively light requests and low levels of commitment from the populace – voting in *Pop Idol*, being part of concert crowds or TV audiences. The views that these sources welcome is the power of celebrity to concentrate voices in the hands of organisations who can then represent their interests at elite gatherings. While the elites at the Brookings Blum roundtable were

Elites and celebrity advocacy **127**

probably among the most genial and egalitarian possible, their enthusiasm is for the elite-privileging politics of post-democracies. Indeed, it would be difficult to find a clearer example of Crouch's depiction of post-democratic politics and public roles that I quoted earlier (p. 35):

> The idea of post democracy helps us describe situations when . . . powerful minority interests have become far more active than the mass of ordinary people in making the political system work for them; where political elites have learned to manage and manipulate popular demands; where people have to be persuaded to vote by top-down publicity campaigns.[78]

There is one more twist to this story, however – and this concerns the nature of public support for and belief in the power of celebrity. Elite interest in and desire to work with celebrity advocates is based partly on the premise that it engages with and represents broader public interest. This is a fair assumption to make, given the way that celebrity fills so much of the news and public domain. But it remains an assumption. It is time to test it and explore how celebrity advocacy can be received.

Notes

1 Chambers, 2005: 85.
2 Source 35.
3 Source 48.
4 Source 77.
5 Erdogan, 1999; Pringle, 2004.
6 Source 55.
7 Source 51.
8 But the dividing line between what can be done freely for the charity, and what must be paid for by the corporation, can be thinly drawn. Public figures can endorse the relationship that companies may have with NGOs but not the company itself. It would be acceptable for a public figure to model a T-shirt saying 'If you go to Debenhams and buy this T-shirt the charity will get £5', but they cannot say, 'I love shopping at Debenhams' (Source 35). Furthermore, some associations with particularly well-known charitable causes can result in further opportunities for (paid) corporate endorsement for the celebrity. Some public figures take the work and endorsement opportunities resulting; others refuse to take on such endorsements saying 'it is an insult to be offered to be paid' as a result of any association that arises out of work for charity (Source 71).
9 King, 2006: 4.
10 Unnamed interviewee from Virgin to Christian Lahusen, 1992. The person being interviewed sounds very like Richard Branson, the company's founder.
11 Source 33 and www.thesun.co.uk/sol/homepage/news/Green/2970915/Lily-Allen-backs-bid-to-save-rainforest.html (viewed 25 August 2012).
12 Source 67.
13 Source 65.
14 Source 76.
15 Source 63.
16 Source 92.
17 Available at: http://codepink.org/blog/2009/08/official-release-oxfam-suspends-ahava-spokeswoman-kristin-davis-from-all-publicity-work (viewed 18 February 2012); www.theguardian.com/film/2014/jan/30/scarlett-johansson-oxfam-quits-sodastream (viewed 3 February 2014).

128 Elites and celebrity advocacy

18 Source 73.
19 Bishop and Green, 2008: 204.
20 Cooper, 2008b.
21 Source 88.
22 Source 88.
23 Source 93. Strine's research shows that when celebrities appear before congressional committees they are treated more gently than other witnesses (Strine, 2006). But then the purpose of their presence is not always so much as to provide robust evidence, as publicity opportunities. The most extreme case of this I have come across was when the House Appropriations Subcommittee on Labor, Health and Human Services and Education called Elmo the muppet to witness before them in 2002 (Hyde, 2010: 123–4).
24 Source 81.
25 Source 48; also Source 119.
26 Source 75.
27 Source 48.
28 The Elders are: Martti Ahtisaari (former Finnish President); Kofi Annan (former UN Secretary-General); Ela Bhatt (Indian activist); Lakhdar Brahimi (former Algerian Foreign Minister); Gro Brundtland (former Norwegian Prime Minister); Fernando H. Cardoso (former President of Brazil); Jimmy Carter (former US President); Graç Machel (UN diplomat); Mary Robinson (former Irish President); Desmond Tutu (Nobel Peace Prize winner). Nelson Mandela was and Aung San Suu Kyi (Burmese dissident) is an honorary Elder and Mohammed Yunnus (founder of the Grameen Bank), a former Elder. See Huijser and Tay, 2011.
29 Other sponsors include the Bridgeway Foundation, which is the charitable foundation of the investment firm Bridgeway Capital Management, receiving half their annual profits as their income, and the Nduna Foundation, set up by Amy Robbins who set up the NY hedge fund, Glenview Capital.
30 Available at: www.theelders.org (viewed 8 January 2013).
31 Crouch, 2004: 122
32 Source 75.
33 Source 14.
34 Lewis, 2010.
35 Source 81.
36 Campbell, 2007: 407; Martin, 2008: 216.
37 Jackson, N., 2008.
38 Campbell, 2007: 407.
39 Campbell, 2007: 407.
40 Busby, 2007. Bono made Helms cry on two occasions; he also did so with respect to funding for HIV/AIDS (Jackson, N., 2008).
41 De Waal, 2008 and De Waal, personal communication, 14 October 2011.
42 Martin, 2008: 357.
43 Hill, 2010.
44 Source 92.
45 Source 46. The interviewee also qualified this statement, recognising the value of broader public support and of building a broader movement that provides the right public climate within which to work.
46 When lobbying in the US, Bono would ask 'who's Elvis?' – i.e. who are the individuals who can get things done (Assayas, 2005: 91)?
47 DATA's successor, the ONE campaign, describes itself as 'ONE is a grassroots campaign of more than 3 million people committed to the fight against extreme poverty and preventable diseases.' Available at: www.one.org (viewed 31 January 2013).
48 They did so when the Republican, Sonny Callahan, representing Alabama, opposed the Foreign Aid Bill in 2001 and when Iowa Republican Jim Nussle proposed a cut that could affect funding for HIV/AIDS medicines (Jackson, N., 2008: 85, 151).

Elites and celebrity advocacy **129**

49 Agrawal and Kamakura, 1995. This is based on 110 firms who announced celebrity endorsement campaigns in the mid-1990s.
50 Pringle, 2004.
51 Amos *et al.*, 2008.
52 The detail of the evidence for this paragraph, and its sources, are discussed in Appendix Two.
53 Bishop and Green, 2008: 196.
54 Brainard and LaFleur, 2007.
55 Brainard and LaFleur, 2007: 4.
56 Brainard and LaFleur, 2007: 5.
57 Brainard and LaFleur, 2007: 16.
58 Brainard and LaFleur, 2007: 35. Bishop and Green repeatedly report a similar tendency among their philanthrocapitalists – a belief that they can solve problems others cannot and a reluctance to listen or learn from that experience (Bishop and Green, 2008: 49, 92, 134).
59 Sireau, 2008. See Chapter 4.
60 Flint and De Waal, 2008; Crilly, 2010; Hamilton, 2011.
61 Brainard and LaFleur, 2007: 16.
62 Brainard and LaFleur, 2007: 18.
63 Brainard and LaFleur, 2007: 6. Geldof expressed a similar view with respect to the authority of pop concerts over traditional marches: 'You may, if you like, consider these [the Live 8 concerts] as marches. Except they don't wander down police prescribed byways fruitlessly. They are vast numbers of people in one place, all day, all over the world, brought together in a community of shared interest and all sympathising with your messaging. They are the vast billions watching. Brought together around the electric hearth of the tv or computer screen by the Pied Pipers of Rock 'n' Roll. Now that's a lobby. That's a vote and a half. That lends legitimacy.' Available at: www.starsuckersmovie.com/bob-geldof-letter (viewed August 2011).
64 cf. Dienst specifically on Live 8: 'The mass mobilization of crowds through media spectacle is fundamentally conservative: it serves the purposes defined from the top down, rather than serving as a means of expression from the bottom up' (2011: 113).
65 Cox authored a major report that analysed development campaigns between 1991 and 2011, which drew on over 300 often high-level interviews (Cox, 2011).
66 Cox, personal communication, 8 January 2013 (my italics).
67 Cox, 2011: 55.
68 Cox, personal communication, 8 January 2013.
69 Ibid.
70 Source 123.
71 Source 123. Later on, however, celebrity can be no simulation but a reflection of public engagement. This is what happened with Make Poverty History, which eventually achieved very high levels of public awareness and involvement.
72 Cox, 2011: 48.
73 Available at: www.starsuckersmovie.com/bob-geldof-letter (viewed August 2011).
74 Cox, personal communication, 8 January 2013.
75 Ibid.
76 This presents a slightly more complicated situation than some of the more condemning analysts of Make Poverty History. Dienst writes that the Live 8 crowds were campaigning, somewhat inertly, for things that governments had already agreed beforehand (2011: 113). This was true for some aspects of the deal (the debt forgiveness that had been agreed the previous June) but clearly not every aspect, otherwise the negotiations Cox refers to would not have been so tense and drawn out. Moreover, agreement was reached in part only because the government negotiators feared the inert crowds' impending demands for/celebration of that agreement. The artificial and shallow politics of the spectacle did exert a force on decision-makers of the moment, perhaps because those decision-makers believed in the power of such a spectacle themselves. But it clearly did not exert a

130 Elites and celebrity advocacy

sufficiently powerful or sustained force, for the concessions won were insufficient, and the promises made were not honoured.

77 In this respect it is possible to see celebrity as an extension and modification of the tools with which modernity allows rulers to see their subjects, and quite possibly the ruled to see themselves. In his essay 'The Work of Art in the Age of Mechanical Reproduction' Walter Benjamin added this note:

> In big parades and monster rallies, in sports events, and in war, all of which nowadays are captured by camera and sound recording, the masses are brought face-to-face with themselves. This process . . . is intimately connected with the development of the techniques of reproduction and photography. Mass movements are usually discerned more clearly by a camera than by the naked eye. A bird's-eye view best captures gatherings of hundreds of thousands. And even though such a view may be as accessible to the human eye as it is to the camera, the image received by the eye cannot be enlarged the way a negative is enlarged. This means that mass movements, including war, constitute a form of behaviour which particularly favours mechanical equipment.
>
> (Benjamin, 1999: 243–4).

By extension, celebrity is a form of media/cultural technology that condenses and represents masses and mass movement. It allows political and corporate elites to discern the mass public – in the form of a single person.

78 Crouch, 2004: 19–20.

8

THE WITCHES' POND

> Nick Couldry has made the point to me that we know very little about to what extent [our culture's appetite for consuming celebrity] is 'industry constructed' rather than the product of some kind of grassroots cultural process (which is how it is customarily understood). It is a fair point and, like him, I am unaware of any empirical work on this area which could answer that question.
>
> Graeme Turner[1]

Some commentators can adopt a curiously extreme position when writing about the consumption of celebrity. Take for, for example, Fred Inglis in his *Short History of Celebrity*. He writes: 'when celebrities are mentioned or flash onto the TV, everyone in the cultivated classes is ready with their dose of denigration, while everyone else watches with more or less envy, admiration, or malice'.[2] I find this a curious notion because Inglis is suggesting that celebrity commands *everyone's* notice. There is no possibility here of just not being interested in celebrity.[3]

I do not think that this view is likely to be accurate. Yet I was not surprised when I read it, for it comes from a social and intellectual milieu which, as Turner observes above, presumes celebrity to have a very broad appeal. Indeed, sometimes thinking about the attractions of celebrity can use a fallacious argument that simply makes it impossible to recognise lack of interest. This argument suggests that we must all feel variously a curiosity, an open fascination with the wealth and intrigue of famous lives, a vicarious enjoyment of their pleasures, physical attraction or a desire to follow the role models the famous provide. But if we profess to none of these, then we must be demonstrating 'disavowed interest', which is precisely the same set of curiosities except that the observer denies them to herself, expressing that denial in criticism or feigned disinterest.

132 The witches' pond

There is no way out. We are all interested in celebrity to various degrees and if you say you are not, that is proof that you are, but that you disavow your actual fascination. This sort of reasoning about celebrity's influence seems to me a throwback to the old medieval test for witchcraft in which suspects were thrown, bound, into a pond. If they drowned they were innocent; if they lived they were burned as a witch.

Indeed, some of the most cerebral writers seem to fall into the trap of exalting the reach of celebrity. Couldry, for example, writes that using celebrity is tempting to media professionals because it 'guarantees high attention'.[4] Marks and Fischer's whole argument about the simulation of consent by celebrity activists hinges upon the invigorated public response they believe (it is not clear why) that celebrities provoke. 'Celebrities thus serve a vital function in re-igniting the political interest of the citizenry and bringing the masses back into the democratic fold.'[5] Even more strangely, Richard Dyer, in a (life's) work riven with sensitivity to the varieties of audience readings, can still baldly assert 'We're fascinated by stars'.[6] Who is the 'we' here?

Celebrity can be absorbing, and interest in it disavowed, but exaggerating either does not allow sufficient possibility for interest in celebrity to vary over time, or between social groups, nations, gender, and so on.[7] I would prefer that our analyses of celebrity culture and of celebrity advocacy have to consider some variety of reaction, and, if I may suggest the obvious, the possibility that some people may indeed not be interested in it. However, in an atmosphere where celebrity is presumed to be ubiquitously interesting, all the evidence we might mobilise to show that people are not particularly bothered about celebrity could be interpreted as disavowed interest to prove that celebrity is interesting. We fall into the trap that the witches suffered.

There are ways out of this methodological dilemma.[8] We can ask indirect questions about celebrity and explore what media people consume. We can compare those answers to more direct questions about celebrity consumption. We can also listen to the way people talk about what they hear about celebrity. For the sorts of conversations they have, and the awareness they display and the responses they have, can also tell us how enthralling, or not, it is for them.

I have attempted all those tasks. I have the answers to indirect questions asked in a 2005 survey by Couldry and Markham, and a repetition of that survey conducted in 2011 on the UK Public Opinion Monitor. I have answers to direct questions asked in another survey in 2012 to the same Monitor. Finally, I have listened to nine focus groups talk about celebrity advocacy.

From that work I present six key findings in this chapter. The first is that interest in celebrity media is varied. It is most prevalent among young women; it does not vary with socioeconomic status. There are lots of people for whom celebrity is relatively unimportant, and whose encounters with it, though frequent, are shallow and light. I provide additional evidence in the form of interview data with media professionals to support this point.

Second, despite the shallow exposure to celebrity that most Britons experience, many are still able to talk about celebrity advocacy with reasonable fluency. They tend to talk, however, about the same examples, and particularly the telethons, not the rich variety of advocacy that exists. This suggests that, while they are aware of celebrity advocacy, it tended to be a low salience issue for them.

Third, there is a clear belief in the popular power of celebrity. Despite the fact that most people are not themselves interested in it, most people think that most other people are. Celebrity thus has a peculiar credibility. It does not occupy the attention and interest of the majority (let alone everyone), but Britons think that it generally does. We may think that the emperor is naked, and looks silly naked, but we like to imagine that everyone else is cheering his wonderful costume.

Fourth, lack of interest in, or even hostility towards, celebrity news does not necessarily result in poor responses to celebrity advocacy. Indeed, there is a general disposition to look kindly on celebrity advocacy, particularly if it involves some sort of public suffering and pain, and even if people do not personally like the celebrity.

Fifth, the main reason for the approbation is that most people associate charitable activity, and particularly development needs, with giving or raising money. They recognise that celebrities are good at raising money and reward them accordingly. They do not look for political lobbying or political change as a means of advancing development causes.

Sixth, the limitations of celebrity advocacy are demonstrated in the way that people talk about it, for they mainly talk about the celebrity, not the cause with which the celebrity is associated. Awareness may well be raised but not the sort that the celebrities were trying to produce. In that respect the main beneficiaries of celebrity advocacy are the celebrities themselves, rather than their causes.

And from these findings there is one important argument. Celebrity advocacy does not demonstrate widespread power. Few people are influenced by it or take much notice of it. But far more important than the actual reach of celebrity advocacy is the clearly widespread belief in its power, influence and effectiveness. Belief in celebrity advocacy confers on it a power that it may not otherwise have. But this means that celebrity, conceived as a means of connecting to, and representing, the public, may not fulfil that role. The means of reaching a disengaged public in post-democratic times turns out to be another means of passing over their heads.

The limited consumption of celebrity media

Let us first examine how interest in celebrity is manifest in answers to indirect questions. These are questions that are not about celebrity per se, but about media consumption. From the 2005 survey, Couldry and Markham produced a cluster analysis of different sorts of engagements in political issues (Figure 8.1). This shows that most people in their survey are interested in mainstream politics (41 per cent) or particular issues (30 per cent). A minority are rather disaffected and not really interested in anything at all (14 per cent), and a similar group are interested in celebrity matters (14 per cent).

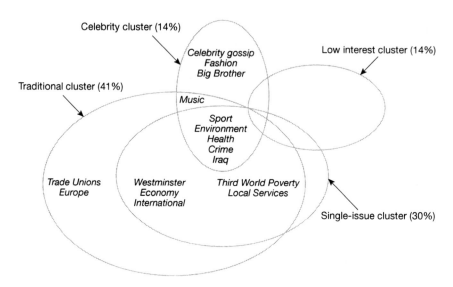

FIGURE 8.1 Survey respondents (2005) grouped according to the things they keep up with

Source: Couldry and Markham, 2007: 412. Reproduced with permission.

These clusters reflect other more basic differences of socioeconomic status, age and gender. People from the social groups ABC1s (wealthier and more educated) tend to be more interested in mainstream politics than C2DEs (poorer and less educated). Fewer ABC1s declare themselves not to be interested in anything. There is, however, no variation in socioeconomic grouping in celebrity affairs (so much for Inglis's 'cultivated classes'). But there are clear differences in interest in celebrity with respect to gender and age. Women are more interested in celebrity affairs than men, and younger people more than older people. Those most interested in celebrity affairs tend to be young women. Some 40 per cent of women of age 18–34 belong to the celebrity cluster, more than any other cluster for that group.[9]

When we repeated these questions in the 2011 survey, and the cluster analysis, a similar set of groupings emerged (Table 8.1). The group that was not interested in much (even the economy) was still there, as was the traditional politics group. Then there was a group interested in most political affairs but somewhat less interested in some issues than the traditional political group, especially with respect to local politics and poverty overseas. Finally, there was a large group of people who were generally disengaged from most issues, but more tolerant of celebrity than any of the others.

The clear finding from both surveys is that celebrity affairs is a minority interest. This accords with the low salience of celebrity in people's lives that was plain in their answers to the direct questions of celebrity use each week that were asked in the 2012 survey (Table 8.2). Over 75 per cent of people reported either not reading celebrity news, or doing so for less than five minutes. Over 35 per cent

The witches' pond **135**

TABLE 8.1 Media use clusters from the 2011 survey

Cluster	Characteristics	% of sample
Highly politically engaged	Interested in all things political, with very small proportions not interested in any single particular topic.	19
Quite politically engaged	This group is almost as interested in political affairs as the highly engaged cluster, but there are some generally low salience issues that do not interest most of its members.	36
Unengaged but celebrity tolerant	Very few issues engage the majority of the members of this cluster (the ups and downs of the UK economy are one). However, it is the most tolerant of all the clusters about celebrity affairs. It accounts for the majority of the interest in them.	31
Hardly interested in anything	Very little moves this group, not that it would be interested in the fact.	14

TABLE 8.2 Engagement with celebrity news in a typical week

Response	Reading about celebrity news (%)	Talking about celebrity news (%)
More than an hour	3	2
Up to an hour	5	4
Up to half an hour	14	11
5 minutes or less	46	46
Not at all	32	37

of people never talk about it, 46 per cent only for a few minutes. Less than 10 per cent of people read about celebrity, or talk about it, for up to an hour or more. Once again, celebrity appears to be a minority occupation.

Moreover, celebrity news is not something people appeared to seek themselves. The majority, 70 per cent, are encountering it incidentally. A total of 17 per cent of people reported deliberately trying to find out about celebrity.[10] Research into patterns of readership of women's magazines in the mid-1990s, which are often characterised by their high levels of celebrity content, reinforces these findings. Even among readers of the magazines, their encounters with the content were relatively light. They are dipped into in spare moments of the day, read in part because they are easily put down.[11]

I conducted a cluster analysis of responses to direct questions about celebrity news which suggested five different groupings. There are two clusters interested in celebrity news, one strongly so (13 per cent of the sample), the other mildly (17 per cent). There are two clusters who were not interested, again, one strongly

136 The witches' pond

TABLE 8.3 Clusters of celebrity news consumption

Category	Proportion of respondents
Strong interest in celebrity	13
Mild interest in celebrity	17
Ambivalent consumers	20
Mildly uninterested in celebrity	31
Strongly uninterested in celebrity	18

so (18 per cent) and the other mildly so (31 per cent). The fifth group is most interesting because they seem to display some of the characteristics of disavowed interest. I call these people 'ambivalent consumers'. They are taking in a lot of celebrity media in diverse forms (watching a lot of television in particular) but they appear not to like what they are hearing and seeing very much. These constitute 20 per cent of the sample (Table 8.3).

We encountered members of these clusters in the focus groups. There were ambivalent consumers who were watching a fair amount of (celebrity-ridden) television while not liking it very much.

> *Sam:* I watch Comic Relief and Sport Relief and I get angry with it and think why am I watching it?[12]

And there were those who were hostile to celebrity and those who welcomed it, which display familiar gender divisions and could co-exist in the same (young) households:

> *Giles:* The missus loves the reality things like TOWIE and things like that, she's just got them constantly lined up.
> *Moderator:* Do you watch them with her, do you enjoy them?
> *Giles:* No, she presses play and I walk out the room to go and have a cigarette outside and then as I walk back in she turns it off, so that's pretty much all I see but it's awful.[13]

The point here is that, contrary to the views I cited in the Introduction, interest in celebrity affairs is not universal. We can recognise people who are interested, and whose interest is disavowed (the ambivalent consumers) but these groups are by no means as all encompassing as the popular accounts would have it. Rather, interest in celebrity varies according to different population groups, according to age, gender (but not socioeconomic grouping).

Consumption of celebrity media: a reality check

We must pause at this point. If celebrity does not resonate with the public, why is it all over the news? Are the media professionals so ignorant of their audiences' needs?

The first point here is that while 'celebrity' might be a minority interest, 'fame' is more widely followed. Some 39 per cent of respondents said that they were interested in famous people and not celebrities. Given that in practice the line between fame and celebrity is hard to draw (when do celebrities become famous?) this gives more leeway for using the famous/celebrities as a means of drawing attention.

The second is that some journalists are indeed ignorant of these data. When I asked them to predict what Couldry and Markham found, one experienced journalist guessed that 60 per cent of the public would belong to the celebrity cluster, not 14 per cent. However, in other cases they are doing the research, and finding similar results. This was apparent in my interviews. There have been cases of newspapers refusing to run development stories with celebrities attached, because they would work better without it.[14] One editor of a popular magazine aimed at young women reported that her focus groups were suggesting that audiences wanted more real-life stories from 'real people' rather than celebrities.[15]

A similar account was reported by the researcher working for a TV broadcaster. He had worked on appreciation index analyses of factual genres and found that programmes that did well among younger people had not been celebrity driven, or glossy, but were rather direct, 'warts and all' programmes. The work led to the commissioning of well-received real-life programmes about issues facing young people that were deliberately not (in a complete reversal of previous policy) presented by celebrities.[16] The point here is not that celebrity is unpopular, but that, for a particular age group, at that time, celebrity-presented genres were in less demand than had been thought.

Another television executive also reported limits to the reach of celebrity. Her comments are particularly interesting because she was aware that there was demand for celebrity from a reality TV and *Heat* magazine generation. She wanted her channel to cater for it, and she had pioneered the introduction of programmes that did so. But, despite this pro-celebrity stance, she also found topics and scenarios where celebrity did not fit well:

> Mostly I've found that a lot of communities who really take their cause seriously don't really care about the celebrity angle . . . If you try and sell that to them as the way that we're getting this story out, a lot of them will say that's not important to us we don't care about that just do the story . . . Or if we say can we reward . . . your young people . . . by bringing a celebrity into meet and greet them, they don't really care and most often will reject the offer saying that's not what's important to us . . . which really puts things into perspective from a showbiz point of view and you think wow we might all be kissing the ground that these people walk on day and night because that's what the industry is used to but when it actually comes to real people's lives and their experiences it makes no difference, what's real is what they're going through.[17]

138 The witches' pond

And finally there is the fact that any interest, or lack of interest, in celebrity will be situated in specific historical, social, political and economic circumstances. We can expect it to vary. Such variation is clear from trends in newspaper reporting on celebrity. I present the detail of those trends in Appendix Three. Suffice to say here that reporting on celebrity does not display a monolithic increase. There was a strong increase in celebrity stories, but that appeared to cease around 2005, and thereafter may even be decreasing. Clearly, newspapers have realised that demand for celebrity may not be as insatiable as it is commonly perceived to be. We cannot tell whether this is a permanent change, but the more important point is that demand for celebrity advocacy fluctuates.[18]

Engagement with celebrity advocacy

The light encounters described above, however, must be qualified by the fact that almost everyone was able to talk about celebrity advocacy in the focus groups. Paradoxically, the only person who was not was a young woman (Rachel, see below) who was too engrossed in celebrity culture to notice the advocacy. But this common conversation was possible partly because the groups came prepared to talk about celebrity advocacy in the warm-up task.[19] Scott reports, for a different research exercise involving twenty-seven focus groups with a different warm-up task, that: 'talk about celebrity humanitarianism seldom emerged, unprompted, as a topic of conversation . . . celebrity humanitarianism was explicitly raised by [the 108] participants themselves on only six occasions'.[20] Furthermore, when forty-eight of Scott's focus group participants were asked to keep media diaries, 'only six percent of all entries were about celebrity humanitarianism – almost all of which were about programmes or advertisements in the build-up to Comic Relief'.[21]

Similarly, in my own groups a common conversation about celebrity advocacy was possible because the same examples kept coming up: the activities of well-televised events such as Comic and Sport Relief, Children in Need and the work of particularly famous people well-known for their advocacy (Geldof, Bono, Jolie, Lumley and Clooney). The prominence of the telethons may be a peculiarly British characteristic of celebrity advocacy. The BBC has run Children in Need telethons since 1980, Comic Relief biannually since 1989, and Sport Relief biannually since 2002. These events marshal hundreds of celebrity supporters and the entire range of entertainment figures to appeal to every sector of the audience. My focus group participants reported that it is hard not to notice those forms of celebrity advocacy which are broadcast so intensively across the nation: 'you sort of have it on in the back ground . . . because there's absolutely nothing else on'.[22]

Apart from the telethons, and despite all the variety of celebrity advocacy, people were not aware of very much of it. Recall that 90 per cent of the most prominent celebrities and 60 per cent of celebrities more generally are involved in celebrity advocacy.[23] In a fragmented fame market, reaching many people, one would expect many different examples of celebrity advocacy to be cited by the different members of the focus groups. This did not happen. Very few people could even name famous

The witches' pond **139**

people associated with charities they supported, even ones with strong celebrity ambassador programmes like UNICEF, Oxfam and the Red Cross.

> *Sacha:* I'm pretty sure that there are ... famous people who ... are associated with the Red Cross but I can't think of any. My interest is in the Red Cross not in any celebrity. [24]

This was also apparent in the survey data. Awareness of associations between the famous and NGOs is low (Table 8.4). This must be contrasted to generally high awareness of the organisations themselves, and all the work that these organisations have put into cultivating teams of celebrity ambassadors (cf. Table 5.1).[25]

Most people supported charities because of personal connections in their lives and families that made these causes important, not because of the celebrities.

> *Miriam:* I don't actually support the charity because [of] celebrity ... I donate to the charity because I want to donate to charity not because somebody is endorsing it ... I don't actually know who does Macmillan because I've never looked into [it] because I've never needed to.[26]

Nevertheless, there were incidents where people (we met five in the sixty who took part in the focus groups) had responded to causes because of celebrity endorsements:

> *Moderator:* Tell me why UNICEF, why is it close to your heart?
> *Graham:* I had heard about it before the programme The Long Way Round with Ewan McGregor and Charley Boorman but I hadn't seen what they did. In that they stopped at different UNICEF camps or places [and] they helped children ... they are ambassadors for UNICEF and I got to see that actually this money has built schools, teaches children and that made me think that's a charity I would like to do something for.[27]

TABLE 8.4 Awareness of famous people working with development organisations

Number of charities for which awareness was claimed	Awareness of listed charities (%)	Awareness of famous people with listed charities (%)
None	<1	66
1	<1	16
2	<1	10
3	1	3
4	4	2
5–7	95	1

The listed organisations were: Action Aid; Amnesty International; CAFOD; Christian Aid; Oxfam; Save the Children; Red Cross. Very similar patterns were displayed for the non-development NGOs included in our questionnaire.

140 The witches' pond

There was also one person who took action other than giving money:

> *Simon:*   When Hugh Fearnley-Whittingstall did the fishing quota thing last year. I signed up for that. I don't think I've ever signed a petition before.[28]

Finally, there was one case of someone whose broader awareness of the world grew as a result of celebrity advocacy:

> *Emily:*   I know Angelina Jolie does the United Nations Ambassador refugee stuff. She wrote a journal when she went to Cambodia and Pakistan and I read it and saw some of the things that she wrote about when I went to Cambodia. I didn't know anything that had happened in Cambodia until I went. It woke me up and it was through seeing what she had talked about that made me think let's put Cambodia on the list of places to go. She just seemed really human. [29]

The generally slight response to celebrity advocacy was reinforced in the survey data. We explored responses in two ways, first examining the lighter responses involving retweeting, clicking 'like' and exploring websites. These can often be associated directly with specific messages from famous people. Most people, over 75 per cent, reported taking no action (Table 8.5). Of the remainder, most tried to learn more about the cause that had been mentioned.

TABLE 8.5 Specific light responses to charitable endorsements by the famous

Reactions	*Proportion of respondents*
Never influenced	79
Negative reaction	1
Positive reaction	20
Negative and positive reactions	<1

TABLE 8.6 Deeper reactions to charitable endorsements by the famous

Reactions	*Proportion of respondents*
Not influenced	75
Giving 'stuff'	18
Giving of 'self'	4
Giving both stuff and self	3

Giving 'stuff': give money in a one-off donation; donate some possessions to the cause.

Giving of 'self' (because the actions below tend to involve more time): set up regular donations; give my time to the cause; change the way I voted in a local or national election; go to a meeting; join a campaign; join an organisation/charity/party.

The witches' pond **141**

Second, we examined deeper responses requiring giving time or money, and which cannot be easily attributed to any particular message. Similar patterns emerge. Most, 75 per cent, give nothing in response to celebrity appeals (Table 8.6). Of those who do respond, the vast majority are giving money in a one-off donation, or possessions. Only 7 per cent claim to have done something more substantial in terms of committing their time due to an appeal from a famous person. Note we cannot conclude from these findings that famous people are an inefficient means of getting people's attention. Reported reactions are few, but they could have been even lower without the celebrity involvement.[30]

To explore patterns in reaction to celebrity advocacy further I conducted cluster analyses of responses to celebrity advocacy which produced similar groupings to the cluster analysis of celebrity news consumption.[31] There was even a group of 'aware and hostile' people who, like the ambivalent consumers, knew much about what was going on with celebrity advocacy (more than those who were more receptive of it) but did not like it. However, there was one key difference – namely, with respect to the age and gender of those who approved of associations between celebrity and charity. Approval of fame and charity associations tends to *increase* with age (61 per cent of the 'pro-fame' group in the fame-charity cluster were over 45). This reverses the pattern of interest in celebrity news (which is greatest among the young). It suggests that younger people tend to be interested in celebrities for their core activities as celebrities (acting, music, sport etc.), whereas older people are more interested in their broader social activities.

Furthermore, it is clear that antipathy to celebrity news does not necessarily produce hostility to interactions between fame and charity or development. One would expect that if people are sympathetic to the work of fame in development, they might also be interested in celebrity news. Liking the latter should warm people up to accept the former. That is not the case. In fact, of those who approved of the work of fame in development, more were hostile to celebrity news (39 per cent) than sympathetic to it (34 per cent). The remaining 27 per cent were ambivalent. The difference is not great, but the point is that it is the opposite of what one might expect. One would expect most people who approved of celebrity advocacy also to be sympathetic at least to celebrity news. Instead, it appears that celebrity news, and celebrity advocacy for development, could provoke very different reactions from the same people.

The lack of correspondence between the reception of celebrity affairs and responses to celebrity advocacy was visible in the focus groups. For example, Rachel, the young woman I mentioned above, exemplified the view of those who are interested in celebrities for their own sake and not for the good works they do. Rachel liked celebrity culture. She would try to 'grab a magazine' at lunch, which might be '*Heat, Hello!, OK!*. Anything that's juicy on the front. If I see Peter Andre I grab that one.'[32] In the middle of a discussion about Bono (and the groups always mentioned him), Rachel had been keeping quiet. The moderator tried to involve her, producing this response:

142 The witches' pond

> *Rachel:* To be honest I'm quite lost in all of this 'cause I don't really keep
> up to date with anything. I don't even know who Bono is. I felt kind
> of stupid not knowing who that is, but to be honest I'm living a life
> where I don't care. Most of my friends are ooh yeah Peter Andre, that's
> nice, he looks quite fit. I know it's quite shallow right now but –
> *Jill:* But would you support something if Peter Andre was involved?
> *Rachel:* If I was totally honest I'd think that's quite good, but it would be
> gone like that [. . .] for me celebrities and charities don't mix very well.[33]

We also met Rachel's obverse, people who kept away from the media, especially
celebrity media, but still responded positively to celebrity charity events:

> *Collin:* I don't watch a lot of TV in all honesty, but . . . I'll watch something
> like Sport Relief or Comic Relief, Children in Need and all things that
> seem to really matter.
> *Moderator:* When you say they matter, what do you mean and why do you
> pick those out in a world of not watching much TV?
> *Collin:* Because I hate things like soaps and stuff, they bore the shit out of
> me, anything that is about like someone else's life or things that are made
> up or are supposed to be real have absolutely no bearing on my life
> whatsoever, but things like this where people are in need, then I find
> that interesting.[34]

Popular belief in celebrity power and approval of celebrity advocates

Despite the fact that most people register little response themselves, they think that
other people will respond more positively to celebrity messages. The clearest result
from this survey is that most people (74 per cent) think that their lack of response
to celebrity is atypical (Table 8.7). When asked if they think they pay more attention
than other people, most reply 'no'; when asked if other people pay more attention
than them, most reply 'yes'. There is a popular, and false, belief that celebrity
resonates broadly with the public.

TABLE 8.7 Beliefs in other people's responses to celebrity advocacy

Category	*Proportion of respondents*
Other people pay more attention than me	43
Other people probably pay more attention than me	31
I am the same as other people	8
I probably pay more attention than other people	2
I pay more attention than other people	1
I don't know	4
Inconsistent answers	10
Total	100

The witches' pond **143**

All the focus groups were characterised by their firm belief in the power of celebrity to command media coverage. In this they reflected the common misunderstandings among NGO employees about the abilities and uses of celebrity.

> *Andrew:* The bottom line is that any celebrity will get a charity media coverage and that has to be good. [35]

Celebrity belonged to the media world and, being associated with the celebrity by definition, pulled a charity into that media world that was glamorous, important, interesting and noticed. From the media coverage (that *any* celebrity is believed to provide) awareness, and especially money, would flow.

It may be because of their presumed effectiveness that negative reactions to celebrity advocacy were rare. Those negative views that were expressed were in response to specific actions perceived to be shallow and uncommitted, such as when celebrities 'just tweeted or put on a pretty dress to go to a UN meeting.'[36] The hypocrisy of celebrities was mentioned, but only twice:

> *Gemima:* Al Gore [. . .] annoys me in how he went straight from being Vice President to saving the world yet he flies around in jets and lives the high life.[37]

> *Mark:* I don't think I've ever given to Comic Relief, I've never picked up the phone, you see these multimillionaires standing there, like oh look at this starving child, well how much money have you put, have you put your hand in your pocket?[38]

There was not much indication that people resented the possibilities that celebrities were benefiting from their charitable acts. Those few who suspected celebrities were getting paid for their television appearances could resent the payment. It made their connection less 'genuine'.[39] But there was only one person who expressed any resentment at celebrities' privilege. In a discussion on Soccer Aid Sarah said:

> Most men who like football and who play football would absolutely kill to play at Old Trafford, Wembley, just to have that experience and these people that have got all that they have got get to do things like that . . . All these wealthy celebrities they all get things given to them they don't have to go out and buy their own clothes.[40]

In contrast to these individual instances of hostility the general tone that greeted celebrity advocacy was approval. Some people were not prepared to criticise it at all:

> *Diane:* No matter who the celebrity is and what their reasons behind it are I just think they are . . . making everyone aware of that particular charity so I think that has got to be a good thing.[41]

144 The witches' pond

Even if the group members did not like a particular celebrity, they were prepared to welcome their advocacy. They were also prepared to welcome them even if the celebrity benefited:

> *Ger:* I don't think you can knock anyone, really. I mean, even if a little bit of them is doing it for themselves, if they're helping someone else it balances it.[42]

However, the welcome was textured in important ways. Action was important, and groups were particularly warm and receptive of celebrities who suffered visibly. The pain proved the authenticity of their commitment:

> *Tracy:* Angelina Jolie, you know she spends months and months getting dirty, not showering.[43]

> *Kieren:* Lenny Henry went and lived with them for a while, like he went the extra mile, he wasn't just saying 'I'll look at that, it's bad', he went and experienced it.[44]

> *Diane:* I liked John Bishop who did that run because he absolutely killed himself doing it.[45]

In fact, there were also instances of people being turned off by the celebrity advocates enjoying themselves too much in their fundraising:

> *John:* I'm a football fan but I hate Soccer Aid . . . I like Robbie Williams and all that [but] I hate it for the reason that they are doing what they want to do. They want to play football with the big boys they are living out their fantasy to play with world class footballers at Old Trafford . . . I'm not knocking that . . . this money is for a good cause but . . . when you do something for a sponsorship it is normally a hard thing that you have to do.[46]

The charitable frame

Above all, the people we talked to valued celebrity advocacy because it raised money. Money was often the currency of supporting charities.

> *Laura:* At the end of the day *that* [money] is it, isn't it? That is the important thing. You can watch somebody and admire them – does that matter at the end of the day you are not giving them the money, which is the whole point of them spending that money paying that celebrity to do that thing.[47]

Money made charity possible:

> *Tracy:* So having the celebrity endorsement gets them awareness and a faster way to earn money than they would for other charities. The celebrity gets the money and without that some of these charities wouldn't even exist.[48]

Even people who were not well inclined towards celebrity felt they should reward fundraising:

> *Moderator:* Are there some sorts of issues which the use of celebrities works well with?
>
> *Martin:* Fundraising, because you don't have to believe them, but you can respect what they've done.[49]

After disagreements about the desert of celebrity advocacy, the common response was 'at the end of the day they are raising money for a good cause'.[50] Some people even hated celebrity fundraising events, but still gave to them:

> *Sarah:* I would do . . . anything not to watch the big events. They drive me absolutely mad. I know that they are doing good . . . I'll give and I did the last Children in Need one by text . . . but to actually sit and watch them for God knows how many hours they are on at night. No, I couldn't think of anything worse.[51]

More than that, charitable actions themselves were equated with raising or giving money, rather than taking some other form of action. Only once did we come across someone taking another form of action (Simon, who signed the petition above). Disapproval of celebrity advocacy was expressed by not giving money:

> *Phil:* (with respect to Angelina Jolie's visits overseas) It's all staged, and because of that I wouldn't give her money.[52]

A lack of money meant that people could not take part:

> *Tricia:* I can't afford to support charities.[53]

Talking about celebrity advocates

The story now becomes a little more complicated, for when you listen to the way in which people talk about celebrity advocacy and what they say about the celebrity advocates, it is clear that celebrity advocacy can be a substantial and positive part of the brand and public image of celebrities. There were numerous such cases across the groups. In some instances it transformed people's relationships with the celebrities:

146 The witches' pond

> *Arthur:* I wasn't a David Walliams fan at first but I am now. How can you do something like that and not be liked? His personality shone through and now he is one of my favourite people.[54]

> *Moderator:* So did you think John Bishop was genuine and committed and someone with integrity before Sport Relief?
> *Edmund:* No, absolutely no.[55]

> *Laura:* John Bishop, when he did the swimming and the running and the cycling I thought that was absolutely fantastic and he has really gone up in my estimation from that . . . now I will watch him as a comedian because I just think that's amazing.[56]

In other instances it made less popular people (problematic footballers, 'tossers') more bearable:

> *Sam:* Didier Drogba, he's got his own Ivory Coast organisation. He gives all his sponsorship money to help people where he was born. Sky Sports did a programme on it and I think it's good that he's not forgotten his roots. It made me look up his foundation on the Internet, but I must admit it didn't make me set up a direct debit or donating.
> *Moderator:* Did you like him anyway?
> *Sam:* As a footballer I'm not too keen, but my respect grew for him after that. [57]

> *Moderator:* Did Jamie Oliver doing that campaign change how you feel or give you more knowledge or did it just fall in line with what you already felt?
> *Graham:* It fell in line with what I believed in but it changed my opinion towards Jamie Oliver, I have to say. I thought actually he is not such a tosser after all.[58]

In other cases it caused people to reverse their thinking on a celebrity:

> *Emma:* I googled Keira Knightley 'cause I don't like her, so I thought she must have done something I don't like. But then I saw something that she'd been supporting and I'm that fickle that I now like her, because . . . she made a film with a charity called *The Cut* about domestic violence.[59]

More than this, however, it was clear that often the attention won, was focused on the celebrity, *not on their cause*. More often than not people were prepared to talk about the celebrity and their feelings about the celebrity rather than the cause that she had supported. Take David Walliams again:

> *Moderator:* What was he doing it for?
> *Mark:* Sport Relief.

The witches' pond **147**

Moderator: And therefore what issue was he doing it for?
Mark: Don't know.[60]
Moderator: What about David Walliams what was he raising his money for?
Chris: I'm not too sure, it was Sport Relief again wasn't it, so I assume it all goes into a pot.
Moderator: What does Sport Relief go to?
Chris: I think it goes to, the erm [sentence unfinished]. The one thing I know it goes to the poorer African countries who want to set up, say, football leagues for kids.[61]

Or Robbie Williams's work with Soccer Aid:

Moderator: What is the cause for Soccer Aid?
Charlotte: I think they are raising money for Africa and that, but I watch it because I'm a big Robbie Williams fan and he is the main organiser. It works well in our house because my husband and sons love the football part of it and I'm interested in the celebrity side of it.[62]

And Ewan McGregor for UNICEF:

Moderator: Who was Ewan McGregor riding for?
Chris: Erm, I'm not too sure. It was famine relief of some description.[63]

It was not just ignorance of the causes that characterises responses here. Hostility or affection for the celebrity's style, rather than anything to do with the cause, could determine the reception of the advocacy:

Joanna: I put Angelina Jolie [in the hells]. I know she's done all that work for refugees but again I just can't stand her. She stole Brad Pitt from Jennifer Aniston [laughter] and I will never like the woman ... [resentfully] she looks beautiful in anything.[64]

The quality of her cause is not an issue here. In responding to celebrity advocacy members of our groups tended to look, talk and think about the celebrity, and not examine the issues about which the celebrities are trying to raise awareness.

Conclusion

These data suggest that there are limits to the interest and preoccupation with celebrity. Only a minority of people will declare themselves, in indirect questions, to be interested in things that we normally associate with celebrity matters. A similarly small proportion of people declare an interest in celebrity if asked about it directly. Likewise, few people report particularly deep engagements with celebrity advocacy.

148 The witches' pond

The generally light and hostile reception of celebrity news does not determine how associations between celebrities and NGOs are interpreted. A different set of rules seems to apply to the public reception of these matters. Indeed, even the typical association of celebrity with the young breaks down. This is not in accordance with the popular idea that working with a celebrity helps charities to make contact with people who would not normally be interested in their work.

When people hear about celebrity advocacy, they are generally prepared to respond positively to it. Celebrity advocacy appears, to use Billig's language (cf. p. 44), well settled in people's minds. It involves little angst or struggle to accommodate the perceived inequalities that celebrity existence, compared to their own, can invoke. But the focus groups add some texture to the nature of the authentic relationships the British public welcomes. Authentic commitment is not just demonstrated through expertise, experience, sympathy or empathy. It can also be demonstrated through pain and suffering. It remains a performance. But is a performance featuring blood, sweat and viruses.

Despite the general lack of interest, and the normally small number of people who watch and participate in activities popularly associated with celebrity culture, there is a widespread belief in the power of celebrity, at the same time as relatively few people demonstrated that power in their lives. There were few incidences of people responding to celebrity advocacy. There was widespread talk of celebrities raising awareness, at the same time as few people had had their awareness raised. There was praise about the power of celebrity to get media attention for good causes at the same time as most people knew of relatively few examples beyond the obvious. Most people are not particularly aware of celebrity advocacy by NGOs with strong ambassadorial programmes. They are only able to talk about the topic because of the work of a few highly committed and famous advocates, and because of the major celebrity telethons that form a staple part of annual entertainment on the BBC.

Responses to celebrity advocacy result in double-talk. People exalted celebrity power while, in the same breath, their discussions demonstrated its lack of reach and influence. We believe that celebrity advocacy is powerful, and if what we say does not support that belief, other people's behaviour will doubtless back us up. We are back at the witches' pond. It is impossible to find limits to celebrities' influence, but we must add a twist to the analogy. When doubters of celebrity are ducked in the pond, they would be jeered by crowds, most of whom shared their doubts.

A critic, however, might be ready to accuse *me* of disavowal at this point. For it is possible to interpret these data as refuting my thesis that some people are not interested in celebrity. The focus groups were prepared to talk at length, and in such glowing terms, about celebrities and their advocacy. When celebrities support causes we take notice, whether we like the celebrity or not. Indeed, the celebrities dominated the attention of the people watching to the exclusion of the causes they were 'raising awareness' about. Does this not demonstrate, after all, considerable interest in celebrity?

However, that objection derives not from these data, but from the prevailing beliefs about celebrity. It ignores the contrived (and prepared) nature of a focus

The witches' pond **149**

group discussion. It ignores the limited repertoire of conversation that these groups, with that preparation, produced. It ignores the prominence of the big events in Britain. It ignores the comparative findings from Scott's groups (in which celebrity did not feature) and the opinions of media professionals I cited above.

The important point is that so many Britons *believe* in celebrity advocates' influence. The belief is partly a consequence of the charitable frame that dominates public understanding of advocacy generally. Celebrity advocacy is welcomed because it raises money, not because it undertakes other forms of political engagement. Indeed, the welcome afforded to charitable fundraising is also a *displacement* of other forms of political engagement. Having raised money, having texted our donation, we have done our bit and can think about other things.

The belief is also partly a reflection of the ordinary world/media world distinction that Couldry described.[65] And this fact helps us to recognise some of the ways in which celebrity advocacy can be immensely powerful and influential, for this entire chapter has concerned the *mediated* presence of celebrities. It describes encounters on television, Twitter, the Internet and newspapers. These I have contended are not as powerful as is commonly believed. But we must treat differently the much more powerful consequences of direct unmediated interactions. These, as we have seen in Chapter 5, can be most useful for building the supporter base of organisations. Media power creates a body of people who make us feel good about ourselves if we meet them.

Unmediated encounters also, as we saw in Chapter 7, work well with elites. Celebrity marshals publics in ways that governments can appreciate, even if, at the same time, it fails to engage them. Note, however, how extraordinary this situation is. Celebrity, which is *unlikely* to indicate public engagement, is taken as an indication of precisely that. Populist form is confused with popular participation. The connection that celebrities enjoy with broader publics is less important than the connection they are *believed* to have. The people's representatives (the politicians) consider the celebrities to be the people's representatives. It does not matter (for this argument) if they are not. It does not matter that the politicians, thinking thus, also cease to be representative. After all, of what import is it in post-democratic politics if the public are not really behind a campaign? As long as they can be invoked, then the campaign will win some moral and political force.

This means that we must modify slightly Marks and Fischer's arguments about celebrities simulating consent (cf. pp. 40 and 132). For they saw the popularity of celebrity, and the passive acceptance and reception of celebrity messages, as being surrogates of consent. The popular appeal of celebrity advocates gave their work legitimacy. But the direction of the appeal is wrong here. It does not work because it invigorates the public and engages them in democratic deliberation and debate. It works because it simulates consent to political elites who believe in that invigoration.

If my interpretation of these data is correct, the post-democratic separation of ruling elites from apathetic subjects is deeper than we have realised. For even the populist elements of it prove to have limited popularity. What, then, does this situation portend for the work of celebrity advocates in international development?

150 The witches' pond

Notes

1 Turner, 2006: 163, note 3.
2 Inglis, 2010: 270.
3 Others are similar. In the early 1990s Jib Fowles claimed '[e]veryone had an opinion on the marriage of Mike Tyson and Robin Givens'. Everyone? (Fowles, 1992: 183; the pair mentioned were a boxer and actress respectively.) Stephen Gundle, in *Glamour*, asserts the universal appeal of glamour and celebrity, without qualification (and without evidence), repeatedly throughout his book (Gundle, 2008: 108, 129, 142). On other occasions in the book he recognises that interest is structured by class and gender.
4 Couldry, 2012: 81. There is also an irony in the way Couldry writes about everyday practices that cement the authority of celebrity power, and the boundaries between the 'celebrity' and the 'ordinary'. One of his examples of these 'everyday' practices is celebrity sightings and the reactions they create (ibid.: 81–2). But these are precisely not an everyday practice; they occur infrequently. If anything it is the labelling of such rare occurrences as 'everyday', rather than the sightings themselves, which cements celebrity power (hence the irony).
5 Marks and Fischer, 2002: 387.
6 Dyer, 2004 [1986]: 15.
7 For a sensitive and nuanced study which does look at audience identification with celebrity, as manifest in copycat suicides, see Stack (1987). For the absorptions, and self-absorption of celebrity, see Giles (2000).
8 They are attempted surprisingly infrequently. Gamson's work remains a touchstone here (Gamson, 1994). Merton (1946) provides a remarkably early example. Halpern's survey of children in Rochester, New York, provides some evidence of the variegated fascination of US teenagers with celebrity (Halpern, 2007).
9 This last fact is particularly important for the analysis of 2011 and 2012 surveys. The panel of respondents to whom the questions are put is nationally representative, but the composition of the sample answering the question is self-selecting, and often *not* representative. In particular, in this case we had a surfeit of older men answering the questions. I have weighted the answers accordingly so that they do not dominate the opinions of the young women (see celebrityanddevelopment.wordpress.com/methods-used-in-the-book-celebrity-advocacy-and-international-development/ for more information).
10 A further 200 people said that they could not remember why they read celebrity news.
11 Hermes, 1995.
12 Group 1.
13 Group 2.
14 Source 62.
15 Source 90.
16 Source 97.
17 Source 98.
18 Rein *et al.*, 1987: seven reported declines in magazine article titles in the US with the word 'celebrity' from 1930 to 1939 and in the mid 1960s before a spectacular increase throughout the 1970s and 80s.
19 The warm-up task asked group members to think about examples of celebrity advocacy they liked and disliked (labelled heavens and hells).
20 Scott, Martin, 2013b: 12.
21 Ibid.
22 Group 5.
23 Thrall *et al.*, 2008.
24 Group 7. Maya, also in that group, wondered out loud 'UNICEF – do I know any [ambassadors]?'.
25 Note also that this finding accords with Samman and colleagues who reported that 'Respondents very rarely named a specific charitable affiliation in association with a celebrity, and when they did, this was often incorrect' (Samman *et al.*, 2009: 140).

26 Group 6.
27 Group 3. Both McGregor and Boorman are actors.
28 Group 9. Fearnley-Whittingstall is a chef.
29 Group 4.
30 Actual studies of how audiences respond to particular instances of celebrity advocacy are rather limited. I have found two papers doing so. Van den Bulck *et al.* examined recognition and support of six Flemish campaigns (three with celebrities, three without) among 7,993 (!) Belgian citizens (Van den Bulck *et al.*, 2011). They found that a campaign without celebrities enjoyed the highest recognition, but two celebrity-endorsed campaigns enjoyed the highest level of NGO recognition, and all three celebrity-endorsed campaigns enjoyed the most support. Robert Wheeler has examined responses to advertisements in a sample of 930 US college students and found that celebrities who are well connected to charities did increase these students' intentions to act (Wheeler, 2009). Samman and colleagues study of 100 commuters in Dublin concluded that most people were aware of at least one celebrity advocate (and this was mostly either Jolie or Bono) and but that few said they were influenced by such activity (Samman *et al.*, 2009).
31 This cluster analysis is available on the website celebrityanddevelopment.wordpress.com/ methods-used-in-the-book-celebrity-advocacy-and-international-development/.
32 Group 4.
33 Group 4. Andre is a musician.
34 Group 2.
35 Group 9.
36 Edmund, Group 1.
37 Group 1. Gore was Vice-President of the US.
38 Group 2. Group 7 also objected to celebrities avoiding tax and then asking the public for charitable donations.
39 Group 4.
40 Group 5.
41 Group 5.
42 Group 2.
43 Group 4.
44 Group 2.
45 Group 5. Bishop is a comedian. Another frequent example was David Walliams (a comedian) who had recently swum the Thames and contracted cholera as a result.
46 Group 5. Williams is a musician.
47 Group 6. Emphasis in the speaker's expression.
48 Group 4.
49 Group 9.
50 Group 5.
51 Group 5.
52 Group 5.
53 Group 4.
54 Group 3.
55 Group 1.
56 Group 6.
57 Group 2. Drogba is, as you have probably guessed, a footballer.
58 Group 3. Oliver is a chef.
59 Group 4.
60 Group 2.
61 Group 8.
62 Group 3.
63 Group 8.
64 Group 6. Aniston is an actress.
65 Couldry, 2001.

9

CHANGING THE WORLD THROUGH CELEBRITY ADVOCACY

When you explore celebrity advocacy it becomes a peculiar and paradoxical entity. We have seen that it is becoming increasingly important in the NGO sector in the UK which has evolved a systematic and well-organised set of relations with the celebrity industries. Work with charities is now an important element of celebrity brand building and news reporting. This is largely carried out on the celebrity industries' own terms. We have seen that a great deal of energy, effort and work is invested in it on all sides. 'Getting' the relationship between celebrity and NGOs is hard. Liaison officers have to negotiate numerous hurdles thrown up by colleagues, the celebrity industries and corporate partners. These efforts at relationship building are generally successful at building interactions that display various forms of authenticity. In fact, the authentic relationships resulting can be much stronger than the traditional means of reporting on them suggest. There can be a depth to celebrities' engagements with international development that will not be well captured in the standard reports about their field-trips.

Another way of summarising these points is that celebrities now constitute a new set of development actors who need to be taken seriously, and around whom the development NGO community, politicians and corporations have significantly reorganised their practices.[1] Indeed, some celebrities' lives have become reordered around their charitable activities. And yet, despite all this, we have seen that public interest in and reception of celebrity news and celebrity advocacy is variable. The appeal of celebrity is surprisingly limited, although publics are generally kindly disposed towards celebrity advocacy. The British public is aware of the major events, but do not have a particularly deep understanding of the diversity of celebrity advocacy.

Finally, we have seen that belief in celebrity power is justified whenever celebrities interact with elites; for corporate and politicians' interest in celebrity can make it a powerful lobbying tool. And yet even that is partly sustained by a false belief in the popularity of celebrity. This is something that campaigners deliberately play upon: in the 'smoke and mirrors' of setting up a campaign, celebrity is an excellent device for simulating a public interest which is absent.

All this activity is an integral part of the actually existing practices of post-democracy. Celebrity advocacy flourishes in elite circles and with elite governance; it reproduces and reinforces the power of those elites. It does so in the presence of publics who are largely disengaged from all this activity, but who do not seem to mind that they have been left out. Elites misrecognise the public's participation in and enthusiasm for their celebrity liaisons. They are partying by themselves, but nobody in or out of the party seems to mind. Everyone may be deceived to varying degrees, but they are quite happily so. This is an illusion that works. Celebrity advocacy, apparently popular and engaging with publics, turns out to be one more tool in the separation of governing elites from their subjects.

What, then, are we to make of celebrity advocacy for international development? I want now to return to the main questions which I asked earlier in the book. After considering public awareness of development and the representation of distant others (Chapter 2) I suggested that we need to ask how celebrity advocacy affects public understandings of development (p. 31). I answer this question in 'Development representations' below.

After examining post-democratic politics and previous critiques of celebrity advocacy (Chapter 3) I suggested we needed to know more about how celebrity advocacy works. Thus informed, I hoped we would be better able to examine how celebrity advocacy alters the economic structures producing and reproducing inequality, and what potential it has to affect meaningful change. Is it too much part of the problem of inequality to make any difference? How egalitarian are the outcomes of celebrity politics and advocacy when applied to international development? I examine these issues in two sections. 'Inequity and accountability' outlines the dangers and problems of trying to change the world using unaccountable elites. 'Working with celebrity elites in post-democracies' presents a more pragmatic approach and considers the possibilities of working through them.

In answering these questions my argument will differ from the normal radical critiques of celebrity. These authors often dismiss celebrity advocates as vapid, unrepresentative, or hypocritical. At its worst, celebrity advocacy allows hugely wealthy and privileged individuals to advance the needs of an oppressive economic regime and restrictive policies, in the name of championing the rights of the silenced, often invisible poor. This is not the stuff of which revolutions are made. And yet, while I find much problematic about celebrity advocacy, I also think that it can be put to good use. Ironically, that might be precisely because of the nature of post-democratic politics which give these unelected representatives more space to speak.

Development representations

There is a nagging question behind this book: why do we not care more about international poverty?[2] Unless there is a widely accepted norm that global poverty

154 Changing the world through celebrity advocacy

is unacceptable there will be little hope of challenging it. What role can celebrity play here?

The data I have presented above suggest that celebrity advocacy for international development is, generally, not marked by any significant beneficial change to awareness of the needs of distant strangers, or development issues. This is partly because the conventions on reporting about them are dominated by the celebrity industries' attention to the image of their clients, and not by an equivalent attention to the development issues that require promoting. My data on the construction and reporting of field-trips suggest that these are ultimately vehicles for building celebrities' brands more than they are vehicles for improving public understanding of development.[3]

It is partly also because of the ways in which the British public noticed and acknowledged celebrity advocacy, which was, generally, just not very much at all. They were aware of the major events and some individuals' personal sacrifices and tribulations undertaken successfully to raise money for causes overseas. But they knew little about those causes, or those lives overseas. Instead, they were much more aware of the celebrity. Celebrity advocacy has resulted in interactions between celebrity and charity in which the purpose of the celebrity's advocacy is often submerged beneath the prominence of the celebrity's own appearance.

It is partly because development causes, as with other NGO activities generally, are so persistently viewed in a charitable frame. The issues of development and humanitarianism are plainly issues of justice and equity that cannot be solved or readily addressed by Western publics giving money. Yet celebrity advocacy prevails in an atmosphere where giving money is equated with taking action and where other forms of political participation are just hardly mentioned. Celebrity advocacy generally reinforces the 'giving money = action' frame. This is despite prominent and deliberate messages surrounding, for example, Live 8 and the ONE campaign which proclaimed 'we do not want your money, we want your voice'. It is difficult for many audiences to understand what that could mean if they are normally asked to give money to tackle injustice, if, as we saw in Chapter 2 (p. 28), campaigns can centre on the 'no brain issues' where 'people will feel comfortable giving money'.[4]

I must balance these sobering conclusions by acknowledging that there are clear cases where awareness has been raised and political activism, rather than merely money, mobilised.[5] We must recognise that celebrity involvement can often be really good for the supporter base, especially where it involves unmediated encounters, when the media world can touch and enliven the ordinary world. However, this is difficult to work at scale, and perhaps more importantly, because it works with supporters, it is working with people who are already converted. It does not challenge or change the attitudes embedded in the broader public which NGOs might want to take on.

Given this assessment it is hard to see how celebrity advocacy advances awareness of development issues in the long-term, or cosmopolitanism more generally. Development representations are ruled by the politics of pity. Celebrity advocacy

Changing the world through celebrity advocacy **155**

appears to be doing little to challenge that.[6] I am not convinced that celebrities will help us to care more about global poverty.

My conclusions, however, come with two caveats, for my methods do not allow me to test two important ways in which celebrity could be bound up with long-term beneficial change and increasing awareness of the needs of distant strangers. First, I have not examined the personal histories and journeys of development NGOs' supporters. I have not examined the extent to which their high levels of engagement, awareness, acknowledgement and activism can be attributed to celebrity influence before they were supporters. The focus groups showed that this was possible. It also suggested that people supported NGOs with whom they had an affinity. If celebrities can build affinity for NGOs on a large scale among their supporters, this could make an appreciable difference to development NGOs' supporters. Second, I have not looked at how fan communities have responded to their stars' activism. Apathy and passivity is unsurprising among members of the public for whom the celebrity is just another famous face. But something different might be possible among people whose identity is more bound up in their star's behaviour.[7] Or, to put this differently, if celebrities are used to narrow-cast to specific audiences rather than broadcasting, they might be more productive.[8]

Inequity and accountability

Let me be heretical for a moment. Ultimately, the opinions of Northern publics about international development are not particularly important. They are a second order problem. What matters more in the first instance is the condition and circumstances of the distant strangers themselves. If they are content with their lives and prospects, what does it matter what other people think of them? If they are not, then what concrete change has development advocacy brought about that would make their lives happier and more prosperous?

What role has celebrity advocacy played in promoting prosperity in the South? In some respects the answer here is simply that it has become an integral part of the development NGO sector, as we have seen in Chapter 5. Celebrity advocates and NGOs are part of the same edifice. Celebrity ambassadors are enrolled and trained by the NGOs; they are their mouthpiece, their spokespeople, and, perhaps most importantly, their fundraisers. To the extent, therefore, that the development NGOs are effectively promoting development, so also are their celebrity advocates. They are one of the means by which NGOs maintain their presence on the world stage.

For sympathetic assessors of development NGOs' achievements, this will suffice. For example, Roger Riddell, an experienced commentator from within the NGO movement, argues that NGOs have played a role in challenging a number of inequitable policies, and that they have supported thousands of effective interventions and projects on the ground.[9] If celebrity advocates are advancing those practical gains directly or indirectly, they are doing as much as could be reasonably expected.

156 *Changing the world through celebrity advocacy*

Other critics of development NGOs are more sanguine about their achievements. Diana Mitlin and her colleagues note strong pressures on development NGOs to become part of neoliberal government agendas, and that concerns and criticisms about their proximity to power, voiced for well over a decade, which appear not to have been addressed by the sector.[10] While they remain alive to the possibility that NGOs could become, and have been, part of valuable alternatives to development, they warn repeatedly against the tendency to be sucked into elite lobbies, creating an 'international civil society elite' that dominates development possibilities and can inevitably distance development NGOs from the people they exist to serve.[11] For such critics, the presence of celebrity in the transnational civil society would be both emblematic, and constitutive, of that danger.

This charge – that NGOs are part of neoliberal agendas, and not promoting alternative development pathways – is serious. For it means that development NGOs may be complicit in promoting policies which inhibit prosperity in the South. This is a complex issue but, put briefly, neoliberal development policies seek to maximise free trade and limit national support for particular industries so that market forces can work internationally with as much freedom as possible. The problem with these measures is that they do not produce much growth in the global South. Ha-Joon Chang calls the promotion of these policies 'kicking away the ladder', for it means that rich countries can prohibit poor countries from following the strategies that they themselves employed when they were prospering.[12] He calls the countries and Bretton Woods Institutions which enforce these policies 'Bad Samaritans' because of the poverty and misfortune they produce.[13] Joseph Stiglitz, Chang's mentor and long-term critic of the IMF, has shown how the IMF was responsible for intensifying and worsening economic crises in East Asia and Russia in the 1990s.[14] Dani Rodrik too insists that the 'hyperglobalisation' strategies are misguided, and that countries need much more freedom from the WTO to define their own tariffs and industrial development policies.[15]

The more severe critics of the role of celebrity advocacy find that current forms of protest and lobbying against this neoliberal hegemony are at best ineffective and may actually be harmful. They identify a number of problems that stem from the character of the transnational civil society elites which Mitlin and colleagues criticised. A general point is that a disconnected transnational elite is problematic because it will have difficulty understanding and adequately representing the forms of development poorer people desire. As Mitlin and colleagues put it: 'some NGOs' unprecedented levels of access to at least part of the policy process . . . also brings challenges, particularly concerning the capacity and legitimacy of NGOs to act as pseudo-democratic representatives of 'the poor''.[16]

A much more serious issue is that it is not clear how such elites can be made accountable for their actions on development issues. Time and again in the annals of celebrity advocacy for international development the gains sought are stymied by elite control of highly complex procedures and the difficulty of holding leaders to account for their failures. This is true even of the highpoints. For example, consider Bono's persuasion of Bush to attend the Monterrey conference in 2002

Changing the world through celebrity advocacy **157**

and promise billions of dollars in extra aid.[17] Unfortunately, these promises, if honoured, would have only left US aid at less than 0.2 per cent of GNP, much less than the 0.7 per cent goal. Sachs's judgement was that the initial optimism he felt after Monterrey was, in hindsight, unwarranted.[18] Make Poverty History resulted in significant pledges with respect to aid that NGOs, while they complained at the time, have vigorously tried to make their governments keep. They have failed to do so. Just over half of the money pledged was given, and there has been no lasting public desire to ensure that pledges were met. As David Hulme observes, these promises 'have made a little difference but they have not been honoured; nor have leaders been held accountable for this'.[19] It produced the illusion of victory at the time, but it did not achieve its goals.[20]

Celebrity advocacy is not good at holding leaders to account for their broken promises. This is visible in the failures of the most powerful advocates. We have already considered the fact that Italian President Silvio Berlusconi once considered increasing Italian aid because he feared a tongue-lashing from Bono (p. 121). But, while it shows that he feared Bono, in the event he resolved to endure Bono's wrath and *decreased* Italian aid by over €200 million. Bono and Geldof responded with an online game which depicted Berlusconi being thrown into the air by an athlete.[21] This was clearly a humiliation which Berlusconi was able to survive.

We cannot see this as a problem of elites having their way despite popular protest. It is possible in part because of popular lack of interest. International development is a low salience issue for Northern electorates. That is why these promises are so easily broken. If the edifice of celebrity advocacy is flawed for its want of accountability, part of the fault lies with publics who do not seek justification or explanation of their leaders' actions. Even the landmine treaty success (with which this book began) is marred by the subsequent decline in funding for clearing up still-existing minefields. The public appeared to think that the job was done.[22]

But, whether the cause be public apathy or elite disregard, the lack of accountability and understanding can be potentially quite dangerous. The most severe critics of celebrity advocacy insist that, far from understanding, representing and lobbying for the needs of the poor, celebrity advocates can lobby for the economic policies which *cause* their problems. Take again the case of the Millennium Challenge Account for which Bono lobbied so strongly in 2002 and which President Bush announced at Monterrey. This was, for Hulme, a high point in poverty reduction's place on the agenda of world leaders and institutions. But its performance since then has been questionable. Emma Mawdsley argues that the compacts signed with countries who will receive funds are 'redolent of the "bare knuckle" neoliberalism that devastated sub-Saharan Africa, Russia and parts of Latin America over the 1980s and early 1990s'.[23] She argues that there is little about poverty reduction in the compacts signed with recipient countries but that, following Susanne Soederberg, they are best interpreted as part of a broader pursuit of US economic hegemony, opening up markets through the 'extension and ever-deepening penetration of neoliberal capitalism . . . [which] precisely undermines the conditions for sustainable profitability, as well as social justice'.[24]

158 Changing the world through celebrity advocacy

In other words, Bono's lobbying has, in Mawdsley's assessment, produced the very problematic globalisation policies that we would need celebrity advocates to fight against if they are to be effective in promoting poverty reduction.[25]

Harry Browne, in a biting critique of Bono's work as a whole, makes a more general point. He contends that the neoliberal restructuring and remaking of the world is led by an unaccountable elite who use celebrity humanitarians, like (and especially) Bono, to legitimate this exercise as a drive for a more just, global society. Bono is, as the title of Browne's book drives home, a 'frontman' of this unpleasant exercise. He is endorsing and supporting politicians, corporations and foundations who are not, in their actions, doing enough to reduce poverty, and may be deepening it.

This fronting role, when taken at face value, gives celebrity humanitarians a moral authority that clearly disturbs many critics. It is not just that their saintliness is allegedly founded on hypocrisy and untruth. It is that the opportunity to strike such a disingenuous pose derives from these structural injustices, and imposes a vision of development that occludes others. As Dienst argues:

> It is not as if 'the poorest and most vulnerable people' do not express themselves, in countless ways, all the time. They are articulate, deliberate, and far too various to be summed up just by their pain or their poverty. They have many representatives, too, in and out of governments. All of them are aching to be heard. None of that seems to matter when Bono goes to the White House. Indeed we should make no mistake about it: he can stand there *precisely because* those people are so absent; he can speak for them exactly insofar as they are silenced . . . What is missing, invisible, off the agenda, is any belief that economic development can be a mode of collective self-determination, opening up a realm of freedom for the poor beyond that envisioned for them by billionaires.[26]

The role of celebrity in promoting neoliberal ideologies in development interventions has been observed in other initiatives.[27] For example, with respect to celebrity lobbying for Fair Trade, Goodman cautions that it builds connection less between consumers and producers, and more with the consumers and celebrity promoters. Similarly, Darnton and Kirk in *Finding Frames* query consumerist strategies because of the more selfish values they promote. Likewise, Richey and Ponte are wary of the 'causumerism' of (Product) RED.[28] They note that this scheme entails weak variants of corporate social responsibility which are not particularly transparent (it is hard to find out how much each company has given) and they do not promote a transformation of business practices which could potentially be undermining the goals that the scheme exists to promote. It also encourages Western consumers to think that HIV/AIDS can be solved in poor countries simply by paying money to deliver pills rather than by also providing the necessary support networks of clinics and assistance that an effective HIV/AIDS programme requires.

Changing the world through celebrity advocacy **159**

It is plain from much of the data that I have presented above that these are potentially telling criticisms. On one hand it is clear that the celebrity advocacy for international development is part of a broader edifice of celebrity support for the NGO sector, and both are now well integrated into the celebrity industries. Indeed, humanitarian and international development causes are leading players in this merging of powerful celebrity and NGO brands. We have seen that the schedules, levels of commitment and the representation of trips are all determined by the celebrity industries, even if the content and messaging is dominated by the NGOs. We have seen that these relations are strongly shaped by a corporate hunger for celebrity, and that even the most mainstream organisations have to be leery about taking too strong a line against government leaders for fear of scaring off corporate sponsors. Viewed thus, celebrity advocacy is very much a business-as-usual approach.

Moreover, when we consider the forms of civic participation that celebrity advocacy encourages, we have seen that this has tended to support rather light forms of participation – attending concerts, texting messages, wearing wristbands. It is too simplistic to view this as a top-down orchestration of spectacle. We have seen with Live 8 that the prospect of the spectacle shaped governments' negotiations. But we have also seen that this massive popular involvement (protest, if you will) did not produce the sustained interest that made leaders keep their promises. For all the power of elite access and interest that celebrity affords, it also signifies part of the disengagement of publics from politics that characterises post-democracy.

Given all this, it would be tempting to turn the question of celebrity advocacy's influence around and ask, Foucault-like, if little is changing as a result of celebrity advocacy for international development, then what is sustained by it? The constants, as opposed to the changes, are easy to point out. One constant is that celebrity advocacy has coincided with a steady growth of income in the revenues of leading development NGOs which is increasing absolutely and relatively in proportion to their share of household income. Another is that the flourishing of development NGOs, and celebrity within development NGOs, has not been matched by any lasting visible change in public opinion about development or development issues. Another is that there has not been much movement with respect to the forces producing global inequality. It would be unfair to blame NGOs for the failings of states' and multilateral institutions. Nevertheless, it still appears that celebrity advocacy is part of a broader and increasingly prosperous development-and-humanitarian-NGO-system whose publicity effectively directs people's attention to their wallets and to themselves, rather than to distant strangers.[29]

For radical critics, then, the rise of celebrity advocacy is a bleak prospect. Celebrity advocacy for international development enhances the distributions of power and inequality that it purports to change. It is its own nemesis, its own contradiction, its own negation. And for that reason it must be shunned, for the world created by neoliberal capitalism is deadly for the poor. Celebrity advocacy merely denotes a co-option by corporate and neoliberal interests and abandonment of radical protest.

160 Changing the world through celebrity advocacy

Working with celebrity elites in post-democracies

From a more progressive (i.e. less radical) point of view, things are not so dismal. There are instabilities and tensions in these processes that could become forces for change. As we saw in the previous section, we do not know very much about the role of celebrity in individuals' journeys into activism. So also we do not know how consumer activism features in those journeys. Attempting to purchase justice through ethical shopping may well be entrenched in neoliberal ideologies of individualistic consumer power. But is that the end of it? How do minds and attitudes change as a result of exposure to these injustices? Or does shopping for change merely reinforce inactivism?

There is currently an unproductive debate about this possibility in academia. Jeremy Youde suggests that shopping for causes could be the start point of more activism, Kapoor says it might be the start and endpoint.[30] Neither has much data to bear on what ethically minded consumers have done or become. Roopali Mukherjee and Sarah Banet-Weiser have recently collated the most helpful set of contributions which tries to eschew the unproductive dichotomies and explore the ways in which consumption provides routes into political engagement.[31] We are still learning about those possibilities.

Another element to consider is the corporate journey involved. Corporate support for international development can evolve and change as business leaders come to understand the nature of the problems they are dealing with. We cannot be too hopeful here; Samantha King's work suggests that, in the long term, corporate journeys in social responsibility tend to bring the charitable activity in line with the brand.[32] Nonetheless, it is a part of the story that needs to be told.

And, finally, if there is no change to consumer, or corporate, thinking, then, as Dan Klooster asked, what are the opportunity costs to development of failing to change consumers' ideologies?[33] If money is being raised from the purchases of a group of consumers who are not thinking reflectively about their purchasing power, then what does it matter that these particular forms of corporate social responsibility are relatively weak? Given that there are groups of people who care very little about aid or poverty, might not initiatives such as (Product) RED be a good way of taking from the uncaring rich and giving to the poor?

In addition to the potential of consumers and corporates there are the celebrities themselves. If their grasp of the issues is sufficiently deep, they may already be effective lobbyists – the nature of post-democratic politics ensures there is the space for that. They will need to recognise the pervasiveness of neoliberal thinking and how it can infect their activism, but they are a potential resource to work with.[34]

This possibility emerged clearly from the interviews I conducted. A persistent theme was that people in the celebrity industries complained of the unimaginative and boring nature of the 'asks' that they were bombarded with by the charitable sector. In the imagination and creativity of the celebrity industries there may yet be sources of new ideas that could further more radical agendas. Conversely, the successful celebrity interventions I was told about resonated with creativity which

Changing the world through celebrity advocacy **161**

made them spectacular or moving to watch or take part in.[35] As one of the more effective operators I met put it:

> What works well is not going in with a lot of preconceived notions and a canned template of what you want the celebrity to do, what works well is to listen to the celebrity and partner with the celebrity and ask her what her vision is and how much time she has to give to it and what her availability is and then collaborate and be mutually respectful, that really works well. And then what often emerges is not what either one of you would have proposed initially but it's a true collaboration . . . It's never a matter of 'we want you to do this appearance or a film or a song on a cd or something.' It's 'we want to change the world, we would like to do that with you, if you share this vision or values lets talk about how we could do that. So shall we brainstorm?' And then the possibilities are endless and then at the end you get something that works for everyone. So we never come in with a preconceived notion of how we would like them to behave.[36]

To put this point differently I suspect that NGOs might be able to make much more interesting use of their celebrity patrons in challenging the British public's ideas and notions of development and the needs of distant strangers. This finding chimes with Martin Scott's rather dismal assessment of the ways in which distant strangers are currently portrayed on British television, and the possibilities of being more creative and entertaining about depictions of distant parts of the world (Chapter 3). Part of the problem of celebrity activism could be that it is an under-exploited resource. Its full potential is not realised. In this sense, as Lisa Richey puts it, the contribution of celebrity advocates is to work development issues into their world, rather than working celebrity into development.[37]

I must be explicit about the dangers here. This is an elitist strategy. It looks to celebrity elites to initiate and pursue meaningful change. It perpetuates the problems of representation and accountability I have just discussed. Indeed, it appears to contradict a number of major authorities' calls to challenge global inequality through more effective democratic processes. Consider, for example, the central premise of Oxfam's recent work – that the world is changed by active citizens and effective states.[38] My call seems to fly in the face of theirs. Likewise, Mitlin and colleagues specifically warn against elite development advocates becoming 'associated with processes that may in themselves undermine broader democratic norms'.[39] And central to Rodrik's arguments about fair global economic policies is the idea that economic policies should be exposed to deliberative democratic debate.[40] For this exposure, he believes, will help to redistribute resources within states in more equitable ways and provide the stability and legitimacy that states require in pursuing their chosen development paths. The emphasis in all these texts is on stronger democratic performance of states, not in trying to produce more genial elites.

How, then, can we reconcile these calls for stronger democratic control over development futures with my suggestion that we need more elite-led work? I think

162 Changing the world through celebrity advocacy

the answer here is to bring post-democracy into the equation. None of the authors I have just mentioned pay much heed to the problems of post-democratic politics. The term 'post-democracy' does not feature in their arguments. Mine is premised on its strictures. In calling for more effective and more just celebrity advocacy, I am doing no more than following Crouch's specific endorsement that we work with existing elite governance structures in pursuit of egalitarian causes. 'Even if the causes supported by egalitarians are always weaker than those of larger corporations, they are weaker still if they stay out of the lobby.'[41] To some extent, therefore, the ideas above that democracies can promote effective development policies require modifying in the light of the constraints of post-democracy. It is quite possible that, en route to promoting stronger democratic deliberation about development policy, *more* elite lobbying may be required.

Conclusion

Celebrity is an integral part of an iniquitous economic system that produces profound inequality. The rules of the game of that system are currently built, on a global scale, in ways that favour the wealthiest nations and that make it harder for the poorer nations to pursue policies that will help them to close the gap on the richer countries. Celebrity is not, however, responsible for these unjust rules, nor is it responsible for the economic thinking that maintains them.

Celebrity is also part of iniquitous political systems in which rule by elite and quiescent publics facilitate inegalitarian politics that favour the interests of the wealthy firms who are able to put more money into furthering their interests than are poorer groups. Celebrity colours and shapes those relationships, but it does not drive them. Their origins lie in the structure of the world economy and the nature of the global economic policies promulgated by states and promoted by corporate interests.

Celebrity is surprisingly ineffective at communicating with publics. It does not command their attention and appears relatively infrequently in their commitments to good causes. Its presence in campaigns simulates public involvement; it does not, necessarily, signify it. And yet celebrity power is believed in. Celebrity belongs to the media world that is somehow by definition glamorous to everyone else, if not necessarily to you.

For all these reasons, therefore, celebrity advocacy for development causes is problematic, but it may be redeemable. It may, or particular individuals may, become a force for egalitarian politics and globally fairer economic structures. The odds of that happening, as I hope this summary makes plain, are slim. Let us see what the architects, directors, designers, backstage staff, actors and audiences of the current celebrity-charity edifice can produce.

Notes

1 Richey and Ponte, forthcoming.
2 cf. Hulme, 2010: 185–9 and Chapter 7 in that book.
3 It is important to remember too that these are general tendencies, not absolute rules.

4 Source 70.
5 Unfortunately one of the clearest cases where celebrity has raised voice, awareness and political activism is the Save Darfur Campaign in the US. This is also one of the more cautionary tales of celebrity activism. For the campaign certainly did successfully raise awareness about a relatively insignificant part of the world that would not normally make the headlines. In doing so it has facilitated interventions whose impact on conflict resolution are at best ambivalent. Its awareness raising has not necessarily also promoted effective understanding of the problems on the ground (cf. Budabin, forthcoming).
6 cf. Nash, 2008.
7 Please see Lucy Bennett's work here for a good point of departure (Bennett, 2012). Jackson also reports that 20,000 U2 fans wrote in support of Bono's lobbying on HIV/AIDS expenditure in 2002 (Jackson, N., 2008).
8 Hulme, having reviewed the processes and institutions that have governed the battles against global poverty in recent decades, argues that we need a gradual change of attitudes so that global poverty in an affluent world becomes abhorrent (Hulme, 2010: 226). He recommends a plethora of strategies to do so, including 'new campaigns, lobbying strategic events, links to religions, re-shaping school curricula, supporting leaders, working with celebrities and other devices (ibid.).' The celebrity strategy may well be one to use carefully.
9 Riddell, 2007: 296–7. Similarly, Hulme takes succour from the way neoliberal economists find it necessary to attack NGOs' lobbying. Previously, they could just ignore them (Hulme, 2008: 338).
10 Mitlin *et al.*, 2007.
11 Mitlin *et al.*, 2007: 1703.
12 Chang, 2003; Chang and Grabel, 2004.
13 Chang, 2007.
14 Stiglitz, 2002.
15 Rodrik, 2007, 2011. David Hulme best puts the damage done by this neoliberal thinking into perspective. The financial crisis caused by subprime mortgages and derivatives, and by implication the financial liberalisation and lack of regulation that underlie them, have caused '[a]round 200 million people have slid back into extreme poverty between 2005 and 2008; preventable infant deaths have increased by 200,000 to 400,000 each year; an estimated 44 million people will suffer permanent damage (physiological or cognitive) caused by malnutrition; and the number of those experiencing hunger is rapidly increasing (from 850 million in 2007 to 960 million by 2008, and probably over 1 billion by late 2009)' (Hulme, 2010: 211).
16 Mitlin *et al.*, 2007: 1708.
17 Mallaby, 2004.
18 Sachs, 2005: 218.
19 Hulme, 2010: 227.
20 It is possible that all the major British political parties retained high aid expenditure in their election promises because of Make Poverty History's public prominence (Source 40). This is, however, a hard proposition to test.
21 Hill, 2010.
22 Scott, 2001: 130.
23 Mawdsley, 2007: 489.
24 Mawdsley, 2007: 504; Soederberg, 2004.
25 Note that Mawdsley also recognises that the poor may well benefit in some way from the moneys donated through the Millennium Challenge Account, through improved transport infrastructure and schooling opportunities. But her point is that these benefits to the poor are not sufficiently explicitly planned by the compacts signed with each recipient country.
26 Dienst, 2011: 117–18. cf. Browne: 'Bono's version of America's idea, in short, is fully in keeping with his own campaigning practice: rich and powerful men making decisions and creating change that they say is in the interests of everyone else – who may or may not get a say in the matter.' Browne, 2013, Kindle location: 2795–7.

27 Goodman, 2010.
28 Richey and Ponte, 2011.
29 cf. Benthall, 2010 [1993].
30 Kapoor, 2012: 73; Youde, 2009.
31 Mukherjee and Banet-Weiser, 2012.
32 King, 2006.
33 At a discussion panel at the Association of American Geographers in 2011 that was debating Richey and Ponte's book.
34 Some of my more radical interviewees were keen to tell me of incidents of celebrity lobbying that they felt were effective ways of being radical and pushing radical causes, just as they were keen to remonstrate against weaker forms. For example, see www.guardian.co.uk/commentisfree/2011/mar/11/cultural-boycott-west-bank-wall (viewed 5 February 2013).
35 Sources 5, 23, 38, 40, 55, 61, 71, 80.
36 Source 93.
37 Richey, personal communication, 13 September 2013.
38 Green, 2008.
39 Mitlin *et al.*, 2007: 1708.
40 For example, with respect to domestic social safeguards (Rodrik, 2011: 254–5) and regulations on international financial transactions (Rodrik, 2011: 264–5).
41 Crouch, 2004: 122.

AFTERWORD

This book came together faster than anything I have ever written. The first draft emerged in a whirlwind of writing, reading and ideas at the end of 2012. It could do so because I was living undisturbed in the backwaters of rural Tanzania. I was going through the slow process of setting up research permissions and contacts during a period of sabbatical research and had time to write. I put the manuscript down after completing all but the concluding chapter and settled into the sort of traditional anthropological programme of research that I first began in this country in 1995. I visited homes, listened to histories, participated in meetings and the business of day-to-day life, enjoyed happenchance discussions and just 'hanging out'. I tried to learn Iraqw (my wife's mother tongue), which proved to be one of the most complex and obstreperous languages I have ever encountered. The work gave my neighbours a time to quiz me on all sorts of issues – what development means to my compatriots, why do we have so much of it, what do Europeans think of Africa (it was embarrassing answering that one), what I was doing here, and why I could not pronounce easy words like *garmawookáheéke*.

All of this gave me a useful distance from the celebrity advocacy that I had been writing about and made the actual business of living in 'developing' countries more prominent in my mind. I am not claiming any special empathetic insight as a result of this time in Tanzania. Empathy is not my strong point. Nor am I claiming the authority of any 'authentic' experience of living through the challenging experiences of life in the rural South. Mine was a comfortable existence – indeed, princely by local standards. I was drawing my university salary and staying in a large comfortable house with decent water supplies, electricity and my own quiet office space. My point is just that this field research on a topic far-removed from celebrity put this book in a different perspective.

One of the joys of anthropological fieldwork is that it does not just look at the world through the lens of 'poverty' or 'development'. Many of my more elderly

166 Afterword

neighbours here grew up in times when their status and fortune was reflected in the vigour of their families, farming and herds. Land, I am told, was plentiful. The forest rivers draining Mount Hanang behind us were full and clean. There were few schools and hospitals, no tarred road or phone coverage. The infrastructure required for a prosperous state was even more parlous than it is now. But elders here did not necessarily define themselves according to modern criteria involving education, large brick houses, aluminium roofs or electricity. They may well have been 'undeveloped', but they were not poor.

There are still elements of that condition present. What the Wilsons, working in this country decades ago, called 'an enlargement of scale' in people's worldviews and terms of reference is still unfolding.[1] Indigenous definitions of wealth and poverty still apply, and apply differently from the framework imposed by the development industries.

But it is also true that many people's scales here are now large. They compare themselves to the Northern lifestyles portrayed in films and Western music videos shown constantly in the smallest settlements, and aspire to different futures from their grandparents. Modernity has been promulgated by the Tanzanian state for over fifty years. Modern understandings of the good life, and of poverty, have been internalised. Most of my neighbours want 'development'. An anthropology of life here is also an anthropology of poverty.[2]

The vast majority of people here know that they do not have *uwezo* (means), that the *watajiri* (the rich) in the village are few and have, comparatively speaking, comfortable and easy lives. They know that getting their children through school, or to clinics and struggling with the dictates of farm labour is hard. Few would call themselves *maskini* (poor), but many recognise that they have to have strategies to become more prosperous (young households) or to delay the decline as their powers wane (the older homes).[3]

So when I came to write the Conclusion that you have just read, doing so was depressing, for all that is missing in it. For I could not summarise from all this research that celebrity advocacy for international development makes any noticeable difference to public attitudes towards development, towards cosmopolitanism and the needs of distant strangers. It has made only a limited difference to the structures of global society and economy which produce poverty and inequality. It has not effectively challenged the thinking and ideas that have continually made it so difficult for poorer countries to pursue viable and coherent development policies.

I would love it to be otherwise. I would love celebrity advocacy to be producing deeper and stronger responses among increasing numbers of the British public. I would love politicians to be listening to NGO messages and lobbying in a way that made a significant difference to economic relations between rich and poor countries. I would love corporate relationships with celebrities and NGOs to be defined by a deep and rigorous concern for others, rather than their deep and rigorous concern for brand. I would love it because these are good things to achieve, whatever the actual personalities involved might be like.

I feel strongly because I write this Afterword still surrounded by the evidence of decades of poverty and failed development, and with my notebooks and brain full of the stories of people who have had to live with it. My children's primary school has classrooms with holes in the walls for windows, no electricity and a shortage of teachers. We have lost my sister-in-law (to AIDS-related complications) and her granddaughter (to pneumonia at just two weeks old) while living here. All around us on the farms most people's time is consumed tending maize and bean fields with hand hoes. Any shortage of labour through sickness, drunkenness or failings in social networks will mean suffering later in the year, for there is no social security or other safety net here. Mentally and physically handicapped children in neighbouring houses, and their families, have no state provision to assist them. Local government institutions are locally renowned for their weakness and failings.

I am surrounded too by stories of resilience and self-reliance, of homes carefully husbanding their resources, planning their families, investing in assets, working hard on their farms, borrowing money to invest in business, setting up loaning associations and, as we say here, *wanapambana na maisha* – they are taking life by the horns.[4] Few people go hungry, many are investing in good houses and children's education. There is colour, laughter, fun, relaxation, freedom and delight in so much of what we do day by day. The home-built church just five minutes from our house rings with song and drumbeats on many evenings, and much of the night over the weekend, drowning out the hyenas calling from the forest reserve. But there is also poverty. This is a part of the world that has much to gain from fair international economic policies.

I am under no illusion that prosperity buys happiness, or that it is likely to reduce intra-country inequality here. Nor will it fix the problematic family relations and qualities of character that shape so strongly the immediate experience and causes of poverty here. But I would still dearly love something powerful, enduring and effective to transform the prospects of my children's friends, and to make the old age of my friends and relatives here as secure as mine is likely to be.

Having examined how celebrity advocacy in so much detail and having explored the development problems it tries to tackle, I find much of the complaint and carping against celebrity dissatisfying. It does not matter how annoying Bono is, or how rich he or any other celebrities happen to be. It does not matter if their diplomacy can appear gauche. Nor does it matter how much nausea *Hello!* magazine induces, or how luxurious Elton John's white tie parties are. What matters, the only thing that matters, is the difference celebrity advocates make to global inequality. They may be symbols of an unequal order and happy to play that role; they may make inequality easier to sustain because they encourage acquiescence, and make it harder to imagine alternatives. Their parties and gatherings may constitute some of the means by which economic inequality leads to inequalities of power and influence. But the issue for me is: are they at the roots of inequality? Or, as I suspect, are they merely a more decorative consequence of more powerful engines of inequality? If there are economic and political relationships at work – trade rules, economic

168 Afterword

policies, taxation regimes – that are more directly responsible for more inequality than celebrity, then celebrity is not the most important thing to be worried about.

However, this reasoning also means that if celebrity advocacy is not targeting the main drivers of inequality, then it is at best a distraction and at worst irrelevant. Thus far I doubt that celebrity advocacy has made a sufficiently appreciable difference to the core development problems it needs to address. This is despite the considerable efforts of the celebrities and NGOs involved. I would love, and certainly my current neighbours would love, for them to be more successful. But if celebrity advocacy cannot support effective development advocacy and policy, then what purpose does it serve?

Dan Brockington
Sagong
15 August 2013

Notes

1 Wilson, 1971.
2 cf. Ferguson, 2006.
3 All the terms in this paragraph are Swahili.
4 The translation (from Swahili) is a loose one.

APPENDIX ONE

Methods

There are many ways to study celebrity. For an excellent introduction, see Jessica Evans and David Hesmondalgh's work.[1] Here I explain what I have been able to do, and what not, and what caution and further work is required with these findings. More information and copies of the questionnaire used are also available on the research website.[2]

Interviews

This book is not based on any personal experience of working with celebrity. Its authority, such that it is, derives in the main from the interviews I conducted, and the methods by which I have checked my findings. NGO employees comprise the bulk of my informants (65 per cent). I talked to most of the major development NGOs in the UK, as well as a large number of smaller ones, and NGOs in other countries. I also talked to NGOs who worked with celebrity but not in development or humanitarian causes. Within these organisations I spoke to celebrity liaison officers, campaign organisers, press officers and directors. I asked them about their work with celebrity in their current organisation and with previous employers. I also asked them to recommend other people I could talk to. The result of this mixture of purposive and snowball sampling was that I learned about experiences of working with celebrity from over 140 individual episodes of employment in 87 different NGOs, as well as talking to over 50 people who had worked as media professionals or in the celebrity industries as agents, managers or publicists (Table A1.1). I also received copies of twenty interviews conducted by Christian Lahusen on celebrity advocacy in the early 1990s.[3]

170 Appendix one

TABLE A1.1 Country and organisation experience of the interviewees consulted in this research

Region	NGOs	Celebrity industries[1]	Media	Other[2]	Total
Australasia	2				2
Asia	2				2
South America	2				2
North America	14	6		2	22
Africa	13	1			14
Europe excl. UK	5				5
UK	109	24	25	14	172
Total	147	31	25	16	219

1 Includes intermediary industries negotiating links between celebrities and NGOs.
2 Includes government officials, researchers and corporate leaders.

The interviews, and my writing-up of them, took place under the constraint that I was writing about a world with which I was not familiar. To ensure the accuracy of the accounts resulting and my interpretation and treatment of interview material I sent my interview notes to my informants before I used them. I also checked my early pieces of writing with them. I did so because I wanted to check that my representation of these interactions was not alien to the people who had told me about it. Fortunately, however, the material coming from the interviews made writing relatively straightforward, and I received strongly positive feedback from my interviewees, who often recognised in other people's words, things that they thought or felt themselves (Box A1.1). There was thus a common experience which, even though I had not observed it directly, I was able to represent. These iterative interview techniques continued by means of the research website I set up (www.celebrityanddevelopment.wordpress.com) which allowed me to release initial findings for comment and criticism.[4] Towards the end of the fellowship new postings would result in hundreds of hits.

These interviews and the engagement with the website gave me some insights into how celebrity advocacy was done and how it worked with elite groups and corporate interests. I also used important contributions to the grey literature, including Cox's report on campaigning which is based on over 300 interviews with high level development professionals, government ministers and some celebrities, and a report of a meeting held at the Brookings Blum roundtable in 1997.[5]

Surveys

To explore public attitudes to celebrity I have reanalysed the 2005 survey (n = 1,017) undertaken by Couldry and Markham on forms of media use (including engagement with celebrity outputs). In collaboration with Spensor Henson of the Institute for Development Studies (IDS) in Brighton, I have replicated that survey

---

BOX A1.1 Interviewee responses to circulated papers

Well – I was just going to have a quick look at that I ended up reading the whole thing! It was a great comfort to know that we are all experiencing the same thing! I kept reading quotes and thinking 'I must have said that!' but it wasn't me.

The bits that you reference me were accurate ... and the other bits from other people were really pretty much things I would happy if I had said!

It's a great read and really interesting to see all the comments from the other charities, so much rings a bell!

Overall, very well-thought out, organised and delivered. Interestingly, I agree with all of it – so great to know that experiences are common.

You shed great light on the age old 'getting it' which is so hard to describe, but interesting that those of us who 'get it' know exactly what you mean. NICE WORK and CONGRATULATIONS!

Well, you have done a great job so far! I don't think I had any great thoughts to feedback, because you had covered everything so thoroughly and fairly.

Sorry to have taken literally months to read your paper. It's excellent. Really a clear argument and very insightful – and also very much reflects my own experience in the field.

Source: Personal emails. Note that in putting this box together I have not been selective and filtered out the negative criticism. This does fairly represent the tone of what I have received with respect to the papers I circulated.

(n = 1,111), and conducted another survey specifically on celebrity advocacy (n = 1,999) on the Public Opinion Monitor, a panel database maintained by the IDS.[6] These populations are skewed to older and male respondents, so answers have been weighted appropriately. The survey questions and sample characteristics are provided on the research website, along with a more detailed discussion of the results obtained from it.

Focus groups

I have complemented those quantitative surveys with qualitative work on nine focus groups, four in London and five in Manchester of different ages, socioeconomic status, gender compositions and attitudes to development (Table A1.2). Altogether

TABLE A1.2 The characteristics of the focus groups

Group no.	No. of members	Gender	Socioeconomic status	Age	Family	Race	Location	Attitude to development	Recruited
1	7	Mixed	(B)C1C2	50–65	'Emptying nesters'	White British	London	Very concerned	Professionally
2	6	Male	C2D(E)	18–30	Pre-family	White British	London	Fairly concerned	Professionally
3	7	Mixed	C2D(E)	30–45	Children at home	White British	London	Fairly concerned	Professionally
4	8	Female	C1C2	18–30	Pre-family	Mostly white British	London	Ambivalent	Professionally
5	8	Mixed	C2D	30–45	Children at home	White British	Manchester	Ambivalent	Professionally
6	7	Female	BC1C2	18–30	Pre-family	White British	Manchester	Ambivalent	Professionally
7	5	Female	ABC1	30–45	Children at home	African and Afro-Caribbean	Manchester	Very concerned	Friendship network
8	7	Male	BC1C2	47+	Post-family	White British	Manchester	Ambivalent	Friendship network
9	5	Male	(B)C1C2	18–30	Pre-family	White British	Manchester	Fairly concerned	Professionally

sixty people took part. This small number of people, and the multiple variables that differentiate them, mean that in no way is this a representative sample. We cannot extrapolate from these findings to particular sectors of the population. That would involve making judgements based on very small numbers. I have, however, drawn attention to views that were rare across all the groups and those that were common or universal. I have spoken to enough people to spot isolated opinions that are not likely to be widely held in a larger sample. When such diverse groups as I have spoken agree on something, that is likely to be important.

The groups started with a discussion of their patterns of media consumption and particularly what television programmes they watched. This allowed us to gauge interest in and awareness of reality TV programmes and the big telethons (Comic Relief, Sport Relief, Children in Need), which we called 'the big events' in the group discussions. We then asked people to name the charities they supported and talked about any famous people they associated with those charities; this merged into a discussion of the pre-group task all had been completed, which was to think of examples of celebrity advocacy which had worked, and not worked, for them. These are referred to as 'heavens' and 'hells' by the groups. Finally, we presented the groups with different examples of celebrity advocacy and asked them to categorise them as they saw fit.

The first four groups (in London) were conducted by Alice Fenyoe of TWResearch, with me in attendance. Alice has many years' experience on groups and particularly on group work for the development sector. She spent much time doing work with Martin Scott and his research with the IBT, as well as with Andrew Darnton when exploring the impacts of Make Poverty History. I then conducted the next four groups in Manchester using the same format. Finally, Alice conducted the ninth group, also in Manchester.

The individuals in these groups were generally characterised by their lack of personal interaction with the famous. One group member had met some musicians while working at a record company. Another encounter was just a tweet. But apart from that, the people we met in these focus groups did not interact with the famous. Their encounters with celebrity and celebrity advocacy were all mediated.

Newspaper and magazine surveys

To examine trends in the portrayal of celebrity I have undertaken three surveys of newspapers and magazines. First, I conducted an electronic search of newspapers' use of the word 'celebrity' (and similar terms). Second, I complemented that with a sample of newspaper coverage of celebrity matters in actual physical copies of papers for one week in May from 1981. These data have helped me to understand the long-term trends in coverage of celebrity affairs. To examine trends in celebrity advocacy specifically I examined a sample of issues of *Hello!* magazine to explore trends of their coverage of development issues. I have also analysed the records of the website Look to the Stars which reports on the charitable actions of celebrities, the weekly reports of *Third Sector* (the trade journal of British NGOs) on the same,

174 Appendix one

and the biweekly reports of the Red Pages which announce new liaisons between celebrities and brands, charities or agencies and publicists. These gave me some insight into the current patterns of celebrity advocacy generally.

Limitations

As Couldry recognises, there are many forms of 'practice' around any given media which could be studied as part of an analysis of media practices.[7] It would be difficult to capture them all in one study. My work misses several aspects, which I hope others will be able to attend to. I have not undertaken participant observation of the parties, fundraising events or field-trips undertaken by celebrity ambassadors. I have not been present during negotiations about celebrity support for good causes. Richer and more detailed accounts than mine certainly may be possible. Also, I have not undertaken specific studies of fan groups with respect to their responses to the celebrity advocacy of their stars.[8] Given the variety of celebrities grouped under the banner of celebrity advocacy, this gap is problematic. Another omission is the lack of textual analyses of celebrity advocacy.

In all instances, the absence of these methods is no comment that I think them somehow unimportant. Quite the opposite, I tend to value them highly and am rather jealous of the insights their practitioners are able to glean. For instance, I am aware that there is a debate in celebrity studies about the importance of textual analysis.[9] However, I am not making an intervention to that debate here by not using those methods. I have learned a great deal from existing textual analyses.[10] I will continue to do so. I felt I could make other contributions. I have tried to do the things I would be better at, and had time to do.

I also hope that others will pursue a more differentiated approach to different celebrities' work than I have been able to. As Dyer notes, celebrities may be manufactured but the process of manufacture is fraught and varied, and the role that celebrities themselves play in that can be equally varied.[11] As I show in Chapter 5, the sheer variety of celebrity activism suggests a prominent role for individual celebrities in shaping this aspect of their public image. I do not think that I have captured that variety well here. My excuse is that I have found more than enough to do examining the structure, history and organisation of the current terrain, and some of the general characteristics of public and elite responses to this generally recognised thing called 'celebrity advocacy'. As Marsh and colleagues observed, there is little systematic work here on which I could build for this study.[12] My hope is that this work can provide the foundations for more variegated work in due course.

There is a danger that these methods could be inferred as offering some sort of dismissal of the study of popular culture or recognition of its importance in people's lives. I have not done the things that those who study popular culture tend to do, and my conclusions that celebrity is, in the round, unengaging, might encourage that inference. Please do not think that. In the first instance this book is itself is a study of popular culture – it is about how celebrity advocacy is constructed and consumed. In the second instance, I myself think that it is vital to study popular culture and have learned a great deal from those who do.[13] In fact, this book builds on one of the basic premises of studies of popular culture – that we cannot generalise responses across generic audiences, but rather we have to explore the specificities of audience response and engagement with popular culture.[14] Doing this, I suggest, could also entail considering the *lack* of response to some forms of popular culture among some audiences. There are good reasons why studies of popular culture, or celebrity, have not dwelled on such lacks. They generally deal with people who engage in these cultural forms. But I think we need to open up a space to think about these non-, or muted, responses. For where the popular is merely populist, and not actually that popular at all, and where it is also overtly political, then lack of engagement becomes interesting. It becomes particularly interesting if this lack of engagement is not recognised.

Notes

1 Evans and Hesmondalgh, 2005.
2 Available at: www.celebrityanddevelopment.wordpress.com/methods-used-in-the-book-celebrity-advocacy-and-international-development (viewed 25 February 2014).
3 Lahusen, 1996.
4 Available at: www.celebrityanddevelopment.wordpress.com (viewed 25 February 2014).
5 Brainard and LaFleur, 2007; Cox, 2011.
6 Actual sample sizes were 1,753 and 2,842 respectively, but age and gender data for the respondents are incomplete and since answers have to be weighted by age and gender, the other answers have been discarded.
7 Couldry, 2012: 43.
8 Lucy Bennett's work on Lady Gaga is particularly interesting in that regard (Bennett, forthcoming). cf. also Fraser and Brown, 2002.
9 Boone and Vickers, 2010; Turner, 2010.
10 Dyer, 2004 [1986]; Yrjölä, 2009; Tester, 2010; Scott, 2011; Brough, 2012; Chouliaraki, 2012; Dogra, 2012; Gotham, 2012; Molina-Guzmán, 2012; Mukherjee, 2012; Sandvoss *et al.*, 2012; Trope, 2012.
11 Dyer, 2004 (1986): 4–5.
12 Marsh *et al.*, 2010.
13 There are many excellent authors but among my favourites are Hermes (1995, 2005), Stacey (1994), Farrell (2012) and Dyer (1979, 2004 [1986]).
14 See, for example, Johansson here with respect to particularities of celebrity consumption (Johansson, 2006).

APPENDIX TWO

Research on celebrity endorsers

There are just three points to make here. The first is that research on celebrity endorsement has been dominated by work on US citizens and especially US college students for much of its history. The evidence for this is presented in at the end of the text of this Appendix (Table A2.3); the sources from which it draws follow that table. Note that *no* research of this type was conducted outside the US before 1998.

The second is that this matters because US citizens and US college students are much more celebrity credible than people who are neither. This fact comes from Amos *et al.*'s meta-study of celebrity endorsement research. They observed that studies of students are much more likely to find significant celebrity effects than studies of non-student populations, and that studies of US consumers are more likely to observe significant effects of celebrity endorsement than consumers living in other parts of the world.[1]

I present below revised data from that study supplied by the authors.[2] These show the distribution of effects by population group. It is clear that student populations are highly likely to respond significantly to celebrity advertisements as 83 per cent of effects are significant among student samples (Table A3.1). Non-students are more evenly split: 53 per cent of effects are significant. In US populations 80 per cent of effects are significant; in non-US populations only 43 per cent are. In both cases these differences in distribution are statistically robust (χ^2 tests on the significance of these differences are reported beneath the table). Or in plain English, US populations and student populations are very likely to respond in significant ways to celebrity advertisements. The presence of celebrity in an advertisement affects the way they respond. Non-US populations are more than likely not to respond in significant ways, whereas non-student populations are more equivocal.

Appendix two **177**

TABLE A2.1 Distribution of effects of celebrity advertising from Amos *et al.*, 2008

Sample characteristics	All effects	Significant effects	Non-significant effects
Student	157	129	28
Non-student	145	77	68
	302	206	96
US	187	150	37
Non-US	127	55	72
	314	205	109

Chi Square test results:
Student/non-student: $\chi^2 = 29.36$; df = 1; p < 0.001
US/Non-US: $\chi^2 = 45.45$; df = 1; p < 0.001

Data courtesy of Clinton Amos, 5 October 2012.

TABLE A2.2 Citation count of different sample types

	Non-student	Student	Total
Non-US	52	78	130
US	725	2,136	2,861
Total	**777**	**2,214**	**2,991**

The third point is that the US-based literature has been more influential among researchers than work outside the US. Papers based on US subjects account for 96 per cent of all citations (Table A2.2). Those based on US students account for 72 per cent of citations, whereas US students constitute 60 per cent of the collective sample. Just 2 per cent of citations refer to articles about subjects who are not US residents and not students.

Such a dominance is to be expected given that papers earlier on in this sequence could only cite US-based work; none other existed. However, since papers based on other countries have begun to be published, they have tended to be cited less than papers published based on US subjects which were published in equivalent years. Papers based on non-US populations are cited on average 0.6 times for each year of their existence, those on US populations 2.1 times per year.

From these three points I conclude that the literature on celebrity endorsement has been strongly influenced by US subjects and by US college students in particular in ways that make it unrepresentative of the rest of the world. Other countries may be more celebrity credible than the US (South Korea, Japan) or less celebrity credible (parts of Europe).[3] But in order to tell we will need surveys that do not employ US subjects.

TABLE A2.3 The sampling of different countries and populations over time in the celebrity advertising literature

Year	Non-US		US		Total	Cum'tive Total	Cumulative totals		Cumulative proportions		
	Non-student	Student	Non-student	Student			Cumulative US subjects	Cumulative US students	US subjects %	US students of US subjects %	US students of all subjects %
1951	–	–	–	223	223	223	223	223	100	100	100
1976	–	–	–	150	150	373	373	373	100	100	100
1977	–	–	200	–	200	573	573	373	100	65	65
1978	–	–	75	166	241	814	814	539	100	66	66
1979	–	–	360	–	360	1,174	1,174	539	100	46	46
1981	–	–	–	99	99	1,273	1,273	638	100	50	50
1982	–	–	–	135	135	1,408	1,408	773	100	55	55
1983	–	–	196	335	531	1,939	1,939	1,108	100	57	57
1985	–	–	–	277	277	2,216	2,216	1,385	100	63	63
1989	–	–	139	–	139	2,355	2,355	1,385	100	59	59
1990	–	–	265	852	1,117	3,472	3,472	2,237	100	64	64
1991	–	–	343	268	611	4,083	4,083	2,505	100	61	61
1992	–	–	100	–	100	4,183	4,183	2,505	100	60	60
1994	–	–	–	1,446	1,446	5,629	5,629	3,951	100	70	70

1996	–	–	–	147	147	5,776	5,776	4,098	100	71	71
1997	–	–	–	1,086	1,086	6,862	6,862	5,184	100	76	76
1998	100	–	–	842	942	7,804	7,704	6,026	99	78	77
1999	–	–	–	200	200	8,004	7,904	6,226	99	79	78
2000	–	–	152	425	577	8,581	8,481	6,651	99	78	78
2001	141	–	–	–	141	8,722	8,481	6,651	97	78	76
2002	–	–	–	864	864	9,586	9,345	7,515	97	80	78
2003	–	880	–	106	986	10,572	9,451	7,621	89	81	72
2004	–	130	218	249	597	11,169	9,918	7,870	89	79	70
2005	280	706	–	232	1,218	12,387	10,150	8,102	82	80	65
2006	–	249	–	339	588	12,975	10,489	8,441	81	80	65
2007	–	500	–	962	1,462	14,437	11,451	9,403	79	82	65
2008	631	342	566	1,556	3,095	17,532	13,573	10,959	77	81	63
2009	100	–	–	1,409	1,509	19,041	14,982	12,368	79	83	65
2010	316	319	–	–	635	19,676	14,982	12,368	76	83	63
2011	1,530	–	700	503	2,733	22,409	16,185	12,871	72	80	57
2012	–	172	–	1,244	1,416	23,825	17,429	14,115	73	81	59
Total	**3,098**	**3,298**	**3,314**	**14,115**	**23,825**	–	–	–	–	–	–

180 Appendix two

The following sources were used to compile Table A2.3 above, listed in order of publication date:

Hovland and Weiss, 1951; Friedman *et al.*, 1976; Fireworker and Friedman, 1977; Friedman *et al.*, 1978; Sternthal *et al.*, 1978; Friedman and Friedman, 1979; Mowen and Brown, 1981; Freiden, 1982; Klebba and Unger, 1982; Atkin and Block, 1983; DeSarbo and Harshman, 1985; Kahle and Homer, 1985; Kamins, 1989; Kamins *et al.*, 1989; Kamins, 1990; Misra and Beatty, 1990; Ohanian, 1990; Langmeyer and Walker, 1991; Ohanian, 1991; Gail *et al.*, 1992; Heath *et al.*, 1994; Kamins and Gupta, 1994; Lynch and Schuler, 1994; Moore *et al.*, 1994; Tripp *et al.*, 1994; Basil, 1996; Basil and Brown, 1997; Nataraajan and Chawla, 1997; O'Mahony and Meenaghan, 1997/8; Till and Shimp, 1998; Till and Busler, 1998; Cronley *et al.*, 1999; Lafferty and Goldsmith, 1999; Goldsmith *et al.*, 2000; Till and Busler, 2000; Erdogan *et al.*, 2001; Lafferty *et al.*, 2002; Louie and Obermiller, 2002; Stafford *et al.*, 2002; Pornpitakpan, 2003; Priester and Petty, 2003; Silvera and Austad, 2003; Batra and Homer, 2004; Bush *et al.*, 2004; Chao *et al.*, 2005; Forehand and Perkins, 2005; Jackson and Darrow, 2005; La Ferle and Choi, 2005; Biswas *et al.*, 2006; Money *et al.*, 2006; Choi and Rifon, 2007; Saleem, 2007; Van der Waldt *et al.*, 2007; Wood and Herbst, 2007; Austin *et al.*, 2008; Chan and Prendergast, 2008; Jackson, D. J., 2008; Klaus and Bailey, 2008; Lee and Thorson, 2008; Marshall *et al.*, 2008; Martin *et al.*, 2008; Siemens *et al.,* 2008; Till *et al.*, 2008; Zahaf and Anderson, 2008; Edwards and La Ferle, 2009; Koernig and Boyd, 2009; Samman *et al.*, 2009; Wheeler, 2009; White *et al.*, 2009; Eisend and Langner, 2010; Ranjbarian *et al.*, 2010; Veer *et al.*, 2010; Hung *et al.*, 2011; Newman *et al.*, 2011; Nownes, 2011; Pughazhendi *et al.*, 2011; Becker, 2012; Choi and Rifon, 2012; Miller and Allen, 2012; Rice *et al.*, 2012; Rossiter and Smidts, 2012.

Notes

1 Amos *et al.*, 2008: 221, 226.
2 Amos, personal communication, 5 February 2012.
3 Choi *et al.*, 2005; Money *et al.*, 2006; Silvera and Austad, 2003.

APPENDIX THREE

Trends in reporting on celebrity advocacy

Trends in reporting on celebrity and charity (a useful proxy for 'NGOs' in newspapers) in British newspapers show a dramatic increase from the early 1990s onwards (Figure A3.1). It is clear that this period has, in the main, been a time of increasing flourishing of relations between the two sectors. There are two important points to note about these dynamics. First, it is the charity sector which has

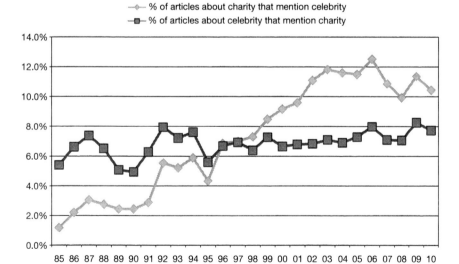

FIGURE A3.1 Trends in reporting celebrity and charity

Source: Lexus Nexus. See http://celebrityanddevelopment.wordpress.com/methods-used-in-the-book-celebrity-advocacy-and-international-development/ (viewed 25 February 2014) for details of how these data were compiled.

TABLE A3.1 Trends in celebrity appearance in a sample of British newspapers

Year	Pages examined	Sample size %	Articles examined	Proportion of articles mentioning celebrity %	First page where celebrity appears (as a proportion of all pages) %	Proportion of celebrity articles with pictures %	Celebrity appearance in *the* Guardian %	Celebrity appearance in *the* Mirror %
1981	310	28	1,689	8	17	67	4	15
1990	336	23	1,487	10	14	72	4	20
2000	361	22	946	16	13	83	16	27
2005	410	18	927	17	17	82	10	28
2008	360	17	846	21	9	85	14	33
2010	348	17	885	16	14	84	16	29
2012	297	18	930	22	10	81	19	28

Source: Author's Survey with Rachel Tavenor. We looked for the appearance of celebrity in *The Times*, the *Telegraph*, the *Guardian, Daily Mail*, the *Sun* and *Daily Mirror* in the first week of May in 1981, 1990, 2000, 2005, 2008, 2010 and 2012.

discovered celebrity more than the other way around. Articles about celebrity have only shown a slight increase in their mentions of charity. They also show that articles about celebrity have only shown a slight increase in associations with charity (the dark grey line). Their subject matter has not changed much. It is still about films, clothes, parties, relationships, and so on.[1] This finding was matched by my survey of development topics (especially field-trips) in *Hello!* magazine. These showed no trend in frequency or size over a twenty-one year period (1988–2009).[2]

Second, the years of increasing associations between celebrity and charities appear to have ceased in about 2005. This is part of a general trend in articles about celebrity which also stop increasing at about the same time. This was a surprising result but confirmed by a sample from the actual newspapers, which found that the proportion of articles on celebrity in these newspapers doubling between 1981 and 2000 (Table A3.1). Thereafter, the proportion has fluctuated, but has not maintained its earlier growth. There may be a slight tendency for articles about celebrity to move closer to the front of the newspaper, but it is not definitive. Nor have articles about celebrity become noticeably better illustrated since about 2000. Patterns vary from title to title (compare the *Guardian* and *Mirror*) but the overall trend is for the increase to cease.

Notes

1   Thrall and colleague's study of celebrity advocacy found that nearly 40 per cent of a random sample of celebrities on Celepedia did not support any particular cause (Thrall *et al.*, 2008). Some of the most famous figures they studied did not. Fame does not require a cause.
2   I really enjoyed spending all those hours in the Bodleian Library reading that magazine to reach such a conclusion.

REFERENCES

Agrawal, J. and W. A. Kamakura (1995) The economic worth of celebrity endorsers: an event study analysis. *The Journal of Marketing*, *59*(3): 56–62.

Alleyne, M. D. (2005) The United Nations' celebrity diplomacy. *SAIS Review*, *25*(1): 175–85.

Amos, C., G. Holmes and D. Strutton (2008) Exploring the relationship between celebrity endorser effects and advertising effectiveness. *International Journal of Advertising Research*, *27*(2): 209–34.

Anderson, A. (2011) Sources, media and modes of climate change communication: the role of celebrities. *WIREs Climate Change*, *2*(July/August): 535–46.

Anderson, N. (2008) Shoppers of the world unite: (RED)'s messaging and morality in the fight against African AIDS. *The Journal of Pan African Studies*, *2*(6): 32–54.

Anonymous (2009) Celebrity diplomacy: the effectiveness and value of celebrity diplomacy. The Norman Lear Center, USC Annenberg.

Anonymous (2012) Government decision-makers' perceptions of the impact of public opinion on international development. Findings from France, Germany, the U.K., and the U.S. *Building Support for International Development*. Washington, DC: InterMedia.

Arulampalam, W., P. G. Backus and J. Micklewright (2009) Donations for overseas development: evidence from a panel of UK charities. Unpublished MS in possession of the author.

Assayas, M. (2005) *Bono on Bono: Conversations with Michka Assayas*. London: Hodder & Stoughton.

Atkin, C. and M. Block (1983) Effectiveness of celebrity endorsers. *Journal of Advertising Research*, *23*(1): 57–61.

Atkinson, A. B., P. G. Backus, J. Micklewright, C. Pharoah and S. V. Schnepf, (2008) Charitable giving for overseas development: UK trends over a quarter century. Working Paper A08/09 Applications and Policy. Southampton Statistical Sciences Research Institute: University of Southampton.

Atkinson, A. B., P. G. Backus, J. Micklewright, C. Pharoah and S. V. Schnepf (2012) Charitable giving for overseas development: UK trends over a quarter century. *Journal of the Royal Statistical Society, Series A 175*(1): 167–90.

Austin, E. W., R. Van de Vord, B. E. Pinkleton and E. Epstein (2008) Celebrity endorsements and their potential to motivate young voters. *Mass Communication and Society*, *11*(4): 420–36.

Barbas, S. (2001) *Movie Crazy: Fans, Stars and the Cult of Celebrity*. New York: Palgrave Macmillan.

Barnett, M. (2011) *Empire of Humanity: A History of Humantarianism*. Ithaca, NY: Cornell University Press.

Barrett, M. (2000) *The World will Never Be the Same Again*. London: Jubilee 2000 Coalition.

Basil, M. D. (1996) Identification as a mediator of celebrity effects. *Journal of Broadcasting and Electronic Media, 40*: 478–95.

Basil, M. D. and W. Brown (1997) Marketing AIDS prevention: the differential impact hypothesis versus identification effects. *Journal of Consumer Psychology, 6*(4): 389–411.

Batra, R. and P. M. Homer (2004) The situational impact of brand image beliefs. *Journal of Consumer Psychology, 14*(3): 318–330.

Bebbington, A. J., S. Hickey and D. C. Mitlin (2008) *Can NGOs Make a Difference? The Challenge of Development Alternatives*. London: ZED Books.

Becker, A. B. (2012) Engaging celebrity? Measuring the impact of issue-advocacy messages on situational involvement, complacency and apathy. *Celebrity Studies, 3*(2): 213–31.

Beer, D. and R. Penfold-Mounce (2010) Researching glossy topics: the case of the academic study of celebrity. *Celebrity Studies, 1*(3): 360–65.

Benjamin, W. (1999) *Illuminations*. London: Pimlico.

Bennett, L. (2012) Fan activism for social mobilization: a critical review of the literature. *Transformative Works and Cultures, 10*: doi:10.3983/twc.2012.0346.

Bennett, L. (2013) 'If we stick together we can do anything': Lady Gaga fans in philanthropic and activist engagement through social media. *Celebrity Studies*. Available at: www.tandfonline.com/doi/full/10.1080/19392397.2013.813778#.UwvE8_YuLtI (viewed 25 February 2014).

Benthall, J. (2010 [1993]) *Disasters, Relief and the Media*. Wantage: Sean Kingston Publishing.

Berman, M. (1970 [2009]) *The Politics of Authenticity: Radical Individualism and the Emergence of Modern Society*. London: Verso.

Biccum, A. (2007) Marketing development: Live 8 and the production of the global citizen. *Development and Change, 38*(6): 1111–26.

Biccum, A. (2011) Marketing development: celebrity politics and the 'new' development advocacy. *Third World Quarterly, 32*(7): 1331–46.

Billig, M. (1998 [1992]) *Talking of the Royal Family*. London: Routledge.

Bishop, M. and M. Green (2008) *Philanthrocapitalism: How the Rich Can Save the World*. New York: Bloomsbury.

Biswas, D., A. Biswas and N. Das (2006) The differential effects of celebrity and expert endorsements on consumer risk perceptions: the role of consumer knowledge, perceived congruency, and product technology orientation. *Journal of Advertising, 35*(2): 17–31.

Black, M. (1992) *A Cause for Our Times: Oxfam, the First 50 Years*. Oxford: Oxford University Press.

Blair, T. (2010) *A Journey*. London: Cornerstone Digital.

Boltanski, L. (1999) *Distant Suffering: Morality, Media and Politics*. Cambridge: Cambridge University Press.

Boone, J. and N. Vickers (2010) Introduction: celebrity rites. *PMLA 126*(4): 900–11.

Boorstin, D. J. (1992 [1961]). *The Image: A Guide to Pseudo-Events in America*. New York: Vintage Books, Random House.

Boudioni, M., J. Mossman, A. L. Jones, G. Leydon and K. McPherson (1998) Celebrity's death from cancer resulted in increased calls to CancerBACUP. *British Medical Journal, 3*(17): 1016.

186 References

Bourdieu, P. (1977 [1972]) *Outline of a Theory of Practice* (trans R. Nice). Cambridge: Cambridge University Press.

Brainard, L. and V. LaFleur (2007) *Making Poverty History? How Activists, Philanthropists and the Public are Changing Human Development*. Washington, DC: Brookings Blum Roundtable.

Brockington, D. (2002) *Fortress Conservation: The Preservation of the Mkomazi Game Reserve, Tanzania*. Oxford: James Currey.

Brough, M. M. (2012) "Fair vanity": the visual culture of humanitarianism in the age of commodity activism. In *Commodity Activism: Cultural Resistance in Neoliberal Times*. R. Mukherjee and S. Banet-Weiser. London, New York: New York University Press.

Brown, W. J., M. D. Basil and M. C. Bocarnea (2003) Social influence of an international celebrity: responses to the death of Princess Diana. *Journal of Communication, 53*(4): 587–605.

Browne, H. (2013) *The Frontman: Bono (In the Name of Power)*. London: Verso.

Budabin, A. C. (2014) Diasporas as development partners for peace? The alliance between the Darfuri diaspora and the Save Darfur Coalition. *Third World Quarterly, 35*(1): 163–80.

Busby, J. W. (2007) Bono made Jesse Helms cry: Jubilee 2000, debt relief, and moral action in international politics. *International Studies Quarterly, 51*: 247–75.

Bush, A. J., C. A. Martin and V. D. Bush (2004) Sports celebrity influence on the behavioural intentions of generation Y. *Journal of Advertising Research, 44*(1): 108–18.

Cameron, J. and S. Fairbrass (2004) From development awareness to enabling effective support: the changing profile of development education in England. *Journal of International Development, 16*: 729–40.

Cameron, J. and A. Haanstra (2008) Development made sexy: how it happened and what it means. *Third World Quarterly, 29*(8): 1475–89.

Campbell, A. (2007) *The Blair Years*. London: Arrow Books.

Cantacuzino, M. (2000) *Out of Hollywood*. The Times Magazine.

Cashmore, E. (2011) Celebrity in the twenty-first century imagination. *Cultural and Social History, 8*(3): 405–13.

Chambers, C. (2006) *Here We Stand: Politics, Performers and Performance*. London: Nick Hern Books.

Chambers, R. (2005) Critical reflections of a development nomad. In *A Radical History of Development Studies*. U. Kothari. London: Zed Books.

Chan, K. and G. P. Prendergast (2008) Social comparison, imitation of celebrity models and materialism among Chinese youth. *International Journal of Advertising, 27*(5): 799–826.

Chang, H.-J. (2003) *Kicking Away the Ladder: Development Strategy in Historical Perspective*. London: Anthem Press.

Chang, H.-J. (2007) *Bad Samaritans: The Guilty Secrets of Rich Nations & the Threat to Global Prosperity*. London: Random House.

Chang, H.-J. and I. Grabel (2004) *Reclaiming Development: An Alternative Economic Policy Manual*. London: Zed Books.

Chao, P., G. Wührer and T. Werani (2005) Celebrity and foreign brand name as moderators of country-of-origin effects. *International Journal of Advertising, 24*(2): 173–92.

Chapin, M. (2004) A challenge to conservationists. *World Watch Magazine*, November/December: 17–31.

Chapman, S. and J. A. Leask (2001) Paid celebrity endorsement in health promotion: a case study from Australia. *Health Promotion International, 16*(4): 333–8.

Choi, S. M., W.-N. Lee and H.-J. Kim (2005) Lessons from the rich and famous: a cross-cultural comparison of celebrity endorsement in advertising. *Journal of Advertising, 34*(2): 85–98.

Choi, S. M. and N. J. Rifon (2007) Who is the celebrity in advertising? Understanding dimensions of celebrity images? *Journal of Popular Culture, 40*(2): 304–25.

Choi, S. M. and N. J. Rifon (2012) It is a match: the impact of congruence between celebrity image and consumer ideal self on endorsement effectiveness. *Psychology and Marketing, 29*(9): 639–50.

Chouliaraki, L. (2006) *The Spectatorship of Suffering.* London: Sage.

Chouliaraki, L. (2012) The theatricality of humanitarianism: a critique of celebrity advocacy. *Communication and Critical/Cultural Studies, 9*(1): 1–21.

Chouliaraki, L. (2013) *The Ironic Spectator: Solidarity in the Age of Post-Humanitarianism.* Cambridge: Polity Press.

Clark, D. J. (2004) The production of a contemporary famine image: the image economy, indigenous photographers and the case of Mekanic Philipos. *Journal of International Development, 16*: 693–704.

Cleasby, A. (1993) *Giving the Broader Picture: BBC TV and the Wider World.* Third World and Environment Broadcasting Project, 3WE.

Cleasby, A. (1995) *What in the World is Going On? British Television and Global Affairs.* Third World and Environment Broadcasting Project, 3WE.

Cleasby, A. (1996) *Watching the World: British Television and Audience Engagement with Developing Countries.* Third World and Environment Broadcasting Project, 3WE.

Cohen, S. (2001) *States of Denial: Knowing About Atrocities and Suffering.* Cambridge: Polity Press.

Collins, C. J. L., Z. Gariyo and T. Burdon (2001) Jubilee 2000: citizen action across the North–South divide. In *Global Citizen Action.* M. Edwards and J. Gaventa. London: Earthscan.

Cooper, A. F. (2007) Celebrity diplomacy and the G8: Bono and Bob as legitimate international actors. The Centre for International Governance Innovation. University of Waterloo, Working Paper 29.

Cooper, A. F. (2008a) Beyond one image fits all: Bono and the complexity of celebrity diplomacy. *Global Governance, 14*: 265–72.

Cooper, A. F. (2008b) *Celebrity Diplomacy.* Boulder, CO: Paradigm.

Corbridge, S. (1994) Post-Marxism and post-colonialism: the needs and rights of distant strangers. In *Rethinking Social Development: Theory, Research and Practice.* D. Booth. Harlow: Longman Scientific and Technical.

Corner, J. and D. Pels (2003) Introduction: the re-styling of politics. In *Media and the Restyling of Politics.* London: Sage.

Cottle, S. and D. Nolan (2007) Global humanitarianism and the changing aid-media field. *Journalism Studies, 8*(6): 862–78.

Couldry, N. (2001) The hidden injuries of media power. *Journal of Consumer Culture, 1*(2): 155–77.

Couldry, N. (2010) *Why Voice Matters: Culture and Politics after Neoliberalism.* London: Sage.

Couldry, N. (2012) *Media, Society, World: Social Theory and Digital Media Practice.* Cambridge: Polity Press.

Couldry, N., S. Livingstone and T. Markham (2010 [2007]) *Media Consumption and Public Engagement: Beyond the Presumption of Attention.* Basingstoke: Palgrave Macmillan.

Couldry, N. and T. Markham (2007) Celebrity culture and public connection: bridge or chasm? *International Journal of Cultural Studies, 10*(4): 403–21.

Cowen, M. and R. Shenton (1996) *Doctrines of Development.* London: Routledge.

Cox, B. (2011) Campaigning for international justice: learning lessons (1991–2011). Where next? (2011–2015). Available at: www.bond.org.uk/data/files/Campaigning_for_International_Justice_Brendan_Cox_May_2011.pdf (viewed 25 February 2014).

188 References

Cram, P., A. M. Fendrick, J. Inadomi, M. E. Cowen, D. Carpenter and S. Vijan (2003) The impact of a celebrity promotional campaign on the use of colon cancer screening. *Archives of Internal Medicine, 163*(13): 1601–5.

Crehan, K. (2002) *Gramsci, Culture and Anthropology*. Berkeley: University of California Press.

Crilly, R. (2010) *Saving Darfur: Everyone's Favourite African War*. London: Reportage Press.

Crompton, T. (2010) Common cause: the case for working with our cultural values. Godalming: WWF, UK.

Cronley, M. L., F. R. Kardes, P. Goddard and D. C. Houghton (1999) Endorsing products for the money: the role of the correspondence bias in celebrity advertising. *Advances in Consumer Research, 26*(1): 627–31.

Crouch, C. (2004) *Post-Democracy*. Cambridge: Polity Press.

Crouch, C. (2011) *The Strange Non-Death of Neoliberalism*. Cambridge: Polity Press.

Dahlgren, P. (2009) *Media and Political Engagement: Citizens, Communication and Democracy*. Cambridge: Cambridge University Press.

Darnton, A. (2006) Make Poverty History: end of year notes. From the 'Public Perceptions of Poverty' research programme. Andrew Darnton Research and Analysis.

Darnton, A. (2007) Global poverty and the public – desk research. Report 2: The UK public's perspective on global poverty. Andrew Darnton Research and Analysis.

Darnton, A. (2009) The public, DFID and support for development – a rapid review. Andrew Darnton Research and Analysis.

Darnton, A. (2011) Aid: why are we still stuck in 1985? *Guardian*.

Darnton, A. and A. Fenyoe (2007) Comic Relief 'Public Perceptions of Poverty'. Story research report. Andrew Darnton Research and Analysis.

Darnton, A. and M. Kirk (2011) Finding frames: new ways to engage the UK public in global poverty. London: BOND.

Davenport, L. E. (2009) *Jazz Diplomacy: Promoting America in the Cold War Era*. Jackson: University of Mississippi Press.

Davis, A. (2010) *Political Communication and Social Theory*. London: Routledge.

Davis, H. L. (2010) Feeding the world a line? Celebrity activism and ethical consumer practices from Live Aid to Product Red. *Nordic Journal of English Studies, 9*(3): 89–118.

DeSarbo, W. S. and R. A. Harshman, (1985) Celebrity and brand congruence analysis. *Current Issues and Research in Advertising, 8*: 17–52.

De Waal, A. (2008) The humanitarian carnival: a celebrity vogue. *World Affairs Fall*. Available at: www.worldaffairsjournal.org/articles/2008-Fall/full-DeWaal.html (viewed 25 February 2014).

Dienst, R. (2011) *The Bonds of Debt*. London: Verso.

Dieter, H. and R. Kumar (2008) The downside of celebrity diplomacy: the neglected complexity of development. *Global Governance, 14*: 259–64.

Doggett, P. (2007) *There's a Riot Going On: Revolutionaries, Rock Stars and the Rise and Fall of '60s Counter-Culture*. Edinburgh: Canongate.

Dogra, N. (2007) Reading NGOs visually: implications of visual management for NGO management. *Journal of International Development, 19*: 161–71.

Dogra, N. (2011) The mixed metaphor of 'third world woman': gendered representations of international development NGOs. *Third World Quarterly, 32*(2): 333–48.

Dogra, N. (2012) *Representations of Global Poverty: Aid, Development and International NGOs*. London: I.B.Tauris.

Douzinas, C. (2007) The many faces of humanitarianism. *Parrhesia, 2*: 1–28.

Dover, C. and S. Barnett (2004) The world on the box: international issues in news and factual programmes on UK television 1975–2003. Third World and Environment Project, 3WE.

References 189

Dowie, M. (2009) *Conservation Refugees: The Hundred-Year Conflict between Global Conservation and Native Peoples*. Cambridge, MA: MIT Press.

Duncombe, S. (2007) *Dream: Re-imagining Progressive Politics in an Age of Fantasy*. New York: The New Press.

Dyer, R. (1979) *Stars*. London: British Film Institute.

Dyer, R. (2004 [1986]) *Heavenly Bodies: Film Stars and Society*. London: Routledge.

Eagleton, T. (1991 [2007]) *Ideology: An Introduction*. London: Verso.

Edwards, M. and D. Hulme (1992) *Making a Difference: NGOs and Development in a Changing World*. London: Earthscan.

Edwards, M. and D. Hulme (1995) *Non-Governmental Organisations – Performance and Accountability: Beyond the Magic Bullet*. London: Earthscan.

Edwards, S. M. and C. La Ferle (2009) Does gender impact the perception of negative information related to celebrity endorsers? *Journal of Promotion Management*, 15(1–2): 22–35.

Eisend, M. and T. Langner (2010) Immediate and delayed advertising effects of celebrity endorsers' attractiveness and expertise. *International Journal of Advertising*, 29(4): 527–46.

Ekbladh, D. (2010) *The Great American Mission: Modernization and the Construction of an American World Order*. Princeton, NJ: Princeton University Press.

Epstein, J. (2005) Celebrity culture. *Hedgehog Review*, 7(1): 7–20.

Erdogan, B. Z. (1999) Celebrity endorsement: a literature review. *Journal of Marketing Management*, 15(4): 291–314.

Erdogan, B. Z., M. J. Baker and S. Tagg (2001) Selecting celebrity endorsers: the practitioners' perspective. *Journal of Advertising Research*, 41(3): 39–49.

Escobar, A. (1992) Planning. In *The Development Dictionary: A Guide to Knowledge as Power*. W. Sachs. Johannesburg, London and New York: Witwatersrand University Press, Zed Books.

Esteva, G. (1992) Development. In *The Development Dictionary: A Guide to Knowledge as Power*. W. Sachs. Johannesburg, London and New York: Witwatersrand University Press, Zed Books.

Evans, J. and D. Hesmondalgh (2005) *Understanding Media: Inside Celebrity*. Maidenhead, Open University Press.

Everett, R. (2006) *Red Carpets and Other Banana Skins*. London: Abacus.

Ewen, S. (1988) *All Consuming Images: The Politics of Style in Contemporary Culture*. New York: Basic Books.

Fall, P. L. and G. Tang (2006) Goodwill ambassadors in the United Nations system. Geneva, Joint Inspection Unit.

Farrell, N. (2012) Celebrity politics: Bono, Product (RED) and the legitimising of philanthrocapitalism. *The British Journal of Politics and International Relations*, 14: 392–406.

Fassin, D. (2012) *Humanitarian Reason: A Moral History of the Present*. Berkeley: University of California Press.

Femia, J. (1975) Hegemony and consciousness in the thought of Antonio Gramsci. *Political Studies*, 23: 29–48.

Ferguson, J. (2006) *Global Shadows: Africa in the Neoliberal World Order*. Durham, NC: Duke University Press.

Ferris, K. O. (2007) The sociology of celebrity. *Sociology Compass*, 1(1): 371–84.

Fielding, H. (1994) *Cause Celeb*. London: Picador.

Fireworker, R. B. and H. H. Friedman (1977) The effects of endorsement on product evaluation. *Decision Sciences*, 8: 576–83.

Fischlin, D. and A. Heble (2003) *Rebel Musics: Human Rights, Resistant Sounds and the Politics of Music Making*. Montreal: Black Rose Books.

Fisher, W. F. (1997) Doing good? The politics and anti-politics of NGO practices. *Annual Review of Anthropology*, 26: 439–64.

190 References

Flint, J. and A. De Waal (2008) *Darfur: A New History of a Long War.* London: Zed Books.

Forehand, M. R. and A. Perkins (2005) Implicit assimilation and explicit contrast: a set/reset model of response to celebrity voice-overs. *Journal of Consumer Research, 32*(3): 435–41.

Foreman, J. (2009) How Hollywood finds its charitable causes. *The Sunday Times,* 4 October.

Fowles, J. (1992) *Starstruck.* Washington, DC: Smithsonian Institution Press.

Franks, S. (2010a) The neglect of Africa and the power of aid. *International Communication Gazette, 72*(1): 71–84.

Franks, S. (2010b) Why Bob Geldof has got it wrong. *British Journalism Review, 21*(2): 51–6.

Fraser, B. P. and W. J. Brown (2002) Media, celebrities, and social influence: identification with Elvis Presley. *Mass Communication and Society, 5*(2): 183–206.

Freiden, J. B. (1982) An evaluation of spokesperson and vehicle source effects in advertising. *Current Issues & Research in Advertising, 5*(1): 77–86.

Friedman, H. H. and L. Friedman (1979) Endorser effectiveness by product type. *Journal of Advertising Research, 19*: 63–71.

Friedman, H. H., M. J. Santeramo and A. Traina (1978) Correlates of trustworthiness for celebrities. *Journal of the Academy of Marketing Science, 6*(4): 291–99.

Friedman, H. H., S. Termini and R. Washington (1976) The effectiveness of advertisements utilizing four types of endorsers. *Journal of Advertising, 5*(3): 22–4.

Frith, S. and J. Street (1992) Rock against racism and red wedge: from music to politics, from politics to music. In *Rockin' the Boat: Mass Music and Mass Movements.* R. Garofalo. Boston: South End Press.

Gabler, N. (1998) *Life: The Movie. How Entertainment Conquered Reality.* New York: Vintage Books.

Gabler, N. (2001) Toward a new definition of celebrity. The Norman Lear Center, USC Annenberg.

Gail, T., R. Clark, L. Elmer, E. Grech, J. Masettie and H. Sandhar (1992) The use of created versus celebrity spokesperson in advertisements. *The Journal of Consumer Marketing, 9*(4): 45–51.

Gamson, J. (1994) *Claims to Fame: Celebrity in Contemporary America.* Berkeley: University of California Press.

Garofalo, R. (1992a) Nelson Mandela, the concerts: mass culture as contested terrain. In *Rockin' the Boat: Mass Music and Mass Movements.* Boston: South End Press.

Garofalo, R. (1992b) Understanding mega-events: if we are the world, then how do we change it? In *Rockin' the Boat: Mass Music and Mass Movements.* Boston: South End Press.

Geldof, B. (1986) *Is That It?* Harmondsworth: Penguin.

Giles, D. (2000) *Illusions of Immortality: A Psychology of Fame and Celebrity.* London: Macmillan.

Gitlin, T. (1980) *The Whole World is Watching: Mass Media in the Making and Unmaking of the New Left.* Berkeley: University of California Press.

Goffman, E. (1959 [1990]) *The Presentation of Self in Everyday Life.* London: Penguin.

Goldman, R. (1994) Contradictions in a political economy of sign value. *Current Perspectives in Social Theory, 14*: 183–211.

Goldsmith, R. E., B. A. Lafferty and S. J. Newell (2000) The impact of corporate credibility and celebrity credibility on consumer reaction to advertisements and brands. *Journal of Advertising, 29*(3): 43–54.

Goodman, M. K. (2010) The mirror of consumption: celebritization, developmental consumption and the shifting cultural politics of fair trade. *Geoforum, 41*(1): 104–16.

Gotham, K. F. (2012) Make it right? Brad Pitt, post-Katrina rebuilding and the spectacularisation of disaster. In *Commodity Activism: Cultural Resistance in Neoliberal Times.* R. Mukherjee and S. Banet-Weiser. London, New York: New York University Press.

References **191**

Graham, B. and R. Greenfield (2004 [1990]) *Bill Graham Presents: My Life Inside Rock and Out*. Cambridge, MA: De Capo Press.

Grainger, A. D., J. I. Newman and D. L. Andrews (2005) Global Adidas: sport, celebrity and the marketing of difference. In *Global Sports Sponsorship*. J. Amis and T. B. Cornwell. New York: Berg.

Gray, J. (2012) The violent visions of Slavoj Žižek. *The New York Review of Books*.

Green, D. (2008) *From Poverty to Power: How Active Citizens and Effective States can Change the World*. Oxford: Oxfam International.

Guignon, C. (2004) *On Being Authentic*. London: Routledge.

Gundle, S. (2008) *Glamour: A History*. Oxford: Oxford University Press.

Habermas, J. (1989 [1962]) *The Structural Transformation of the Public Sphere: An Inquiry into a Category of Bourgeois Society*. Cambridge: Polity Press.

Halpern, J. (2007) *Fame Junkies: The Hidden Truths Behind America's Favourite Addiction*. Boston: Houghton Mifflin.

Hamilton, R. (2011) *Fighting for Darfur: Public Action and the Struggle to Stop Genocide*. New York: Palgrave Macmillan.

Harding, P. (2009) The great global switch-off: international coverage in UK Public Service Broadcasting. Polis, Oxfam, International Broadcasting Trust.

Hardstaff, J. (1991) Getting the full picture: the complementary roles of television news, current affairs and documentary programmes on the coverage of international issues. Third World and Environment Broadcasting Project, 3WE.

Harrison, G. (2010) The Africanisation of poverty: a retrospective on 'Make Poverty History'. *African Affairs*, *109*(436): 391–408.

Hawkins, V. (2011) Creating a groundswell or getting on the bandwagon? Celebrities, the media and distant conflict. In *Transnational Celebrity Activism in Global Politics: Changing the World?* L. Tsaliki, C. A. Frangonikolopoulos and A. Huliaras. Bristol: Intellect.

Heath, T. B., M. S. McCarthy and D. L. Mothersbaugh (1994) Spokesperson fame and vividness effects in the context of issue-relevant thinking: the moderating role of competitive setting. *Journal of Consumer Research*, *20*(4): 520–34.

Heble, A. (2003) Take two/rebel musics: human rights, resistant sounds and the politics of music making. In *Rebel Musics: Human Rights, Resistant Sounds and the Politics of Music Making*. D. Fischlin and A. Heble. Montreal: Black Rose Books.

Heinich, N. (2011) La culture de la célébrité en France et dans les pays anglophones. *Revue Française de sociologie*, *52*(2): 353–72.

Hermes, J. (1995) *Reading Women's Magazines: An Analysis of Everyday Media Use*. Cambridge: Polity Press.

Hermes, J. (2005) *Re-reading Popular Culture*. Oxford: Blackwell.

Hettne, B. (2009) *Thinking About Development*. London: Zed Books.

Hilary, J. (2010) The arrogance of Saint Bob. *Guardian*. Available at: www.theguardian. com/commentisfree/2010/apr/05/geldof-arrogance-poverty-agenda-starsuckers (viewed 25 February 2014).

Hill, A. (2010) WikiLeaks cable reveals Berlusconi's efforts to duck Bono tongue-lashing. *Guardian*, 17 December.

Hitchens, C. (1995) *The Missionary Position: Mother Teresa in Theory and Practice*. London: Verso.

Hochschild, A. (2006 [1998]) *King Leopold's Ghost: A Story of Greed, Terror and Heroism in Colonial Africa*. Basingstoke – Pan Books.

Hodkinson, S. (2005a) G8 – Africa Nil. *Red Pepper*. Available at: www.redpepper.org.uk/ G8-Africa-nil/November (viewed 25 February 2014).

Hodkinson, S. (2005b) Inside the murky world of the UK's Make Poverty History campaign. Available at www.zcommunications.org/inside-the-murky-world-of-the-uks-make-poverty-history-campaign-by-stuart-hodkinson (viewed 25 February 2014).

192 References

Horkheimer, M. and T. Adorno (1972) *Dialectic of Enlightenment*. New York: Herder & Herder.

Hovland, C. I. and W. Weiss (1951) The influence of source credibility on communication effectiveness. *Public Opinion Quarterly*, 15(4): 635–50.

Hudson, D. and J. van Heerde-Hudson (2012) 'A mile wide and an inch deep': surveys of public attitudes towards development aid. *International Journal of Development Education and Global Learning*, 4(1): 5–23.

Huijser, H. and J. Tay (2011) Can celebrity save diplomacy? Appropriating wisdom through 'the Elders'. In *Transnational Celebrity Activism in Global Politics. Changing the World?* L. Tsaliki, C. A. Frangonikolopoulos and A. Huliaras. Bristol: Intellect.

Huliaris, A. and N. Tzifakis (2010) Celebrity activism in international relations: in search of a framework for analysis. *Global Society*, 24(2): 255–74.

Hulme, D. (2010) *Global Poverty: How Global Governance is Failing the Poor*. London: Routledge.

Hulme, D. and M. Edwards (1997) *NGOs, States and Donors: Too Close for Comfort?* London: Macmillan.

Hung, K., K. W. Chan and C. H. Tse (2011) Assessing celebrity endorsement effects in China: a consumer-celebrity relational approach. *Journal of Advertising Research*, 51(4): 608–23.

Hyde, M. (2010) *Celebrity: How Entertainers Took Over the World and Why We Need an Exit Strategy*. London, Vintage Books.

Hyde, M. (2012) We're all poorer when we seek Kim Kardashian's take on poverty. *Guardian*, 8 June.

Igoe, J. and T. Kelsall (2005) *Between a Rock and a Hard Place: African NGOs, Donors, and the State*. Durham, NC: Carolina Academic Press.

Inglis, F. (2010) *A Short History of Celebrity*. Princeton, NJ: Princeton University Press.

Inthorn, S. and J. Street (2011) 'Simon Cowell for prime minister?' Young citizens' attitudes towards celebrity politics. *Media, Culture and Society*, 33(3): 1–11.

Jackson, D. J. (2008) Selling politics. *Journal of Political Marketing*, 6(4): 67–83.

Jackson, D. J. and T. I. A. Darrow (2005) The influence of celebrity endorsements on young adults' political opinions. *The Harvard Journal of Press/Politics*, 10(3): 80–98.

Jackson, N. (2008) *Bono's Politics: The Future of Celebrity Activism*. Saarbrücken: VDM Verlag.

Johansson, S. (2006) 'Sometimes you wanna hate celebrities': tabloid readers and celebrity coverage. In *Framing Celebrity: New Directions in Celebrity Culture*. S. Holmes and S. Redmond. London: Routledge.

Kahle, L. R. and P. M. Homer (1985) Physical attractiveness of the celebrity endorser: a social adaptation perspective. *Journal of Consumer Research*, 11(4): 954–61.

Kamins, M. A. (1989) Celebrity and non-celebrity advertising in a two sided context. *Journal of Advertising Research*, 29(3): 34–42.

Kamins, M. A. (1990) An investigation into the 'match-up' hypothesis in celebrity advertising: when beauty may only be skin deep. *Journal of Advertising*, 19(1): 4–13.

Kamins, M. A., M. J. Brand, S. A. Hoeke and J. C. Moe (1989) Two-sided versus one-sided celebrity endorsements: the impact of advertising effectiveness and credibility. *Journal of Advertising*, 18(2): 4–10.

Kamins, M. A. and K. Gupta (1994) Congruence between spokesperson and product type: a matchup hypothesis perspective. *Psychology and Marketing*, 11(6): 569–86.

Kapoor, I. (2012) *Celebrity Humanitarianism: The Ideology of Global Charity*. London: Routledge.

Kelly, S. (2012) The X factor: what motivates celebrities to support third sector organisations? Masters thesis. Sheffield Hallam University.

King, S. (2006) *Pink Ribbons, Inc: Breast Cancer and the Politics of Philanthropy*. Minneapolis: University of Minnesota Press.

Klaus, N. and A. A. Bailey (2008) Celebrity endorsements: an examination of gender and consumers' attitudes. *American Journal of Business*, *23*(2): 53–61.

Klebba, J. M. and L. S. Unger (1982) The impact of negative and positive information on source credibility in a field setting. *Advances in Consumer Research*, *10*: 11–16.

Kleinberg, A. (2011) Are saints celebrities? Some medieval Christian examples. *Cultural and Social History*, *8*(3): 393–97.

Koernig, S. K. and T. C. Boyd (2009) To catch a tiger or let him go: the match-up effect and athlete endorsers for sport and non-sport brands. *Sport Marketing Quarterly*, *18*: 25–37.

Kuehn, K. M. (2009) Compassionate consumption: branding Africa through Product RED. *Democratic Communiqué*, *23*(2): 23–40.

Kurzman, C., C. Anderson, C. Key, Y. O. Lee, M. Moloney, A. Silver and M. W. Van Ryn (2007) Celebrity status. *Sociological Theory*, *25*(4): 347–67.

La Ferle, C. and S. M. Choi (2005) The importance of perceived endorser credibility in South Korean advertising. *Journal of Current Issues and Research in Advertising*, *27*(2): 67–81.

Lafferty, B. A. and R. E. Goldsmith (1999) Corporate credibility's role in consumers' attitudes and purchase intentions when a high versus a low credibility endorser is used in the ad. *Journal of Business Research*, *44*: 109–16.

Lafferty, B. A., R. E. Goldsmith and S. J. Newell (2002) The dual credibility model: the influence of corporate and endorser credibility on attitudes and purchase intentions. *Journal of Marketing Theory and Practice*, *10*(3): 1–12.

Lahusen, C. (1996) *The Rhetoric of Moral Protest: Public Campaigns, Celebrity Endorsement and Political Mobilisation*. Berlin: Walter de Gruyter.

Lancaster, C. (2007) *Foreign Aid: Diplomacy, Development and Domestic Politics*. Chicago: University of Chicago Press.

Langmeyer, L. and M. Walker (1991) A first step to identify the meaning in celebrity endorsers. *Advances in Consumer Research*, *18*: 364–71.

Larson, R. J., S. Woloshin and L. M. Schwartz (2005) Celebrity endorsements of cancer screening. *Journal of the National Cancer Institute*, *97*(9): 693–95.

Lay, S. and C. Payne (1998) World out of focus: British terrestrial television and global affairs. Third World and Environmental Broadcasting Project, 3WE.

Layard, R. (2006) *Happiness: Lessons from a New Science*. London: Penguin.

Lee, J.-G. and E. Thorson (2008) The impact of celebrity-product incongruence on the effectiveness of product endorsement. *Journal of Advertising Research*, *48*(3): 433–49.

Lewis, P. (2010) Bob Geldof condemns lame and ineffective anti-poverty campaigners. *Guardian*, 2 April 2010.

Lindholm, C. (2002) Authenticity, anthropology and the sacred. *Anthropological Quarterly*, *75*(2): 331–38.

Lindholm, C. (2008) *Culture and Authenticity*. Oxford: Blackwell.

Littler, J. (2008) "I feel your pain": cosmopolitan charity and the public fashioning of the celebrity soul. *Social Semiotics*, *18*(2): 237–51.

Livingstone, S. and T. Markham (2008) The contribution of media consumption to civic participation. *The British Journal of Sociology*, *59*(2): 351–71.

Lomax, A., W. Guthrie and P. Seeger (1999 [1967]) *Hard Hitting Songs for Hard-Hit People*. Lincoln: University of Nebraska Press.

Louie, T. A. and C. Obermiller (2002) Consumer response to a firm's endorser (dis)association decisions. *Journal of Advertising*, *31*(4): 41–52.

Lynch, J. and D. Schuler (1994) The matchup effect of spokesperson and product congruence: a schema theory interpretation. *Psychology and Marketing*, *11*(5): 417–45.

194 References

Lynskey, D. (2010) *33 Revolutions per Minute: A History of Protest Songs.* London: Faber & Faber.

MacCannell, D. (1973) Staged authenticity: on arrangements of social space in tourist settings. *The American Journal of Sociology, 79*(3): 589–603.

MacCannell, D. (1999 [1976]) *The Tourist: A New Theory of the Leisure Class.* Berkeley: University of California Press.

MacCannell, D. (2008a) Staged authenticity today. In *Indefensible Space: The Architecture of the National Security State.* M. Sorkin. London, Routledge: 259–76.

MacCannell, D. (2008b) Why it never really was about authenticity. *Society, 45:* 334–37.

Magee, C. (2009) Representing Africa? Photography, Celebrity and Vanity Fair. In *Celebrity Colonialism: Fame, Power and Representation in Colonial and Postcolonial Cultures.* R. Clarke. Newcastle upon Tyne: Cambridge Scholars Publishing.

Magubane, Z. (2008) The (Product) Red Man's Burden: Charity, Celebrity, and the Contradictions of Coevalness. *The Journal of Pan African Studies, 2*(6): 102, 101–25.

Mallaby, S. (2004) *The World's Banker: A Story of Failed States, Financial Crises, and the Wealth and Poverty of Nations.* London: Penguin.

Manzo, K. (2008) Imaging humanitarianism: NGO identity and the iconography of childhood. *Antipode, 40*(4): 632–57.

Marcus, G. E. (2002) *The Sentimental Citizen: Emotion in Democratic Politics.* University Park: The Pennsylvania State University Press.

Marks, M. P. and Z. M. Fischer (2002) The king's new bodies: simulating consent in the age of celebrity. *New Political Science, 24*(3): 371–94.

Marsh, D., P. 't Hart and K. Tindall (2010) Celebrity politics: the politics of the late modernity? *Political Studies Review, 8:* 322–40.

Marshall, P. D. (1997) *Celebrity and Power: Fame in Contemporary Culture.* Minneapolis: University of Minnesota Press.

Marshall, R., N. Woobong, G. State and S. Deuskar (2008) Endorsement theory: how consumers relate to celebrity models. *Journal of Advertising Research, 48*(4): 564–72.

Martin, B. A. S., D. Wentzel and T. Tomczak (2008) Effects of susceptibility to normative influence and type of testimonial on attitudes toward print advertising. *Journal of Advertising, 37*(1): 29–43.

Martin, P. (2008) *Hell or High Water: My Life in and out of Politics.* Toronto: McClelland & Stewart.

Mawdsley, E. (2007) The millennium challenge account: neo-liberalism, poverty and security. *Review of International Political Economy, 14*(3): 487–509.

McFarren, A (2000) Famous disasters in the famine zone. *The Sunday Times,* 10 December.

Merton, R. K. (1946) *Mass Persuasion: The Social Psychology of a War Bond Drive.* New York: Harper & Brothers.

Meyer, D. S. and J. Gamson (1995) The challenge of cultural elites: celebrities and social movements. *Sociological Inquiry, 65*(2): 181–206.

Micklewright, J. and S. V. Schnepf (2009) Who gives charitable donations for overseas development? *Journal of Social Policy, 38*(2): 317–41.

Miller, F. M. and C. T. Allen (2012) How does celebrity meaning transfer? Investigating the process of meaning transfer with celebrity affiliates and mature brands. *Journal of Consumer Psychology, 22:* 443–52.

Misra, S. and S. E. Beatty (1990) Celebrity spokesperson and brand congruence. *Journal of Business Research, 21:* 159–73.

Mitlin, D., S. Hickey and A. J. Bebbington (2007) Reclaiming development? NGOs and the challenge of alternatives. *World Development, 35*(10): 1699–720.

References   **195**

Mole, T. (2008) Lord Byron and the end of fame. *International Journal of Cultural Studies*, *11*(3): 343–61.

Molina-Guzmán, I. (2012) Salma Hayek's celebrity activism: constructing race, ethnicity and gender as mainstream commodities. In *Commodity Activism: Cultural Resistance in Neoliberal Times*. R. Mukherjee and S. Banet-Weiser. London, New York: New York Free Press.

Money, R. B., T. A. Shimp and T. Sakano (2006) Celebrity endorsements in Japan and the United States: is negative information all that harmful? *Journal of Advertising Research*, *46*(1): 113–23.

Moore, D. J., J. C. Mowen and R. Reardon (1994) Multiple sources of advertising appeals: when product endorsers are paid by the advertising sponsor. *Journal of the Academy of Marketing Science*, *22*(3): 234–43.

Moore, M. (2010) Shrinking world: the decline of international reporting in the British Press. London: Media Standards Trust.

Morgan, S. (2010) Historicising celebrity. *Celebrity Studies*, *1*(3): 366–68.

Morgan, S. (2011) Celebrity: academic 'pseudo-event' or a useful concept for historians? *Cultural and Social History*, *8*(1): 95–114.

Mouffe, C. (2005) *On the Political*. London: Routledge.

Mowen, J. C. and S. Brown (1981) On explaining and predicting the effectiveness of celebrity endorsers. *Advances in Consumer Research*, *8*: 437–41.

Mukherjee, R. (2012) Diamonds (are from Sierra Leone): bling and the promise of consumer citizenship. In *Commodity Activism: Cultural Resistance in Neoliberal Times*. R. Mukherjee and S. Banet-Weiser. London, New York: New York Free Press.

Mukherjee, R. and S. Banet-Weiser (2012) *Commodity Activism: Cultural Resistance in Neoliberal Times*. London, New York: New York Free Press.

Nash, K. (1996) Post-democracy, politics and philosophy: an interview with Jacques Rancière. *Angelaki: Journal of the Theoretical Humanities*, *1*(3): 171–78.

Nash, K. (2008) Global citizenship as show business: the cultural politics of Make Poverty History. *Media Culture & Society*, *30*(2): 167–81.

Nason, S. and D. Redding (2002) Losing reality: factual international programming on UK television 2000–01. Third World and Environment Broadcasting Project, 3WE.

Nataraajan, R. and S. K. Chawla (1997) "Fitness" marketing: celebrity or non-celebrity endorsement? *Journal of Professional Services Marketing*, *15*(2): 119–29.

Newman, G. E., G. Diesendruck and P. Bloom (2011) Celebrity contagion and the value of objects. *Journal of Consumer Research*, *38*(2): 215–28.

Niekerk, M. v. (2008) (Red) Mythology. *The Journal of Pan African Studies*, *2*(6): 55–67.

Njoroge, D. (2011) Calling a new tune for Africa? Analysing a celebrity-led campaign to redefine the debate on Africa. In *Transnational Celebrity Activism in Global Politics: Changing the World?* L. Tsaliki, C. A. Frangonikolopoulos and A. Huliaras. Bristol: Intellect.

Nownes, A. J. (2011) An experimental investigation of the effects of celebrity support for political parties in the United States. *American Politics Research*, *40*(3): 476–500.

Ohanian, R. (1990) Construction and validation of a scale to measure celebrity endorsers' perceived expertise, trustworthiness, and attractiveness. *Journal of Advertising*, *19*(3): 39–52.

Ohanian, R. (1991) The impact of celebrity spokespersons' perceived image on consumers' intention to purchase. *Journal of Advertising Research*, February–March: 46–54.

Olsen, G. R. (2001) European public opinion and aid to Africa: is there a link? *Journal of Modern African Studies*, *39*(4): 645–74.

O'Mahony, S. and T. Meenaghan (1997/8) The impact of celebrity endorsements on consumers. *Irish Marketing Review*, *10*(2): 15–24.

196 References

Otter, M. (2003) Domestic public support for foreign aid: does it matter? *Third World Quarterly*, *24*(1): 115–25.

Ouellette, L. and J. Hay (2008) *Better Living through Reality TV*. Oxford: Blackwell.

Padania, S., S. Coleman and M. Georgiou (2006) Reflecting the real world 2: how we connect with the wider world. CBA; Concern Worldwide; IBT; One World.

Paxton, P. and Knack, S. (2008) Individual and country level factors affecting support for foreign aid. World Bank, Development Research Group.

Peck, J. (2010) The secret of her success: Oprah Winfrey and the seductions of self-transformation. *Journal of Communication Inquiry*, *34*(1): 7–14.

Peck, J. (2012) Looking a gift horse in the mouth: Oprah Winfrey and the politics of philanthropy. *Celebrity Studies*, *3*(1): 106–8.

Pettifor, A. (2006) The Jubilee 2000 campaign: a brief overview. In *Sovereign Debt at the Crossroads: Challenges and Proposals for Resolving the Third World Debt Crisis*. C. Jochnick and F. A. Preston. Oxford: Oxford University Press.

Philo, G. and L. Henderson (1998) What the audience thinks: focus group research into the likes and dislikes of UK wildlife viewers. Glasgow: Glasgow Media Group.

Phu, C. N. (2010) Save Africa: the commodificaton of (PRODUCT) RED campaign. *Kaleidoscope*, *9*: 107–25.

Poniewozik, J. (2005) The year of charitainment. *Time*, 19 December.

Pornpitakpan, C. (2003) The effect of celebrity endorsers' perceived credibility on product purchase intention: the case of Singaporeans. *Journal of International Consumer Marketing*, *16*(2): 55–73.

Priester, J. and R. H. Petty (2003) The influence of spokesperson trustworthiness on message elaboration, attitude strength, and advertising effectiveness. *Journal of Consumer Psychology*, *13*(4): 408–21.

Pringle, H. (2004) *Celebrity Sells*. Chichester: John Wiley & Sons.

Pughazhendi, A., R. Thirunavukkarasu and S. Susendiran (2011) A study on celebrity based advertisements on the purchase attitude of consumers towards durable products in Coimbatore city, Tamil Nadu, India. *Far East Journal of Marketing and Management*, *1*(1): 16–27.

Rancière, J. (1998) *Disagreement*. Minneapolis: University of Minnesota Press.

Ranjbarian, B., Z. Shekarchizade and Z. Momeni (2010) Celebrity endorser influence on attitude toward advertisements and brands. *European Journal of Social Sciences*, *13*(3): 399–407.

Rein, I. J., P. Kotler and M. R. Stoller (1987) *High Visibility: The Professional Guide to Celebrity Marketing*. Oxford: Heinemann Professional Publishing.

Repo, J. and Yrjölä, R. (2011) The gender politics of celebrity humanitarianism in Africa. *International Feminist Journal of Politics*, 13(1): 44–62.

Rice, D. H., K. Kelting and R. J. Lutz (2012) Multiple endorsers and multiple endorsements: the influence of message repetition, source congruence and involvement on brand attitudes. *Journal of Consumer Psychology*, *22*: 249–59.

Richey, L. A. and S. Ponte (2011) *Brand Aid: Shopping Well to Save the World*. Minneapolis: University of Minnesota Press.

Richey, L. A. and S. Ponte (2014) New actors and alliances in development. *Third World Quarterly*, *35*(1): 1–21.

Riddell, R. C. (2007) *Does Foreign Aid Really Work?* Oxford: Oxford University Press.

Rist, G. (2008 [1996]) *The History of Development: From Western Origins to Global Faith*. 3rd edition. London: Zed Books.

Rodrik, D. (2007) *One Economics, Many Recipes: Globalization, Institutions, and Economic Growth*. Princeton, NJ: Princeton University Press.

Rodrik, D. (2011) *The Globalization Paradox: Why Global Markets, States and Democracy Can't Coexist*. Oxford: Oxford University Press.

Rojek, C. (2001) *Celebrity*. London: Reaktion Books.

Ross, E. (1998) *The Malthus Factor: Population, Politics, and Poverty in Capitalist Development*. London: Zed Books.

Rossiter, J. R. and A. Smidts (2012) Print advertising: celebrity presenters. *Journal of Business Research, 65*: 874–79.

Rutherford, K. R. (2011) *Disarming States: The International Movement to Ban Landmines*. Santa Barbara, CA: Praeger.

Sachs, J. (2005) *The End of Poverty: How We Can Make it Happen in Our Lifetime*. London: Penguin.

Sachs, W. (1992) Introduction. In *The Development Dictionary: A Guide to Knowledge as Power*. W. Sachs. Johannesburg, London and New York: Witwatersrand University Press, Zed Books.

Saleem, F. (2007) Effect of single celebrity and multiple celebrity endorsement on low involvement and high involvement product advertisements. *European Journal of Social Sciences, 5*(3): 125–32.

Samman, E., E. M. Auliffe and M. MacLachlan (2009) The role of celebrity in endorsing poverty reduction through international aid. *International Journal of Nonprofit and Voluntary Sector Marketing, 14*: 137–48.

Sandvoss, C., M. Real and A. Bernstein (2012) *Bodies of Discourse: Sports Stars, Media and the Global Public*. New York: Peter Lang.

Schickel, R. (2000 [1985]) *Intimate Strangers: The Culture of Celebrity in America*. Chicago: Ivan R. Dee.

Schlesinger, P. (2006) Is there a crisis in British Journalism? *Media, Culture and Society, 28*(2): 299–307.

Schweiger, H. (2009) Between the lines: George Bernard Shaw as cultural and political mediator. In *Internationalism and the Arts in Britain and Europe at the Fin de Siècle*. G. Brockington. Oxford: Peter Lang.

Scott, M. (2008) Screening the world: how UK broadcasters portrayed the wider world in 2007–8. Department for International Development; International Broadcasting Trust.

Scott, M. (2009) The world in focus: how UK audiences connect with the wider world and the international content of news in 2009. Commonwealth Broadcasting Association; Department for International Development; International Broadcasting Trust.

Scott, M. (2011) How distant others are mediated by UK Television. PhD thesis. University of East Anglia.

Scott, M. (2013a) More news is bad news: expanding the scope of studies of 'The Public Faces of Development' and 'Media and Morality'. In *Popular Representations of Development: Insights from Novels, Films, Television and Social Media*. D. Lewis, D. Rodgers and M. Woolcock. London: Routledge.

Scott, M. (2013b) 'It's actually real and not just the news': the role of celebrities in mediating distant others. Forthcoming in *International Journal of Cultural Studies*.

Scott, M., S. M. R. Rojas and C. Jenner (2011) Outside the box: how UK broadcasters portrayed the world in 2010 and how international content can achieve greater impact with audiences. UKAID; International Broadcasting Trust.

Scott, M. J. O. (2001) Danger – landmines! NGO-government collaboration in the Ottawa process. In *Global Citizen Action*. M. Edwards and J. Gaventa. London: Earthscan.

Seu, B. I. (2003) 'Your stomach makes you feel that you don't want to know about it': densensitization, defence mechanisms and rhetoric in response to human rights abuses. *Journal of Human Rights, 2*(2): 183–96.

198 References

Seymour, E. and S. Barnett (2006) Bringing the world to the UK: factual international programming on UK public service TV, 2005. Third World and Environment Broadcasting Project, 3WE.

Siemens, J. C., S. Smith, D. Fisher and T. D. Jensen, (2008) Product expertise versus professional expertise: congruency between an endorser's chosen profession and the endorsed product. *Journal of Targeting, Measurement and Analysis for Marketing, 16*(3): 159–68.

Silvera, D. H. and B. Austad (2003) Factors predicting the effectiveness of celebrity endorsement advertisements. *European Journal of Marketing, 38*(11/12): 1509–26.

Silverstone, R. (2007) *Media and Morality: On the Rise of the Mediapolis.* Cambridge: Polity Press.

Sireau, N. (2008) *Make Poverty History: Political Communication in Action.* London: Palgrave Macmillan.

Sklair, L. (2001) *The Transnational Capitalist Class.* Oxford: Blackwell.

Smith, J., L. Edge and V. Morris (2006) Reflecting the real world: how British TV portrayed developing countries in 2005. Commonwealth Broadcasting Association; Department for International Development; International Broadcasting Trust; Open University; Voluntary Service Overseas.

Smith, M. (2004) Mediating the world: development, education and global citizenship. *Globalisation, Societies and Education, 2*(1): 67–81.

Smith, M. and J. Donnelly (2004) Power, inequality, change and uncertainty: viewing the world through the development prism. *Studies in Qualitative Methodology, 7*: 123–45.

Smith, M. B. (2008) International non-governmental development organizations and their Northern constituencies: development education, dialogue and democracy. *Journal of Global Ethics, 4*(1): 5–18.

Smith, M. B. and H. Yanacopulos (2004) The public faces of development: an introduction. *Journal of International Development, 16*: 657–64.

Smith, S. (2007) Angelina Jolie wants to save the world. *Newsweek.* Available at: www.newsweek.com/2007/2006/2024/angelina-wants-to-save-the-world.print.html (viewed 25 March 2011).

Soederberg, S. (2004) American empire and 'excluded states': the millennium challenge account and the shift to pre-emptive development. *Third World Quarterly, 25*(2): 279–302.

Sommerlad, N. (2009) Charity balls up: do celebrity fund-raisers short-change the causes they boast about backing? *Daily Mirror,* 25 June http://blogs.mirror.co.uk/investigations/2009/06/charity-balls-up-do-celebrity.html (viewed 25 February 2014).

Stacey, J. (1994) *Star Gazing: Hollywood Cinema and Female Spectatorship.* London: Routledge.

Stack, S. (1987) Celebrities and suicide: a taxonomy and analysis, 1948–1983. *American Sociological Review, 52*(3): 401–12.

Stafford, M. R., T. F. Stafford and E. Day (2002) A contingency approach: the effects of spokesperson type and service type on service advertising perceptions. *Journal of Advertising, 31*(2): 17–35.

Sternthal, B., R. Dholaika and C. Leavitt (1978) The persuasive effect of source credibility: test of cognitive response. *Journal of Consumer Research, 4*(4): 252–60.

Stiglitz, J. (2002) *Globalisation and its Discontents.* New York: Norton.

Stirrat, R. L. and H. Henkel (1997) The development gift: the problem of reciprocity in the NGO World. *Annals, AAPSS 554* (November): 66–80.

Stone, J. (2000) Losing perspective: global affairs on British terrestrial television 1989–1999. Third World and Environment Broadcasting Project, 3WE.

Street, J. (1986) *Rebel Rock: The Politics of Popular Music.* Oxford: Basil Blackwell.

Street, J. (2002) Bob, Bono and Tony B: the popular artist as politician. *Media, Culture and Society, 24*: 433–41.

Street, J. (2003) 'Fight the power': the politics of music and the music of politics. *Government and Opposition*, *38*(1): 113–30.

Street, J. (2004) Celebrity politicians: popular culture and political representation. *British Journal of Politics and International Relations*, *6*: 435–52.

Street, J. (2012) Do celebrity politics and celebrity politicians matter? *The British Journal of Politics and International Relations*, *14*: 1–11.

Street, J., S. Hague and H. Savigny (2008) Playing to the crowd: the role of music and musicians in political participation. *British Journal of Politics and International Relations*, *10*: 269–85.

Strine, H. C. N. (2006) Your testimony was splendid: the treatment of celebrities and non-celebrities on congressional hearings. Paper prepared for the 2006 Annual Meeting of the Southern Political Science Association, 5–7 January. Atlanta, Georgia.

Tait, S. (2011) Consuming ethics: conflict diamonds, the entertainment industry and celebrity activism. In *Transnational Celebrity Activism in Global Politics. Changing the World?* L. Tsaliki, C. A. Frangonikolopoulos and A. Huliaras. Bristol: Intellect.

Taylor, C. (1989) *Sources of the Self: The Making of Modern Identity*. Cambridge: Cambridge University Press.

Taylor, C. (1991) *The Ethics of Authenticity*. Cambridge, MA: Harvard University Press.

Tester, K. (2010) *Humanitarianism and Modern Culture*. University Park, PA: Pennsylvania State University Press.

Thrall, A. T., J. Lollio-Fakhreddine, J. Berent, L. Donnelly, W. Herrin, Z. Paquette, R. Wenglinski and A. Wyatt (2008) Star power: celebrity advocacy and the evolution of the public sphere. *International Journal of Press/Politics*, *13*(4): 362–85.

Till, B. and T. A. Shimp (1998) Endorsers in advertising: the case of negative celebrity information. *Journal of Advertising*, *27*(1): 67–82.

Till, B. D. and M. Busler (2000) The match-up hypothesis: physical attractiveness, expertise, and the role of fit on brand attitude, purchase intent and brand beliefs. *Journal of Advertising*, *29*(3): 1–13.

Till, B. D. and M. Busler (1998) Matching products with endorsers: attractiveness versus expertise. *Journal of Consumer Marketing*, *15*(6): 576–86.

Till, B. D., S. M. Stanley and R. Priluck (2008) Classical conditioning and celebrity endorsers: an examination of belongingness and resistance to extinction. *Psychology and Marketing*, *25*(2): 179–96.

TNS (2010) Public attitudes towards development. TNS Report prepared for COI on behalf of DFID. MS in possession of the author.

Trilling, L. (1971) *Sincerity and Authenticity*. Cambridge, MA: Harvard University Press.

Tripp, C., T. D. Jensen and L. Carlson (1994) The effects of multiple product endorsements by celebrities on consumers' attitudes and intentions. *Journal of Consumer Research*, *20*(4): 535–47.

Trope, A. (2012) Mother Angelina: Hollywood philanthropy personified. In *Commodity Activism: Cultural Resistance in Neoliberal Times*. R. Mukherjee and S. Banet-Weiser. London, New York: New York University Press.

Tuck, S. (2010) *We Ain't What We Ought To Be: The Black Freedom Struggle from Emancipation to Obama*. Cambridge, MA: The Belknap Press of Harvard University Press.

Turner, G. (2004) *Understanding Celebrity*. London: Sage.

Turner, G. (2006) The mass production of celebrity: 'celetoids', reality TV and the 'demotic turn'. *International Journal of Cultural Studies*, *9*(2): 153–65.

Turner, G. (2010) Approaching celebrity studies. *Celebrity Studies*, *1*(1): 11–20.

United Nations Development Programme (UNDP) (2011) *Human Development Report 2011 Sustainability and Equity: A Better Future for All*. Basingstoke: Palgrave Macmillan.

200 References

Van den Bulck, H., K. Panis, A. Hardy and P. Van Aelst, (2011) Een bekende smoel voor het goede doel: de effectiviteit van Bekende Vlamingen in non-profitcampagnes. *Tijdschrift voor Communicatiewetenschap, 39*(2): 4–20.

van der Gaag, N. and C. Nash (1987) *Images of Africa*. Rome: Food and Agriculture Organization.

Van der Waldt, D. L. R., N. E. A. Schleritzko and K. Van Zyl (2007) Paid versus unpaid celebrity endorsement in advertising: an exploration. *African Journal of Business Management, 1*(7): 185–91.

van Heerde, J. and D. Hudson (2010) 'The righteous considereth the cause of the poor?' Public attitudes towards poverty in developing countries. *Political Studies, 58*: 348–409.

van Zoonen, L. (2004) Imagining the fan democracy. *European Journal of Communication, 19*(1): 39–52.

Varga, S. (2011) The paradox of authenticity. *TELOS 156* (Fall): 113–30.

Veer, E., I. Becirovic and B. A. S. Martin (2010) If Kate voted Conservative, would you? The role of celebrity endorsements in political party advertising. *European Journal of Marketing, 44*(3/4): 436–50.

Voluntary Service Overseas (VSO) (2002) The Live Aid legacy: the developing world through British eyes – a research report. London: Voluntary Service Overseas.

Weberling, B. (2010) Celebrity charity: a historical case study of Danny Thomas and St. Jude Children's Research Hospital, 1962–1991. *Prism, 7*(2): 1–15.

West, D. M. (2008) Angelina, Mia and Bono: celebrities and international development. In *Global Development 2.0: Can Philanthropists, the Public and the Poor Make Poverty History?* L. Brainard and D. Chollet. Washington, DC: Brookings Institution Press.

West, D. M. and J. Orman (2003) *Celebrity Politics*. Upper Saddle River, NJ: Prentice Hall.

Wheeler, M. (2011a) Celebrity diplomacy: United Nations' Goodwill Ambassadors and Messengers of Peace. *Celebrity Studies, 2*(1): 6–18.

Wheeler, M. (2011b) Celebrity politics and cultural citizenship: UN Goodwill Ambassadors and Messengers of Peace. In *Transnational Celebrity Activism in Global Politics: Changing the World?* L. Tsaliki, C. A. Frangonikolopoulos and A. Huliaras. Bristol: Intellect.

Wheeler, M. (2012) The democratic worth of celebrity politics in an era of late modernity. *The British Journal of Politics and International Relations, 14*: 407–22.

Wheeler, M. (2013) *Celebrity Politics: Image and Identity in Contemporary Political Communications*. Cambridge: Polity Press.

Wheeler, R. T. (2009) Nonprofit advertising: impact of celebrity connection, involvement and gender on source credibility and intention to volunteer time or donate money. *Journal of Nonprofit & Public Sector Marketing, 21*: 80–107.

White, D. W., L. Goddard and N. Wilbur (2009) The effects of negative information transference in the celebrity endorsement relationship. *International Journal of Retail and Distribution Management, 37*(4): 322–35.

Whitlock, G. (2009) Not on our watch: celebrity campaigns from Hollywood to Darfur. In *Celebrity Colonialism: Fame, Power and Representation in Colonial and Postcolonial Cultures*. R. Clarke. Newcastle upon Tyne: Cambridge Scholars Publishing.

Wilson, J. (2011) A new kind of star is born: Audrey Hepburn and the global governmentalisation of female stardom. *Celebrity Studies, 2*(1): 56–68.

Wilson, M. (1971) *Religion and the Transformation of Society*. Cambridge: Cambridge University Press.

Wolfe, T. (1970) *Radical Chic and Mau-Mauing the Flak Catchers*. New York: Farrar, Straus & Giroux.

Wood, N. T. and K. C. Herbst (2007) Political star power and political parties: does celebrity endorsement win first-time votes? *Journal of Political Marketing, 6*(2/3): 141–58.

References **201**

Youde, J. (2009) Ethical consumerism or reified neoliberalism? Product (RED) and Private Funding for Public Goods. *New Political Science*, *31*(2): 201–20.

Yrjölä, R. (2009) The invisible violence of celebrity humanitarianism: soft images and hard words in the making and unmaking of Africa. *World Political Science Review* 5(1): Article 14.

Yrjölä, R. (2011a) From street into the world: towards a politicised reading of celebrity humanitarianism. *The British Journal of Politics and International Relations*, *14*(3): 357–74.

Yrjölä, R. (2011b) The global politics of celebrity humantarianism. In *Transnational Celebrity Activism in Global Politics*. L. Tsaliki, C. A. Frangonikolopoulos and A. Huliaras (eds). Bristol: Intellect.

Zahaf, M. and J. Anderson (2008) Causality effects between celebrity endorsement and the intentions to buy. *Innovative Marketing*, *4*(4): 57–65.

INDEX

Page numbers in italics refer to figures and tables. Page numbers followed by 'n' refer to notes.

accountability 119, 153, 156–7, 161
Adorno, Theodor 38, 53
advertising 53, 64, 71n65, 122; US response to celebrity 176, *178–9*
Africa: aid for 66, 73n105, 73n107, 74n110, 121; child poverty 34, 50n72; damaging views of 42–3; fundraising for 62, 64; public perception of 66
Ahearn, Michael 111n60
aid: Bono and Geldof lobbying for 120–1; famine relief 15n6, 59, 62, 96; from G8 countries 66, 74n110, 121, 157, 163n20; public attitudes toward 24–5, *26–7*, 31; trends in giving *29*
AIDS *see* HIV/AIDS
Ali, Muhammad 63, 71n71, 72n86
Allen, Lily 115
altruism 10–11, 115; voyeuristic 23
Amnesty International 72n77, *88*; Human Rights Now tour 62, 111n60; Secret Policeman's Ball 59, 115
Annan, Kofi 64
anti-racism 52, 71n69
Arendt, Hannah 19–20
Arulampalam, Wiji 33n37
Assayas, Michka 72n80
Atkinson, Anthony B. *29*, 83
authenticity 10–12, 23; of performance 11, 96, 107–9, 112n92, 144, 148;

of relationships 96–8, 109, 152; sources of 106–7
awareness: of celebrity advocacy 133, 138–40, *139*, 146–7; of development issues 24–5, *26*–7, 153–4; of Make Poverty History campaign 66, 129n71; raising 8, 148; *see also* public engagement

Band Aid 38, 51, 62
Banet-Weiser, Sarah 160
Barnett, Michael xxiii, 54, 69n5
Beatles 59
Belafonte, Harry 62
Benjamin, Walter 130n77
Berlusconi, Silvio 157
Biccum, April 74n126
Billig, Michael 44, 148
Bishop, John 144, 146, 151n45
Bishop, Matthew 123, 129n58
Blair, Tony 1, 54, 68; African Commission 64, 66, 121; Bono and Geldof and 72n91, 73n105, 74n113, 120–1, 125
Bodleian Library 183n2
Boltanski, Luc 19–20
Bono 50n70, 50n72, 51, 128n46, 163n7; Berlusconi's fear of 157; criticism of 158; DATA and ONE campaigns 64, 121, 128n47; George W. Bush and

156–7; Jesse Helms and 121, 128n40;
Millennium Challenge Account
lobbying 156–8; Muhammad Ali and
63, 72n86; personal brand 64, 72n95;
press coverage 41; Tony Blair and
72n91, 120–1
Boorman, Charley *86*, 139, 151n27
Boorstin, Daniel xxi, 53
Bourdieu, Pierre 49n65
branding: celebrity 11, 64, 80–1, 109, 114,
117, 152; of Make Poverty History 66;
of NGOs 80–1, 115, 117, 159, 166;
'voice' concept of 112n89; of
Woodstock Festival 71n68
British Broadcasting Corporation (BBC)
25, 76; telethons 62, 72n75, 138, 148
Brookings Blum Roundtable 123, 126–7,
170
Browne, Harry 158, 163n26
Bush, George W. 42, 120–1, 156

CAFOD *88*
Campbell, Alastair 72n91, 120
capitalism: celebrity advocacy and 44–6;
commodities and 54; consumer 53;
history of development and 54–5;
neoliberal 157, 159; NGO-celebrity
relations and 75; post-democracy and 35
Cause Effect Agency 79
'celanthropists' 123–4
Celebrities Worldwide 53, 77
celebrity: altruism 10–11; definitions of
xxi–ii; democracy and 38–9;
diplomats/diplomatic power 34, 37,
120–1; elites 8, 46, 160–1; encounters
with 76, 90, 132, 149; history of 52–4;
influence 10, 41–2, 49n51, 56, 113;
interest/disinterest in 131–6, 147–8;
popularity of 8, 114, 121, 149, 153; as
populist 9, 10, 149; public engagement
with 8, 9, 41, 114, 125–6, 129n71, 149;
and public intellectuals 64; rise and fall
of 56–8; role in negotiations 119–20;
and spectator 23; supporters 7, 13, 82,
109, 138, 154; *see also* celebrity
advocacy; fame; power of celebrity
celebrity advocacy: achievements 13, 37,
83, 89–91; advantages of 101; belief in
41, 110, 133, *142*, 142–4; creativity and
160–1; debates and critiques 13, 34–5,

40, 49n51, 156–9; definition of xxii;
development and xxiv, 7, 22, 168; as
divisive 34; failings/limitations xxiv,
133, 168; history of 13, 37, 69;
interest/disinterest in 132–3, 138–42,
147–8; misconceptions of 102; negative
reaction to 133, 143–4; payment for
102, 111n54, 114, 143; political
influence 41–2, 118–21; popularity 8–9,
14; post-democracy and 9, 35–7; public
perception of 146–7; statistics on 15n8,
183n1; studies of 41–6; textual analyses
174; *see also* field-trips; NGO-celebrity
relations
Chambers, Colin 58
Chambers, Robert 113
Chang, Ha-Joon 156
Chaplin, Charlie 58
charitable activities: celebrity
ambassadors/supporters of 7, 82–3,
84–8, 97, 116–17; and death of Princess
Diana 63; events 115, *116*, 142;
foundations promoting 77, *78*; media
coverage 143, 181, 183; motivations for
pursuing 10–11, 139; musicians and
musical events 62–4; publicity from
10–11, 80; role of liaison officers in 77,
79–80
charitable donations: celebrity advocacy
and 89, 144–5, 149, 154; celebrity
endorsements and 139–41, *140*, 151n30;
by household income 25, *28*; marketing
strategies 115; public engagement and
14, *26*; trends in 25, *29–30*, 33n37
Cheadle, Don 67, 74n20
China 67
Chouliaraki, Lilie xxiii, 17, 37; on
celebrity performance strategies 22–3,
108, 112n87; on forms of news
reporting 21; on post-humanitarianism
23, 37, 44
Christian Aid *85*
civil rights movement 52, 59–60, 70n56
civil society 9, 14, 55–6, 156
Clapton, Eric 59, 71n69
Clinton, Bill 1, 64, 68, 72n93
Clooney, George 51, 67, 74n120
Cohen, Stanley 18–20, 43, 49n55
college students (US) 123, 151n30, 176–7,
177, *178–9*

Comic Relief 62, 65, 72n75, 138, 143; donations for *30*, 89
commerce xxi, 57, 60
commodities 53–4, 57
compassion 19, 31n4
consent, simulation of 40, 132, 149
conservation policies xxiv(n16)
Conspiracy of Hope tour 62, 111n60
consumers: activism 60, 160; ambivalent 136, 141; and celebrity promoters 158; US 176
consumption 11, 16n17, 53; of celebrity media 10, 12, 131–8, *136*, 173; political engagement and 160
Cooper, Andrew 16n18, 34, 37, 56, 117
Corner, John 39
corporations: endorsements 122–3; interests in celebrity 14, 114–17, 126, 159, 162; power xxiv, 9, 33, 36–7, 55; social responsibility 46, 55, 77, 115, 158, 160
corruption *26*, 31
cosmopolitanism 43, 46, 67, 154, 166
Cottle, Simon 32n24
Couldry, Nick 16n17, 131–2, 170; on everyday practices 150n4, 174; on media power 12, 45; ordinary-media world distinction 50n69, 149; on political engagement 39–40, 48n37, 133; on public interest in celebrity 41, 48n44
Couric, Katie 89, 93n48
Cowell, Simon 68
Cox, Brendan 7, 15n4, 66, 73n109, 126; observations on campaigns 8, 15n3, 63, 125, 129n65
Crehan, Kate 49n65
Crompton, Tom 28, 33n41
Crouch, Colin 47n4, 48n41, 126; on post-democracy 35–7, 46, 68, 119, 127, 162
culture industries 38, 53
Curtis, Richard 62, 65

Dahlgren, Peter 39
Daily Mirror 115, *182*, 183
Darfur 123–4; Save Darfur Coalition 51, 67, 163n5
Darnton, Andrew 25, 66, 158, 173
Darrow, Thomas 42
Davis, Kristin 117

debt relief 63, 65–7, 72n93
democracy: celebrity advocacy and 8, 42; celebrity history and 52, 54; development and 161–2; enthusiasm for 47n4; inequality and 18, 40–1; media and 38–9; outcomes of 40–1; paradoxes of 69n10; *see also* post-democracy
denial 19–21, 23
development: charitable donations for 25, *28*; definition/meaning of xxiii–iv, 52; elite advocates 123, 161; fame in 141; goals of 55; history of 54–6; and humanitarianism differences xxii–iii; inequality and 18, 23–4; neoliberalism and 157–8; overseas (1980s & 90s) 61–4; policies xxiv, 25, 33n35, 156, 162, 166; public awareness of 13, 17, 24–5, *26–7*, 66, 153; representations of 153–5; studies 113; in Tanzania 165–7; values 28, 31; *see also* aid; NGOs
Diana, Princess of Wales: charities and 63; involvement in landmine campaigns 1–8, 15n3; paparazzi 16n19; public persona and voice 6, 10–11, 112n89
Dienst, Richard 50n70, 129n64, 129n76, 158
disaster relief 24, *26*, *29*
distance: and needs of others 19–20; pity and 20; proper 21
distant strangers 47, 50n75; connection with 112n87; giving money to 25; inequality of 17; media portrayal of 161; needs of 13, 18, 21, 154–5, 166
Doggett, Peter 60, 71n65
Dogra, Nandita 22, 43
Duncan, Isadora 58
Dyer, Richard 132, 174
Dylan, Bob 51, 59, 71n68

economic growth xxiv
economic policies 157; global 14, 36, 161–2, 167
Ecorazzi website 79
egalitarian politics 36, 46, 153, 162
Ekbladh, David 55
Elders, the 119, 128nn28–9
elites: accountability 153, 156–8; belief in celebrity power 122, 124–5; celebrity 8, 46, 160–1; as development advocates 123, 161; encounters with celebrities

206 Index

109–10, 113–14, 117–19, 126; governance and lobbying 14, 114, 119, 121, 126, 153, 162; NGO 9; political imaginations of 8–9, 41; and post-democratic politics 13, 35–7, 96–7, 127; power of 34, 37, 46, 119, 159; transnational 156
emotion–reason divide 39
empathy 106–7
empire building 74n126
endorsements: charities and 77, 127n8, 139–41, *140*, 151n30; corporate belief in 122–3; NGO branding 115, 117; of politicians 42; and publicity 41; television 53; US dominance in research on 122–3, 176–7, *177*, *178–9*, 180
Enough Project 74n120
Everett, Rupert 99–100, 108

fame: and celebrity differentiation 53; and development 13; prominent figures in British history 56–7; protests and 59; public interest in 137, 141; term usage xxi–ii; *see also* celebrity
famine relief 15n6, 59, 62, 96
Fassin, Didier 18, 31n4, 32n5, 49n63
Fenyoe, Alice 173
Ferris, Kerry 38
Fielding, Helen 95–6
Fields, Gracie 58
field-trips, celebrity 13, 97–9, 102; media coverage of 96, 100, 103–6, 108, 152
Fiennes, Ralph 81
Fischer, Zachary 40, 132, 149
Fonda, Jane 59, 64
Ford, Harrison 41
Fowles, Job 150n3
Friedman, Tom 47n10
Fulk of Neilly 52
fundraising 25, 28, 33n37, 133; for Africa 62, 64; liaison officer's role in 98; NGO 59; public reaction to celebrity 143–5, 149; *see also* charitable donations

G8 summit (Gleneagles) 47n1, 65–6, 74n113, 121, 125–6
Garofalo, Reebee 72nn76–7
Geldof, Bob 15n6, 34, 51, 62, 72n76; 8 Miles Fund 64; Live 8 concerts 65, 129n63; Make Poverty History and 65,

73n105; reaction to *Starsuckers* film 73n106, 125; Tony Blair and 64, 66, 72n91, 74n113, 120–1
gifts, receiving of 49n65
Gitlin, Todd 60
Glaser, Elizabeth 62
globalisation 36, 156, 158
Global Philanthropy Group 79
Gollancz, Victor 57
Goodman, Michael K. 158
Gore, Al 68, 123–4, 143
Graham, Bill 111n60
Grainger, A. D. 16n18
grants *29*
Green, Michael 123, 129n58
Greenpeace 62
Gretzky, Wayne 42
Guardian 77, *182*, 183
Guignon, Charles 69n20
Gundle, Stephen 150n3
Guthrie, Woody 51, 59, 70n55

Halliwell, Geri 94n62
Halpern, Jake 69n8, 150n8
Harrison, Graham 66
Hay, James 16n18, 53
Heerde, Jennifer van 22, 32n23
hegemony 156; inequality and 44–5, 49n65; US 157
Hello! magazine 167, 173, 183
Hepburn, Audrey 22, 108
Hettne, Björn 54
Hilary, John 73n106
Hill, Joe 58
HIV/AIDS: awareness 81, 158, 163n7; benefit concerts 72n77; foundations 62, 64
Horkheimer, Max 38, 53
Hudson, David 22, 32n23
Hulme, David 73n107, 157, 163n15, 163nn8–9
humanitarianism: celebrity 7, 42–4, 138; common-sense 42; and development differences xxii–iii; elites and 123; history of 54–7, 69n5; inequality and 18, 32n5; overseas (1980s & 90s) 61–4; post- 23, 37, 44, 109; theatricality of 17, 23, 32n24
humanitarian organisations 18, 54, 58, 82
Hyde, Marina 38, 48n16, 91, 94n62

Igoe, Jim 32n12
imagery 38
inequality/inequity 32n5, 49n54; of
    celebrity/celebrity advocacy 42–6, 148,
    153, 159, 162, 167–8; economic 59,
    153, 167–8; policies 155; and post-
    democracy 35; of poverty 17–18, 36;
    royalty and 44–5
Inglis, Fred 131
International Campaign to Ban Landmines
    (ICBL) 1–2, 8, 15n4
international development: apathy toward
    157; celebrity advocacy for 7, 14, 46,
    153–5, 159, 166; corporate support
    for 160; planning and activities 17, 59;
    term usage xxiii; see also development
International Monetary Fund (IMF) 72n89,
    99, 156
Inthorn, Sanna 42
Islamic Relief 88

Jackson, David 42
Jackson, Nathan 120, 163n7
Jebb, Eglantyne 57
Jesus 19
John, Elton: Aids Foundation 62, 93n39;
    white tie parties 116, 167
Jolie, Angelina 117, 124, 140, 147;
    branding 64; performance strategy 22–3,
    108, 144
Jones, Rene 77
Jubilee 2000 campaign 61, 63, 72n86,
    72n93, 120
justice, politics of 19, 43

Kapoor, Ilan 50n72, 160; on celebrity
    advocacy 34, 43, 45, 50n75
Kardashian, Kim 48n16
Kaye, Danny 59, 61, 70n53
Kelly, Sean 11
Khan, Salman 81
King, Martin Luther 60
King, Samantha 115, 160
Kirkley, Leslie 58
Kleinberg, Aviad 52
Klooster, Dan 160
Kouchner, Bernard 58
Kragen, Ken 62
Kutcher, Ashton 75, 92n13

labour movement 58
landmines: Princess Diana's role in 1–8,
    15n3; treaty to ban 1–2, 15n4, 15n12,
    157
Landmine Survivor's Network (LSN) 1
land reform 55
Larson, Robin 93n48
Law, Jude 94n62
Leibovitz, Annie 72n95
Lennon, John 59
liaison officers 7, 13, 92n14, 95, 118;
    celebrity field-trips 98–100; constraints
    and limitations of 97; duties/roles of
    79–83, 96–8, 101, 109; growth of 76,
    76–7; relations with agents 103, 110n21
Littler, Jo 43–5
Live 8 124, 129nn63–4, 154, 159;
    government negotiations and 125–6,
    129n76, 159; Make Poverty History
    conflict 47n1, 65
Live Aid 38, 51, 72n74, 75, 111n60;
    viewers 62, 74n123
Live Earth 68, 74n123, 124
Livingstone, David 56–7
Livingstone, Sonia 48n37
Look to the Stars website 79, 82, 93n37,
    173
Louis, Joe 58
Lovett, Adrian 73n106
Luke, Gospel of 19
Lumley, Joanna 15n7, 68, 83
Lynskey, Dorian 59–60, 68, 70nn55–6

McGrath, Rae 2–6, 15n5, 112n89
McGregor, Ewan 139, 147, 151n27
Madonna 92n13
Make Poverty History (MPH) 47n1, 64,
    73n106, 124–5; altercations 65, 73n105;
    goals 66; pledges 157, 163n20; public
    awareness of 66, 129n71
Malthusian theory 55
Malvolio xxi
Mandela, Nelson 119, 128n28; birthday
    concerts 61–2, 72n77
marginalisation 40–1
markets 36, 55, 157
Markham, Tim 41, 48n37, 48n44, 133,
    170
Marks, Michael 40, 132, 149
Marsh, David 47n8, 174

208 Index

Marshall, P. David 91n2
Martin, Paul 121
mass movements 129n64, 130n77
Mawdsley, Emma 157–8, 163n25
Médecins Sans Frontières 58, *88*
media: democracy and 38–41; glamour in
   world of 14, 45, 90, 143; international
   news reporting 21–2; NGO publicity
   101; and ordinary world distinction
   50n69, 149, 154; political engagement
   48n37, 133–4; portrayal of poverty 17,
   31; power 12, 45, 149; protest leaders
   and 60; public interest in celebrity 125,
   132–6, *134*, *135*, *136*, 141, 148;
   reporting on celebrity field-trips 103–6,
   108; representations of celebrity
   advocacy 107, 109–10; *see also*
   advertising; newspapers; television
methodology: focus groups 171, *172*, 173;
   interviews 169–70, *170*, *171*; limitations
   to 174–5; newspapers and magazine
   surveys 173–4; public opinion surveys
   170–1, 175n6
Micklewright, John *29*, 33n37
military intervention 54
Millennium Challenge Account 157,
   163n25
Mines Advisory Group (MAG) 1–6
Mitlin, Diana 156, 161
Mole, Tom 52–3
Moore, Demi 92n13
Morel, Edward 56–8
MTV 79, 124
Mukherjee, Roopali 160
Murs, Olly 15n7
music industry 60–1, 63, 71nn65–6

Nansen, Fridtjof 57
Nash, Kate 66–7
needs of others: post-humanitarianism and
   23, 109; recognition and denial of
   18–20; *see also* distant strangers
neoliberalism 40; celebrity and 158–9;
   development issues and 157–8; and
   economic changes 53; inequality and
   49n54; markets and 55; NGOs and 156
newspapers: international news coverage
   21–2; reporting on celebrity/celebrity
   advocacy 41, 53, 138, 181, *182*, 183;
   surveys 173–4

New York Times 41
NGO-celebrity relations: awareness of
   139, 139–40, 148; constraints 100–2;
   contact databases 77, *78*, 79; corporate
   sponsorship 36, 113–17, 126; increase
   in 110n7, 159; inequality of 96, 102–3;
   and politicians 118; relationship-
   building 96–8, 100–3, 108–9, 110n5,
   152; rise of 36–7, 64; supporters and
   ambassadors 82–3, *84–8*; as
   systematically organised 7, 13–14, 75,
   91; *see also* field-trips; liaison officers
NGOs: access to elites 9, 14, 37, 113–14,
   119; achievements 155–6; branding
   80–1, 115, 117, 159, 166; corporate
   power and 55–6; *Finding Frames* report
   28, 31, 66, 158; fundraising 59;
   landmine campaigns 2, 4–5; military
   relations 54; neoliberalism and 156;
   popularity and 11; publicity 5, 22–3,
   101; revenues 159; role of xxiii;
   supporters 155; values 28, 31, 33n41
Nicaraguan Solidarity Campaign 61
Nightingale, Florence 56–7
Nixon, Richard 70n45
Nolan, David 32n24
non-governmental organisations *see*
   NGOs
Nownes, Anthony 42

Obama, Barack 42
Olsen, Gorm Rye 47n13
Omidyar, Pam 67
ONE campaign 64–5, 124, 128n47, 154;
   followers of 89
Orman, John 38, 40
Otter, Mark *27*, 33n39
Ouellette, Laurie 16n18, 53
Oxfam 161; celebrity ambassadors *85*, 100,
   117; fundraising 59

Pate, Maurice 70n53
Pels, Dick 39
performance: authenticity of 11, 96,
   107–9, 112n92, 144, 148; strategies
   22–3
Pilger, John 58
Pitt, Brad 89, 117
pity, politics of 19–20, 23, 37, 154

policymaking 33n35; by elites 25, 68
political styles 39
politics, celebrity xxii, 10, 46, 47n8, 153; democracy and 38–40
Ponte, Stefano 158
popular culture 174–5
populism 42; and popular distinction 8–11, 14, 149, 175
post-democracy: celebrity advocacy and 9, 35–7; description of 8–9; elite lobbying and governance in 13–14, 114, 119, 121, 126, 153, 162; inequality and 35–6, 40–1; politics 46, 61, 68, 127, 149, 153; rise of 36; writers 40
post-humanitarianism 23, 37, 44, 109
Postman, Neil 38
poverty: awareness 24–5, *26*, 32n23, 33n36, 66, 123–4; celebrity advocacy and 153–5, 157–8, 163n8; celebrity as causing 45; economic growth and xxiv; increase in 66, 163n15; inequality and 17–18, 36; media coverage of 17, 22, 31; in Tanzania 165–7
power: consumer 160; corporate xxiv, 9, 33, 36–7, 55; elite 34, 46, 119, 159; inequality and 42, 45, 167; media 12, 45, 149; NGOs and 156; political 62–3; state 54, 56
power of celebrity, belief in: advertising and 122; advocacy and 101, 110, 133; corporate 122–3; elite 8, 10, 41, 122, 124–5, 152; popular 126–7, *142*, 142–4, 149; widespread 133, 148
protest: commerce and 60; as fashionable 59; leaders 60; singers and songs 51, 58–61, 68
public engagement: with celebrity/celebrity advocacy 8, 14, 41, 114, 125, 138–41, 152–4; with celebrity media 89, 133–8, *134*, *135*, *136*, 141; government elites and 37; politics and 9, 39–40, 48n37, 133–4, 149, 159; with popular culture 175; simulation of 125, 129n71, 162; *see also* awareness
publicity 9, 81, 128n23; from charitable activities 10–11, 80; NGO 5, 22–3, 101; for politicians 118
Public Opinion Monitor (UK) 12, *27*, *30*, 132, 171

racism 58, 68, 70n56, 71n69
radicalism 55, 71n58, 71n67, 164n34
Rage Against the Machine 68
Rancière, Jacques 35
Rathbone, Eleanor 57
Reality TV: *American Idol* 124; *Big Brother* 39, 80; publicity and 80; in the US 16n18, 53–4; viewer demand for 137
Red Cross *86*, 139
Redgrave, Vanessa 64, 72n80
Red Pages, The 53, 77, *78*, 79, 93n37, 174
representations: of celebrity advocacy 107–10; development 153–5; of needs of others 23, 25, 43, 153
Richey, Lisa Ann 158, 161
Riddell, Roger 155
Rist, Gilbert xxiii
Robeson, Paul 58, 64
Rock Against Racism 71n69
Rodrik, Dani 47nn9–10; on development policy xxiv, 161; on globalisation 36, 156
Rojek, Chris xxi, 52, 69n10
Rolland, Romain 57
Ross, Eric 55
Royal Geographical Society (RGS) 5, 8
royalty 44–5
Rutherford, Kenneth 1, 5, 8, 15n3, 16n19

Sachs, Jeffrey 64, 157
saints 52
Samman, Emma 150n25, 151n30
Save Darfur Coalition 51, 67, 163n5
Save the Children 57, *87*
Schnepf, Sylke V. *29*, 33n37
Schweitzer, Albert 57
Scott, Martin 21, 138, 149, 161, 173
Seeger, Pete 59, 70n55
Seu, Bruna 32n25
Shaw, George Bernard 57
Short, Clare 5
Sightsavers *86*–7
Silverstone, Roger 21
Sireau, Nicky 65
Smith, Matt Baillie 32n25
Soccer Aid 143–4, 147
social media 89
solidarity 17, 18, 32n5, 66

210 Index

South Africa 51, 61
sponsors/sponsorship: celebrity advocacy and 46, 80; of the Elders 119, 128n29; of NGOs 55, 113–17, 126, 159
Starsuckers (Atkins) 65, 73n106, 125
state power 54, 56
Stead, William 56
Stiglitz, Joseph 64, 156
Sting 62, 112n60
stock market 122
Street, John 71n66; on celebrity politics xxii, 38–9, 42, 47n8
Strine, Harry C. 128n23
Sudan 51, 67

Tanzania 165–7
television: advertisements 53; *Dr Phil* 53, 69n20; game shows 79; international news coverage 21–2; MTV 79, 124; portrayal of distant strangers 161; telethons 133, 138, 148; viewer preferences 137, 173; *see also* media; Reality TV
Teresa, Mother 58, 70n46
Tester, Keith 42–3, 49n51
text, decline of 38
Third Sector 79, 93n37, 173
Thrall, A. Trevor 15n8, 41, 74n123, 183n1
Time magazine 65
Tomas, Danny 70n54
trade: fairer 46, 65–6, 158; free 156; relations 18, 66–7
Truman, Harry 54–5
Tuck, Stephen 60, 70n45
Turner, Graeme xxi, 12, 131
Twelfth Night (Shakespeare) xxi

U2 72n80, 163n7; *see also* Bono
UK government 2, 27, 65, 125–6
Ullman, Liv 59
UNICEF 70n53, 81, 139, 147; celebrity ambassadors 61, 71n72, *83, 86*; fundraising 59

United Nations (UN): celebrity ambassadors 22, 64, 140; peacekeepers 67
United Talent Agency 77
Ure, Midge 62
USA for Africa 62
US government 58, 67, 126
US population 176–7, *177, 178–9*, 180
Ustinov, Peter 59, 61

values 28, 31, 33n41
Van den Bulck, Hilde 151n30
Varga, Somogy 11
Veer, Ekant 41
Victorian era 11, 13, 52, 56
Vietnam War 51, 59, 122
volunteers 11, 90

Waal, Alex de 67, 121
Walliams, David 146–7, 151n45
War Child 63, 72n80, 93n39
Washington, Booker T. 58
Water Aid *87*
wealth gap 35–6, 162
Wedgwood, Josiah 57
welfare state 35
West, Darrell 38, 40
Wheeler, Mark 46, 56
Wheeler, Robert 151n30
Wilberforce, William 56
Williams, Robbie 144, 147
Wilson, Monica 166
Winfrey, Oprah 42
witchcraft 132
Wolfe, Tom 59, 71n58
Woodstock Festival 60, 71nn68–9
World War Two 52, 57–9

Yorke, Thom 90
Youde, Jeremy 160
Yrjölä, Riina 43–4, 49n51

Žižek, Slavoj 50n74
Zoonen, Liesbet van 39